MG

HAYNES CLASSIC MAKES SERIES

MG

BRITAIN'S FAVOURITE SPORTS CAR

MALCOLM GREEN

Second and third edition updated by Andrew Roberts

First edition published in November 1998
Second edition published in May 2005
Third edition published in October 2011

A catalogue record for this book is available from the British Library

ISBN 978 0 85733 107 6

Library of Congress control no 2011927868

Published by Haynes Publishing, Sparkford, Yeovil, Somerset BA22 7JJ, UK
Tel: 01963 442030 Fax: 01963 440001
Int.tel: +44 1963 442030 Int.fax: +44 1963 440001
E-mail: sales@haynes.co.uk
Website: www.haynes.co.uk

Haynes North America Inc.,
861 Lawrence Drive,
Newbury Park,
California 91320, USA.

Designed and typeset by Dominic Stickland

Printed in the USA by Odcombe Press LP,
1299 Bridgestone Parkway, La Vergne, TN 37086

contents

MG
introduction

As generations of car-mad schoolboys quickly learned, the well-known initials that have come to symbolise a sports car for enthusiasts were derived from the name of the original parent company, The Morris Garages. This was owned by William Morris, being the successor to the original motor car hire and repair business he started well before moving into manufacturing motor cars. Morris had built his first cars in 1913 and, by the time he employed one Cecil Kimber as Sales Manager of Morris Garages in 1921, he was established as one of the leading car producers in the country. The Morris Garages were the Oxford retail outlet for quite a number of different makes of car, including Morris, but Kimber felt that he would like to be able to offer customers something a little different – a better product for which he could charge a higher price.

Given the encouragement of William Morris, he designed and marketed a special version of the Morris Cowley to sell alongside the standard range of cars. Called 'The Morris Garages Chummy', sufficient numbers of these modified cars were sold for the venture to be deemed successful and for Morris themselves to introduce a similarly styled model into their range – at a much lower price! With his niche in the market thus stolen from him, Kimber had a small number of chassis fitted with two-seater Raworth bodies, and this was the first car to be advertised as an 'MG'.

Cecil Kimber had a considerable aptitude for drawing and painting and it was probably this that gave him the ability to influence the styling of all the cars he produced. The detail design was the work of others, but it seems that we have him to thank for the particularly fine lines possessed by all the pre-war MGs. With his

The Bullnose 14/28 MG was an elegant car and one can see why people were prepared to spend quite a bit more money to buy one in preference to a standard Morris.

Raworth-bodied car selling very slowly, as buyers probably balked at paying £350 for one when a mechanically similar two-seater Cowley could be bought for just £195, Kimber therefore turned his mind to building a car rather more worthy of bearing the MG octagon.

The 1924 model Morris Oxford featured a revised mechanical specification, including a 13.9hp engine, and Cecil Kimber turned to this as the basis for a car to appeal to sporting motorists. A specially designed and luxurious saloon body

The M-Type was the first of its kind and set a new trend in sports car design

with a 'V' windscreen and aluminium panelling was fitted to the Morris chassis. Marketed as an MG Four-door Saloon Morris Oxford, this was priced at £460. Other body styles soon joined what was now called 'The MG Super Sports' range. Late in 1924 the Morris chassis was lengthened and gained better brakes, and these benefits became available on the chassis used by MG. The team at Morris Garages flattened springs, lowered steering columns and tuned engines, in order to improve both the performance and roadholding of their cars.

The early MGs were fitted with the familiar Bullnose Morris radiator, as was a special built by Kimber and used on the 1925 Land's End Trial to gain a Gold Medal. Since revered as 'Old Number One', this car was assembled using modified Morris chassis components, an ohv Hotchkiss engine, and a body by Carbodies of Coventry. It was not the first MG, although it was certainly the first to be specially built with competition in mind, but it is an interesting and important part of MG history. Nearly 400 of the standard model Bullnose

MGs were built between 1924 and 1926 and these gained an enviable reputation as attractive and quick sporting cars.

Towards the end of 1926 Morris revised their cars drastically. The attractive, rounded radiator fitted to every model since 1913 was replaced by one of a plain and undistinguished design. Unfortunately, although the new chassis was wider and stronger, it was also a lot heavier. To make matters worse, the engine, gearbox and back axle were transferred unmodified, so performance suffered. Kimber and his team struggled to make the best job they could of the new chassis, but the 1927 model MG 14/28 did not look as good, or go as well, as the previous cars.

Things improved a little as modifications were introduced late in 1927. Changes to the engine and brakes, as well as small alterations to the bodywork and the addition of a covering over the front dumb irons, saw the car re-launched as 'The MG Mk IV', or 14/40, in time for The London Motor Show at Olympia. Both the 14/28 and 14/40 MGs were good, solid cars, endowed with style and performance that lifted them above

MG 18/80s were large and imposing machines. The De luxe saloon had metal-panelled coachwork and many luxury features, like blinds on the windows and vanity sets and mirrors for the rear-seat passengers.

the average run of machines available in the 1920s. However, in the eyes of many they were really only modified Morris Oxfords, and Kimber had far more ambitious plans for the MG marque.

Being keen to build cars that differed from standard Morris products, late in 1928 Kimber started to produce the 18/80 Sports Six. Probably at his instigation, Morris Engines Branch had built a 2,468cc six-cylinder unit, ostensibly to power a larger Morris but perhaps with MG use in mind. Morris first fitted the engine to a poorly designed chassis that luckily never made it into full production, all but three of the initial batch of cars being dismantled. A stronger and wider chassis was designed and the car joined the range in 1928 as the Morris Six. MG had one of the three original cars for evaluation, discarding pretty well everything but the power unit and designing a new, strong chassis frame

The C-Type Montlhéry Midget was an effective racing car with an impressive string of successes to its credit.

with suspension and steering appropriate for a sporting car. Construction standards were high, and the cast aluminium bulkhead incorporated the MG octagon in the side brackets even though this was hidden with the body fitted! Most imposing was the new radiator: the 18/80 had a specially designed shell with the MG octagon sitting on a crest-shaped nose-piece. This classic radiator was to hallmark MGs for many years.

With hindsight, the decision to build a larger and more expensive car for sale in 1929, the year of the stock market crash in the USA which precipitated the Great Depression, was ill-timed and comparatively few cars were sold. As good a car as the 18/80 undoubtedly was, MG as a marque survived almost entirely due to the announcement at the 1928 Olympia Motor Show of an entirely new type of car.

The M-Type Midget was the first MG of its type and was to establish a completely new trend in sports car design. Based as closely as the earlier cars on a standard Morris product, the M-Type was fortunately just the right sort of vehicle to launch at that time. Just as in later years, with the Suez

crisis and the 1970s oil price shock, the economic situation in the late 1920s and early 1930s did not encourage the purchase of outwardly extravagant and thirsty motor cars. The Morris Minor was introduced by Morris to compete with the light car built by their greatest rivals at the time, the Austin Seven. Endowed with a jewel of a Wolseley-designed, 847cc ohc engine, the Minor was transformed by MG, who made slight chassis changes, lowered and lengthened the steering column, and fitted a rakish, two-seater body that gave the occupants a minimum of weather protection and the maximum amount of style and fun for their £175.

So successful did the Midget become that the larger car was almost entirely eclipsed by its tiny sibling. At first, much of the company's advertising and promotional effort was directed towards the larger cars, but this was to change. They had moved in late 1927 into a purpose-built factory in Edmund Road, Oxford, that had been designed around the volumes of car production then envisaged. However, orders for the Midget were so numerous that by 1929 the search for larger premises started. Late the same year MG production was moved a few miles south to Abingdon, where it was to remain for the next 50 years.

Kimber had become convinced of the benefits of the publicity engendered by competition success, and early in its life the M-Type was made available to selected entrants in the 1929 Land's End Trial, where it proved suitable, two earning Gold Medals. From that point certainly up until the outbreak of the Second World War, there was hardly any such event that did not have an MG Midget of some sort in the entry list.

Although the modest engine power of the early M-Types was insufficient for serious motor racing, some owners entered club events. Things improved once the MG chief designer, H. N. Charles, designed a new camshaft to

Right Top – EX 120: a friend of Kimber, Jimmy Palmes, wanted to make an attempt on the 750cc 24-hour world speed record using a car based on the M-Type Midget. Kimber thought that the standard chassis was unsuitable and offered the use of a new one under development. This was fitted with an engine reduced to 743cc, and special bodywork. With a Powerplus supercharger it became the first 750cc car to exceed 100mph (161kph). The car caught fire at Montlhéry, injuring George Eyston.

Right Middle – EX 127: after the record-breaking attempts with EX 120, a new car was constructed using a C-Type chassis, brakes, front axle and springs. The offset rear axle and transmission allowed the driver to sit lower in the car, reducing the total frontal area and wind resistance. Fitted with a streamlined body and surface radiator, the car was driven at Montlhéry by Ernest Eldridge, without much success. Back at Abingdon the supercharger drive was modified and a conventional radiator installed. The team returned to France and in the hands of George Eyston the car took four records at speeds of over 114mph (183kph). The ultimate goal, however, had been to set a record as the first car in its class to reach 2 miles per minute, and this was finally achieved in late 1932 when he raised the mile, kilometre and 5-kilometre records to speeds of over 120mph (193kph).

Right Bottom – EX 135: in 1938 the company decided to assist the well-known record-breaker 'Goldie' Gardner in an attempt on the 1,100cc world record. The ex-Eyston K3 was purchased, the chassis rebuilt at Abingdon, and a special body designed by Reid Railton was fitted. A modified K-Type engine, fed from a Centric supercharger running at 26lb boost, produced 194bhp at 7,000rpm. In Germany, Gardner took the Class G flying-start records for the kilometre and mile at over 186mph (299kph). The following year, with a higher-ratio final drive installed, the team returned to Germany and took a string of records in the 1,100cc class at speeds of up to 203.5mph (327kph). An overnight rebore with portable equipment saw the capacity of the engine enlarged to take it just within the 1,500cc class. A fresh attempt saw more records fall at speeds of over 200mph (322kph).

increase power output. Cars were prepared for the 1930 Double Twelve-Hour race at Brooklands and fitted with the improved engines, together with other minor mechanical and bodywork modifications. There were six Midgets in that race, three of them taking the Team Prize, and, in a way that was later to become company practice, replicas of the 'Double-Twelve' M-Types were sold to the general public.

As with the earlier models, using the standard Morris components had its limitations. Although the channel-section Morris chassis used for the M-Type was fairly rigid, it had a short wheelbase and a high centre of gravity. To improve matters the springs were flattened by MG to lower the car, but it was still really not particularly well suited to coping with any increase in power, and it was decided that a new chassis for exclusive use of MG should be designed. This had the two main chassis members set parallel to each other, passing under the rear axle. Tubular cross members linked the side frames and also formed mounting points for the springs, each of which was pivoted at the front and held at the rear by bronze trunnions. This chassis was used in the EX 120 record-breaker and in the C-Type Montlhéry Midget, a car designed primarily for competition use.

The first production model to use the new chassis was the D-Type. The C-Type chassis had a 6ft 9in (2m) wheelbase and for the D-Type it was increased to 7 feet (2.1m) for the first 100 cars, and later to 7ft 2in (2.2m). Powered by the M-Type engine, the longer chassis gave room for the fitting of four-seater open and closed bodywork. Once production of the M-Type moved to Abingdon there was also a closed, coupé version on offer, although this was still really just a two-seater. The D-Type was bigger, and heavier, with a consequent performance disadvantage, and for those prepared to find a little more money the six-cylinder F-Type Magna was introduced.

The six-cylinder engine, also used in the Wolseley Hornet, shared the overhead camshaft and vertical dynamo layout of the four-cylinder version. Sheet-metal side covers were fitted to disguise its humble origins, but they could not conceal that the 1,271cc engine had a modest power output of just 37bhp. In spite of this, the car performed tolerably well with quite a number being sold in chassis form to specialist coachbuilders. Being really little more than a stretched D-Type chassis fitted with the larger power unit and an ENV gearbox, the Magna had initially the same puny 8-inch (203mm) brake drums as the four-cylinder cars; these were replaced by 12-inch (305mm) drums when a revised F-Type was announced in October 1932, and at that time a two-seater version appeared to join

The slab-tanked J2 set the style for the 1930s sports car. Weaknesses include 8-inch (203mm) brakes and a two-bearing crankshaft, but a good J2 is a joy to drive.

Both the K1 and KN chassis carried this saloon body. The 'pillarless' design allows easy access to the interior as there is no central pillar between the front and rear doors.

the four-seater open and closed models in the range.

In August 1932 a totally redesigned Midget arrived in the showrooms. The J-Type replaced the four-seater D-Types and the outdated M-Type Midget, and the classic shape of the two-seater J2 model was to set a style for MG sports cars that was to endure for 23 years. The chassis was similar to that used for the later D-Type, and the car still had 8-inch (203mm) brakes and a 3ft 6in (1.07m) track. However, the 847cc engine was fitted with a crossflow cylinder head and a four-speed gearbox. The new model was available as the J1 four-seater open tourer and closed salonette, similar in appearance to the superseded D-Type, and in J2 guise as a two-seater replacement for the M-Type. The competition fraternity were catered for by the J3 supercharged 750cc version of the J2 and eventually by the out-and-out racing J4 – of which only nine were built.

Sharing the MG stand at the 1932 Motor Show was another entirely new car, this time designed to appeal to a rather different market. The Magnette range offered models to cover the needs of both the family man and the motor-racing enthusiast. The K1 was available with either an open four-seater body or as a four-door saloon. The latter had no pillar between the front and rear doors, giving easy access for rear seat passengers when both the front and rear doors were open. The K2 chassis was a two-seater sports car and the K3 a racing car destined to become the most famous of all MGs.

The K chassis was altogether more substantial than those for the Midget and Magna, and the track, at 4 feet (1.22m), gave the cars a much heavier look. Two lengths of chassis were available, the longer for the K1 saloon and open tourer, and the shorter for the K2 and K3 models. A divided track rod was fitted, designed to overcome the transfer of 'kick-back' from the front wheels to the steering wheel. The engine was an entirely new design, based on the features of the six-cylinder F-Type engine but built for use exclusively in MG cars. Virtually every component was modified and strengthened, and the cylinder head was totally redesigned and given

Cecil Kimber (1888–1945)

Born in London and educated in the North of England, Cecil Kimber can be considered to be the father of MG. At first he was employed in his father's printing ink business, but the Rex motorcycle he bought from his earnings fostered an interest in motorised transport. Unfortunately, on a borrowed motorcycle he was involved in a serious accident with a car that so badly damaged his right leg that it took many months and a number of operations before he could use it again. This injury resulted in one leg being a couple of inches shorter than the other, and a transfer of allegiance to four-wheeled transport in the form of a Singer purchased with his compensation money.

Having decided to follow a career in the motor industry, Kimber worked for AC Cars at Thames Ditton and for the component suppliers E. G. Wrigley of Birmingham, before being taken on by William Morris as Sales Manager of Morris Garages. The effect this appointment was to have for the sports car enthusiast cannot be overestimated, nor can the support he received in the early 1930s from William Morris. Relations with Morris were soured by the break–up of Kimber's first marriage, and Morris failed to support him in the argument with Nuffield Organisation Managing Director Miles Thomas that led to Kimber's dismissal from the company in 1941. A period of ill–health followed, although he did secure another post in the motor industry before a tragic railway accident in 1945 robbed the country of one of its brightest talents.

crossflow porting and triple carburettors to improve efficiency. As a result, the 1,086cc engine produced more power than had the previous 1,271cc unit. Significantly, the new engine fell conveniently within the 1,100cc category for international motor racing events and was strong enough to withstand considerable tuning.

The K3 used a modified version of the shorter chassis and this was fitted with an engine boosted by a front-mounted supercharger and mated to a pre-selector gearbox. Following a remarkably short development period, a team of three K3s under the control of Earl Howe was entered in the 1933 Mille Miglia. One of these, in the hands of Sir Henry Birkin and Bernard Rubin, was driven flat out from the start and before retiring with valve trouble managed to force the Maserati opposition into breaking their cars. The other two K3s, driven by George Eyston, Count Lurani, Earl Howe and 'Hammy' Hamilton, finished the race, taking first and second places in class and winning the Team Prize. Further success for the K3 followed, the best remembered being the overall win by Tazio Nuvolari in the 1933 Tourist Trophy race.

No matter how good the K3 was as a racing car, the standard Magnettes were less successful. Later in the year mounting criticism led to the factory fitting longer-stroke, 1,271cc versions of the K-Type engine, while vociferous complaints from customers running the 1,100cc version led to a programme of engine replacements once supplies of the larger units were available. The Magnettes sold in comparatively small numbers and appealed to the sort of people who might previously have run larger-engined vehicles. This meant that the company had to deal with disgruntled buyers who felt that they performed less well than expected, and it seems unlikely that they contributed much to company profits.

The Midget range, however, continued to sell well and the J-Types were updated in September 1933, the small cycle wings giving way to elegant swept wings that provided the occupants with far more protection from the elements. Earlier that year the Magna model had also been revised. Using a chassis of similar design to the previous model, the L-Type Magna enjoyed a twin-carburettor version of the 1,100cc K-Type engine and a manual four-speed gearbox. Again, swept wings were now the fashion and the open four-seater tourer and closed

Fitting redundant K2 bodies to the N-Type chassis produced the two-seater ND, which was built in small numbers and usually sold to customers who wanted a competition car.

The NA Allingham. The open car was of a design unique to this model and could be used either as a pure two-seater, with the rear seat concealed by closing a rear deck panel, or as a four-seater when this panel was opened.

salonette looked particularly attractive cars, the sloping Magna radiator shell blending well with the long bonnet and gently curved wings. Later a two-seater L2 and oddly styled Continental Coupé joined the range.

In March 1934 it was the turn of the Midget to undergo a transformation. The sort of internal redesign carried out on the six-cylinder engine the previous year was now applied to the four-cylinder unit. The capacity remained 847cc, but three main bearings, stronger valve gear, and a revised cylinder head design produced a stronger and more refined engine. The chassis was beefed up and the body made larger, producing in the P-Type what was one of the prettiest cars of the decade. Once again, there were four-seater tourers and a closed Airline Coupé model. This had radical styling, the two-seater body following the 1930s obsession with 'streamlining' by having a steeply sloping tail section.

In an effort to rationalise the range, the Magna and K Magnettes were replaced by a new Magnette, the N-Type. The 1,271cc KD engine was modified to incorporate main bearings of similar design to those used in the new P-Type, and the cylinder head was revised. In this form power was 56bhp, 8bhp up on the earlier engine. A revised chassis was fitted with two- and four-seater bodies, these being mounted on subframes to improve passenger comfort. As additional models, an Airline Coupé similar to the P-Type and an open two/four-seater were also on offer. The larger K chassis was still available as the KN saloon, now fitted with the N-Type engine and manual gearbox.

Competition successes continued, with an unsupercharged racing car based on the new Magnette winning the 1934 Tourist Trophy in the hands of Charlie Dodson. The NE, as the racer was called, was developed solely to circumvent the ban on superchargers that had been introduced largely to make an MG victory unlikely! The factory produced another four-cylinder racing car, the Q-Type, which had many components in common with the 1934 K3. The handling of the racing models was becoming more suspect as power outputs increased, and a radical solution being worked on

John Thornley OBE (1909–94)

Thornley is one of those lucky people who managed to turn their leisure interest into a full-time job. He spent the first three years of his working life as an accountant in the City of London, during which time he bought an M-Type Midget and became one of the founder members of The MG Car Club. His spare-time activities as an official of the club led to frequent visits to the Abingdon factory and to the offer of a job by Cecil Kimber in the Service Department. At Abingdon he was to have an ever-increasing influence on the course of MG development.

His considerable talent for dealing with people was recognised in his appointment as Service Manager in 1934 and in his subsequent duties running the 'Cream Cracker' and 'Musketeer' trials teams. The writing skills honed by the thousands of letters written to smooth the ruffled feathers of aggrieved customers and irate dealers led to his authorship of the standard work on MG racing history, *Maintaining the Breed*. Returning to Abingdon after war service, he was appointed Sales and Service Manager in 1947, Assistant General Manager in 1950, General Manager in 1952, and Director and General Manager in 1956 – a position he was to hold until his retirement in 1969. Thornley would have succeeded whatever his chosen career – witness his rise to the rank of Lieutenant-Colonel in the army and the OBE he was awarded for services to the Air Training Corps. That he chose to spend his working life with the MG Car Company, and much of his spare time on MG Car Club business and for other charities, was to the ultimate benefit of us all.

by the development department was the adoption of a completely new chassis with independent suspension. The R-Type racing car with the all-independent suspension chassis arrived in April 1935, but before this could be fully developed the whole racing programme was cancelled.

The MG Car Company was owned privately by William Morris, and in 1935 he decided to sell it to Morris Motors Ltd. As a result Kimber was no

The NB models introduced in 1935 were the last of the six-cylinder ohc MGs and can be distinguished from the earlier N-Types by the front-hinged doors. This is a four-seater open tourer.

longer Managing Director, merely General Manager, his place being taken by Leonard Lord, who was on the board of the main company. The outcome for MG was a loss of autonomy, hence the racing ban, and a directive to ensure that future production cars used a greater number of components common with cars produced elsewhere within the group. Design henceforth was to be undertaken at Cowley and almost immediately the Abingdon Development Department closed with some of the staff being transferred and others dismissed. Only a small team remained at Abingdon to liaise with the main office.

Modifications to the existing cars were undertaken with the 847cc P-Type

being joined by a PB model that featured a larger-capacity engine, now 939cc, and a slatted radiator grille. There were also minor revisions, like the provision of a separate speedometer in place of the combined speedometer/tachometer fitted to the PA. Similarly, the N-Type also gained the new grille and speedometer; in addition the scuttle was slightly lowered and the doors were hinged at the front rather than at the rear.

The first entirely new car produced under Cowley direction was the 2 litre SA saloon. Vastly different from the N-Type it was meant to replace, its bulk and luxurious appointments were more reminiscent of the long-dead 18/80. However, this was to be a mass-produced car and rather more affordable than its predecessor. The inclusion of a four-door open tourer and a Tickford folding-head coupé in the range widened its appeal.

The TA, introduced in June 1936 as a replacement for the P-Type Midget, was rather more acceptable to existing customers. Although the 1,292cc ohv engine developed from the side-valve Morris Ten unit was of less exciting specification than those fitted to previous Midgets, the new car was still an attractive sporting machine and was to sell in reasonable numbers. The addition of a Tickford coupé version in 1938 widened its appeal and in 1939 it received a much-improved engine and the TB designation. Tickford were also supplying bodies for the SA and for the 1,549cc VA that had arrived on the scene soon after the TA. Designed to appeal to those who had previously bought the Magnette, the VA looked like a scaled-down version of the 2,288cc six-cylinder SA. Although less overtly sporting than the previous cars, the saloon, tourer and Tickford versions of the new mid-sized MGs sold in reasonable numbers, over 2,400 having been delivered by the time production was halted in 1939.

By the end of the 1930s, MG were fully established as Britain's premier builder

of sporting cars. The rationalisation process begun in 1935 had seen the introduction of a range of cars that spread from the two-seater TB to the 2,561cc WA. The latter model had been added to the range for 1939; it was a slightly enlarged SA and was available with the same range of bodies, saloon, tourer and Tickford. Agreed, there was less of the excitement of the early 1930s, with new models appearing every few months and the marque always making headlines, but the company must have been rather more profitable. Nevertheless, competition had not been altogether forgotten, with factory-supported trials cars scoring a number of successes and further speed records to celebrate before war broke out.

MG faced stiff competition for sales in the late 1930s. Although they claimed to be purely sports car manufacturers, in truth many of their products were no more sporting than those of their rivals. The TA/TB Midgets were inheritors of the following for small sports cars built up by the earlier small MGs, but they certainly did not have everything their own way. Singer had made serious attempts on the market with their 972cc and 1,493cc sports models, the two-seater cars having bodywork very reminiscent of that used on MGs. Austin were also in the picture, especially in the early 1930s. Sports versions of the Austin Seven, the Ulster, Nippy and Speedy were good fun and cheaper than an MG, but by 1938 they merely produced open versions of sedate saloons. Rileys always had a following amongst sporting motorists with the stunningly attractive Imp and MPH featuring in every schoolboy's list of 'dream cars'. There were quite a number of other sports car manufacturers competing for the same market – AC, HRG, Morgan, etc. – but most built cars in small quantities and more expensively.

In a way, the larger MGs, the SA, VA and WA, faced far stiffer competition.

Of similar specification, if not performance and style, were the larger Morris and Wolseley models. Buying purely by engine size, these were around two-thirds the price of the equivalent MG, as were the larger-engined saloons from the other volume manufacturers like Ford and Vauxhall. The Ford V8s were relatively light and powerful, if a little unsophisticated, and gained quite a good reputation in sporting trials and rallies at the time. Triumph had built some cars with sporting pretensions but these appeared in small numbers, with development severely hampered by cash problems. Like Kimber, William Lyons had an exceptional eye for good styling. His SS1 was a striking car with reasonable performance at a remarkably low price. The 1½ litre and 2½ litre SS Jaguar saloons competed directly with MG on price, performance and styling; they were popular and substantially outsold the Abingdon products.

The large SA and WA MGs were elegant and comfortable cars, as demonstrated by the cockpit of a Charlesworth open tourer.

The TA and TB Tickford drophead coupés are desirable little cars, the three-position hood making them suitable for use in all weather conditions.

The TC *midget*

The TC was the last of the traditional, cart-sprung MG Midgets. The chassis closely resembles the one designed in 1931, used for the EX 120 record-breaker and D-Type Midget. Despite its lack of sophistication, a TC is still a nice car to own and one of the prettiest 1940s sports cars.

In common with most of British industry, the arrival of peace in 1945 presented the motor manufacturers with a huge problem. Since the outbreak of war six years earlier, the whole emphasis had been on producing an ever-increasing volume of armaments to sustain the war effort and little time had been spent on preparing for the return of more normal conditions. The Abingdon MG factory, for example, had been employed producing tanks for the army, parts for aircraft manufacture, and had even built complete cockpit fuselage sections for the Albemarle bomber. Successful though the factory had been at undertaking this work, there was no guarantee of a resumption of car production when peace returned, and certainly no funds to develop new models.

It must have been a time of uncertainty for the large workforce employed to produce the tools of war. As the military work dried up, many of the largely female assembly line workers were told that they would not be needed when current contracts ended. At the same time, the nucleus of the pre-war Abingdon team were being joined by colleagues returning to take up their old jobs after a spell in the forces. The pressure on management to organise a return to car production must have been immense, and a corner of the factory was soon devoted to developing a post-war sports car that could be brought into production as rapidly as possible.

Before all car building at Abingdon had ceased, the last two-seaters produced had been TBs, so it was to

EAJ 591

this model that the company looked for its post-war sports car. Developed from the successful TA, the TB had a flexible ladder chassis frame that followed traditional MG practice in having bronze trunnions to locate the rear ends of the leaf springs. When designing the replacement, it was decided that these had too short a service life and a change was made to conventional rubber-bushed shackles.

The most important feature that sold any MG was its appearance. Almost every car they had built in the 1920s and 1930s relied on looks to appeal to potential customers, and this was unlikely to be different in 1945. For the post-war car, few changes were made to the basic design of the ash-framed, metal-panelled TB body. There had always been some who had said that cockpit space was too limited, and to address this problem the body was widened by 4 inches (102mm) between the pillars at the rear of the doors. To keep the same overall width, the running boards were narrower.

The TB had used the engine designed originally for the Series M Morris Ten, and for the sports car it had been enlarged to 1,250cc and fitted with twin SU carburettors and a modified camshaft. Power output had been a relatively modest 54.4bhp in standard form, but its free-revving nature had endeared it to sporting drivers, and this XPAG engine was specified for the 1945 car. It was the engine as much as anything else that was to make the car such an enduring success. The TB had been fitted with twin 6-volt batteries placed alongside the rear axle, but these were often neglected by owners, so for the revised Midget they were replaced with a much more conveniently situated 12-volt unit mounted under the bonnet, alongside the toolbox.

So the new MG, which it had been decided would carry the name 'TC Midget', was really just a slightly

modified version of a car that had first seen the light of day as the TA nearly ten years earlier. However, in reverting to a pre-war design, the company were only doing the same as the rest of the British motor industry. In a world starved of new cars, and with the continental European factories in ruins, almost anything they produced would sell; for the new Midget this was certainly to prove the case.

Production of the TC started slowly, with much effort needed just to locate sufficient materials and organise the manufacture of parts before the cars could start rolling off the lines in any quantity. Colour choice was limited to Black, but upholstery could be in Vellum Beige, Shires Green or Regency Red leather. This was a purely temporary measure, and by June 1946 Regency Red and Shires Green had joined Black as options for the paintwork. The interior of red cars was red and the green cars green, but Black cars were still available with any of the three previous colour options. By 1948 the colours available were extended to include Sequoia Cream and Clipper Blue, with the same range of upholstery options. Green cars could have either green or beige trim, red cars either red or beige, cream cars red or green, but blue cars were only fitted with beige trim. As previously, buyers of black cars could choose any of the three colours.

So what is the TC like to drive? For those used to modern saloons or sports cars the first thing you notice is that getting into a TC requires practice. With the doors hinged at the back it is necessary to approach the seat rather differently, and taller drivers can easily get part of their anatomy jammed under the steering wheel rim. However, once in the car most find that there is sufficient room provided the seat is set well back. Adjusting this does involve a degree of co-ordination between driver and passenger as both the seat bases

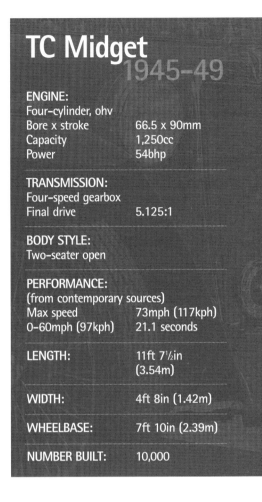

TC Midget 1945-49

ENGINE:
Four-cylinder, ohv

Bore x stroke	66.5 x 90mm
Capacity	1,250cc
Power	54bhp

TRANSMISSION:
Four-speed gearbox

Final drive	5.125:1

BODY STYLE:
Two-seater open

PERFORMANCE:
(from contemporary sources)

Max speed	73mph (117kph)
0–60mph (97kph)	21.1 seconds

LENGTH: 11ft 7½in (3.54m)

WIDTH: 4ft 8in (1.42m)

WHEELBASE: 7ft 10in (2.39m)

NUMBER BUILT: 10,000

The timeless good looks of the TC are exhibited by this well-maintained example. The radiator grille was always painted to match the upholstery colour, in this case red. This car has been fitted with 7-inch (179mm) sealed beam headlight units within the original 8-inch (203mm) shells; even in the 1950s this was a popular modification.

must be moved together; the seat backrest can be adjusted once the wing nuts on the brackets attached to both rear wheel arches have been slackened. The bench seat is surprisingly comfortable and the wide range of adjustment enables most drivers to find just the right combination of seat base and backrest position to make even quite long journeys a pleasure. Some restored cars, however, have poorly shaped and inadequately padded reproduction seats.

The brake master cylinder is fixed to the chassis and the brake pedal sprouts from the floor alongside the direct-acting clutch pedal. The accelerator pedal is pivoted to the firewall and has a roller instead of a conventional pad. Simultaneous operation of the brake and throttle pedals is easy, but there is no place

to rest the left foot, save on the clutch pedal, the whole area being a little restricted for those wearing large shoes. The original steering wheel was a black-covered, three-spoked affair, but the majority of cars seem now to be fitted with Bluemel 'Brooklands' wheels, quite acceptable as these were period accessories used on many TCs from new.

Although the driver sits low in the cockpit, with the car open one is immediately aware that the top edges of the doors fall away quite steeply. Those more used to having higher doors and winding side windows to protect them from the elements will initially feel a little exposed, but this feeling passes as the car becomes more familiar. The amount of wind that works its way past that small screen must have worried drivers, as pivoting 'windwings' fixed to the sides of the windscreen were popular accessories. A better solution is to leave the sidescreens in place in cold weather; these stow in a felt-lined compartment at the rear of the luggage area, and with them installed the cockpit is very snug. The lowered hood and frame remain attached to the rear of the body and are covered by the standard half-tonneau cover, a neat touch being the provision of slots at the sides to allow it to remain in place with the rear side screens erected. A full tonneau cover was an optional extra.

Sports cars are built more to give pleasure to the driver than to provide a means of transport, and the layout of the instruments and minor controls is a very important element in separating them from everyday machinery. In this area MGs seldom

disappoint and the TC dashboard is particularly pleasing with the large tachometer placed ahead of the driver and the speedometer on the left-hand side of the dashboard. The other instruments and switches are set in a central panel that is neatly sculptured to mirror the shape of the dashboard. The attractive, chromed map-reading lamp and 30mph warning light, set on each side of the centre panel, add to the appeal.

For the driver, it is the view past the close-set dashboard, delicately shaped to follow the curvaceous double-humped scuttle, that most excites. The starter pull operates a cable attached to a switch fixed directly on the starter motor, while the mixture knob alongside richens the twin SU carburettors. Less familiar to many is the slow running

The one-piece bench seat is remarkably comfortable. The half-tonneau cover neatly encloses the luggage area and the leather patches on this surround holes that are provided to allow the rear sidescreens to be fitted with the cover in place.

EAJ 591

Although the body on the TC was larger than on earlier Midgets, the space behind the seats was really only large enough to take a small amount of luggage. The twin rear stop/tail lights, and the flashing indicators, are modern requirements – a single D-shaped lamp sufficed when the car was built.

control. On the TC the mixture control does not raise the idle speed when it is pulled; this is achieved by winding out the slow running control knob.

On the move, the long bonnet bobs up and down as the tautly sprung chassis follows every road bump; the chromed radiator cap, separate headlamps and neat side lights gently vibrate in tune with the buzzing engine. Magic indeed! With the engine being firmly rubber-mounted to the chassis, some vibration is also transmitted through the steering wheel and body, and can also be felt through the clutch pedal as this is mounted directly to the bell-housing. The clutch has a smooth, snatch-free action and the engine revs freely and is quite capable of keeping up with modern traffic, aided by a superb gearbox, which has well spaced ratios and synchromesh on all but first gear. Changes can be made fairly quickly, but if rushed too much the gear teeth will protest.

The standard TC rear axle ratio gives just under 16mph (26kph) per 1,000 revs in top gear. A popular modification is to fit the TA rear axle ratio (4.875:1), which gives nearly 1mph extra per 1,000 revs. As the engine spins so freely it is quite comfortable cruising at around 4,000rpm, although a careful watch on the oil pressure gauge is prudent as a fracture of one of the vulnerable oil pipes, a not uncommon occurrence, could lead to the rapid loss of a sump full of oil. The absence of a fuel gauge could be a worry, but a warning lamp on the right-hand

side of the dashboard starts to flash when about three gallons are left in the tank, remaining permanently lit when this falls below two gallons.

The bench seats insulate the driver and passenger quite well from bumpy roads. The ride is firm, and the beam front axle is not as forgiving as independent front suspension. However, the car holds the road well in spite of having narrow-section, 19-inch (483mm) wheels and tyres. The Bishop Cam steering box on the TC does suffer from wear; a good TC will have a small amount of free movement at the steering wheel but will steer accurately, and, although heavy when parking, the steering lightens up at speed. The car will not be upset by smaller bumps provided that the front axle is straight, is fitted correctly, and the taper wedges installed by the factory to later TCs are removed. Removing the wedges may be controversial, but many find that the greater degree of self-centring that this gives the TC steering is of benefit. Worn dampers, steering gearbox and track rod ends can, however, make a TC very difficult to drive.

Although the TC feels different from more modern sports cars, it is still an easy car to master and enjoy. Like many cars of pre-war design, the steering is certainly the weak point with most TCs, requiring the driver to take account of large bumps and changes in the camber of the road, especially on corners. In spite of this, driving the car gives great satisfaction and, as confidence builds, it is surprising how quickly a good TC can be hustled along winding roads. The brakes are good, although they do need a hard push on the pedal, and the 'fly-off' handbrake is satisfying to use; the button on the end of the lever is pressed to set the brakes, while to free them the lever is merely pulled upwards and released.

Now to actual performance. Although road tests carried out by the

motoring magazines in the 1940s were nowhere near as comprehensive as they are today, the published results do make interesting reading. A report carried in *The Autocar* for October 1945 said that the top speed was 80mph (129kph), but when a full test was carried out by *The Motor* in 1947 they gave the timed maximum speed as 72.9mph (117kph) with the windscreen erect. Acceleration to

The mechanical simplicity and pre-war styling of the TC recall an earlier age of sporting motoring

60mph (97kph) took 21.1 seconds, hardly quick now but quite fast for a 1,250cc car in 1947. Typically, fuel consumption was around 30mpg. To give some comparison for the performance figures, it was not uncommon for the average small family car of the time to take as long as 45 seconds to reach 50mph (80kph), giving the sports car quite an advantage on uncluttered roads. All the contemporary tests speak of the good roadholding and handling of the car, something still apparent once the rather different feel of the TC has been mastered.

There were a number of changes made to the TC during the four years it was in production. While none were in any way major, they are significant when looking to see just how well, and accurately, a particular car may have been restored. Like most other classic cars, the most valuable TCs are those that are either totally original, or have been restored to as near original condition as possible. With many of the cars having undergone a number of rebuilds in their long life, much of the original car might have been replaced over

The Le Mans TC

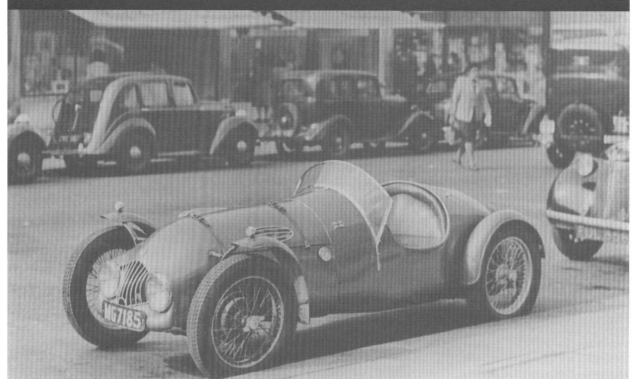

Autosport journalist and photographer George Phillips had bought a TC from University Motors and started using it in competition, but without a lot of success. Frustrated by this, he first tried to improve the power output to make the car faster, before deciding that more drastic measures were needed. The TC is a heavy car, a lot of the weight being accounted for by the body tub and the large wings. Phillips stripped the car down to the chassis over the winter and disposed of the bodywork, replacing this with a lightweight, streamlined body built by Harry Lester, with cycle wings.

To make the car reliable, a full mechanical rebuild was undertaken and the engine modified. The changes included fitting larger valves and stronger valve springs and having the crankshaft and pistons balanced by Laystall. In spite of now having a much faster car, he found at first that race entries were hard to obtain as most events were

oversubscribed. However, he did manage to enter the car in the Manx Cup and various sprints before driving it in a 12-hour race at Montlhéry, near Paris, where the car finished fourth in class.

He then ambitiously decided that he would like to drive it in the 24-hour sports car race at Le Mans and luckily secured an entry in the 1949 event. The TC special was fitted with headlamps, required as the race ran through the night, and these were neatly blended into the front of the body. A special curved windscreen provided a modicum of protection from the elements.

Driven to the circuit by George and his wife, Barbara, the car performed faultlessly for most of the race before breaking down some distance from the pits while being driven by co-driver Dryden. Owing to a misinterpretation of the instructions, the car was disqualified after

The Le Mans TC driven by George Phillips.

receiving outside assistance – quite a disappointment after all that effort.

In 1950 the car was again entered for the race, and this time George and co-driver Eric Winterbottom were rewarded by finishing second in the 1,500cc class after averaging 73mph (117kph) for the whole 24 hours. This was quite an achievement for a private entry, especially with an engine of just 1,250cc. The car also competed in many other races, in the hands of George Phillips and later owners. These efforts brought George into close contact with the MG factory and he was to drive factory-entered cars in a number of events. For the 1951 Le Mans Abingdon built up a TD chassis fitted with a streamlined body that looked very like that eventually used in 1955 for the MGA.

The cockpit of the TC is very comfortable for both driver and passenger. The bench seat has a wide range of adjustment and all the controls are well placed. The speedometer sits ahead of the passenger, leaving him or her to worry about the speed while the driver concentrates on the all-important tachometer.

the years and often these replacements do not match the components on the car when it left the factory.

To illustrate this, look at the situation of the later TCs built especially for the American market. These carried the EX-U chassis plate designation and incorporated a number of significant changes in specification to suit them for use in that country. For direction indicators, relays were incorporated that flashed the front side lights and the special rear stop/tail lamps mounted on either side of the petrol tank when a dashboard-mounted switch was operated. Smaller headlights were fitted so that sealed beam units could be installed to comply with American regulations. There was no fog lamp and the front-mounted horn was replaced by two-tone units fitted under the bonnet. The instrument

panel was slightly changed to reflect the electrical modifications. To protect against parking knocks, there were bumpers front and rear, with the one at the back having a central MG badge. A numberplate lamp was also fitted. Unfortunately a number of these rare versions of the TC have later been restored to standard specification by owners who did not realise that they were built this way by the factory.

The fabric-covered dashboard of a late model TC. Note that the instrument panel is painted tan, while on earlier cars with a wood-veneered dashboard it was black. On either side of the centre panel are lamps: that on the left is a map-reading light, lit by turning the chromed cover, while that on the right is the 30mph warning light.

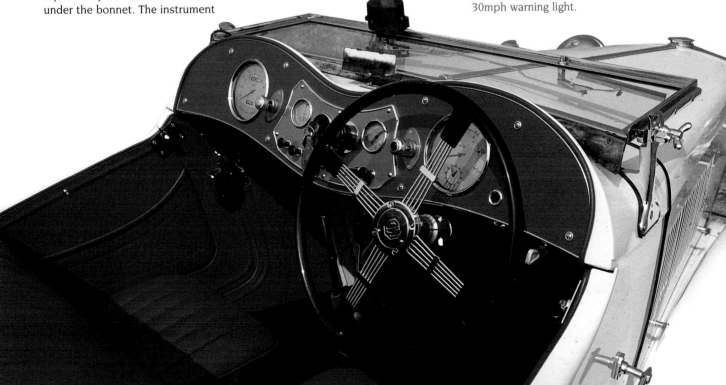

With the battery placed in a box on the bulkhead, space was found behind it for a tool compartment, accessible from either side of the car. This TC has the later, smaller voltage regulator and a heat shield for the carburettors.

The most noticeable change to the specification of the standard TC came after about half of the total number of cars had been built. The exact chassis numbers for each and every change are not recorded, but in general terms it is safe to say that the cars built before mid-1948 had the attractive, walnut-veneered dashboard, while those built later had them covered in fabric to match the upholstery, with a change from black to tan for the bases of the dash lamps and the centre of the instrument panel; incidentally, the fixing studs for this remained black. About the same time as this change was made, a modification in production methods saw the firewall/bulkhead receiving shallower pressed flutes, and it was now painted to match the body colour, rather than grey/green. Also from that time the engine was painted dark red rather than grey.

Around chassis number TC 1850 the headlights changed from those with the flat, pre-war type of glasses to some with much more rounded glass that incorporated diamond-pattern diffusers. At chassis TC 4739 the spot lamp changed from a Lucas FT27 (the type with a raised rim) to the more rounded SFT463 lamp. Early hoods seemed to be black, while these and the tonneau cover were later made from tan material. Early cars had twin rear windows and later cars single ones.

All these small changes are of far more importance when a car is to be shown in concours events than when it is just being driven for enjoyment. With the alterations being relatively insignificant, it is far more likely that the general mechanical and body condition of the car, and the way it drives, will separate a good TC from a bad one. A TC that performs well and looks right is a joy to own. Its mechanical simplicity and pre-war styling recalls an earlier age of sporting motoring, which can be enjoyed without any of the problems associated with running a car for which spare parts are more difficult to obtain.

The tachometer is cable-driven from the dynamo through an often troublesome gearbox. The aluminium rocker cover is a later accessory, although a small number of cars left the factory with similar ones fitted.

Buying Hints

1. TCs are fairly plentiful with quite a number for sale at any one time, so there is no pressure to buy the first car viewed.

2. Chassis rusting is seldom a problem with cars that have been in constant use, but look for accident damage; this is difficult with body and wings in place, but possible if a ramp is available. The front axle beam and chassis dumb irons often suffer and occasionally the chassis can be 'out of square'. Rectification of most chassis problems is only possible with the car dismantled.

3. XPAG engines leak oil and seepage is to be expected on most cars; however, look for signs of heavy leakage from the bottom of the bell-housing as this indicates that it is getting past the rear main bearing, and repairs will require removal of the engine. The good news is that a modern lip seal kit has been developed to effect a permanent cure. Leakage from the front of the crankshaft is easily remedied by fitting a lip seal to the timing chain cover.

4. The bodywork is continually stressed by chassis flexing, as well as suffering from the wood rot and rust usual with this type of construction. Look at the fit of doors and also see that the locks hold them closed on bumpy roads. Rocking the rear door pillars will reveal weak woodwork. Some rubbing of the paintwork around the door frame and edges of the bonnet top and sides is inevitable and can be ignored.

5. The line and fit of the wings and running boards are vitally important. Some replacement wings are badly made and running boards have the wrong profile. Looking down each side of the car from the front will

The TC chassis.

verify that both sides match or reveal misalignment. A number of slightly differing wing shapes were produced by the factory, and fitting a car with one early and one later wing would look a little odd.

6. On the road the car should steer straight and true and should not feel is if it wants to veer off course every time it hits a bump. The engine should pull well and the gearbox and back axle should not be excessively noisy. Wheel bearings and king pins can be checked with the car jacked up; remember that front

stub axles do fail and should be crack tested as a matter of course when a car is rebuilt.

7. Most of the main engine components – crankshafts, bearings, pistons, valves, camshafts, etc – are available. Valve gear wear is common, but ignore the minor tappet noise usual from this unit. Vaporisation with modern fuels can cause misfiring, but a heat shield and brass rather than plastic valves in the float chambers will cure this.

The Y-Type *saloon*

If the TC was built in the tradition of early 1930s sports car design, the first saloon to emerge from Abingdon after the war was altogether a product of a more modern age. That said, the car was still about eight years late arriving, as the basic design work had been completed during 1938 and 1939; the car was due for launch around the time that all car production ceased for the factory to convert to building the tools of war.

In 1938 it was realised that a new small MG saloon would be a desirable addition to the range and work commenced at Cowley on a car that was provisionally called the MG Ten.

At that time Alec Issigonis and Jack Daniels had been working on an independent front suspension layout for a proposed new Morris Ten, but eventually this was not used on the grounds of cost. However, it was thought that the sort of person attracted to buying an MG would not be averse to paying a little extra to gain the advantages offered by the new suspension, so a prototype chassis was constructed.

To keep costs to a minimum, the Morris parts bins were raided to provide many of the other components. The engine was from the Morris Ten, as also used for the TB

The neat and attractive lines of the YA saloon ensure a loyal following for these comfortable little cars. This original low-mileage example has a 1951 Festival of Britain car badge on the front. These were available at the time for 27s 6d (£1.38p), but would cost rather more now!

Midget, and most of the main pressings for the body, including the doors, were taken from the Morris 8 Series E with only minor modifications. The wings, boot panels, bonnet and running boards were specially made for the MG. Pictures of this prototype reveal that it differed only in detail from the car eventually built in 1947.

Once car assembly had resumed at Abingdon, the plans of the MG Ten were brought out of mothballs and work resumed on preparing it for production. The chassis consisted of welded, closed box-section side rails and tubular cross members. The side rails ran under the rear axle, which was suspended on leaf springs and had a Panhard rod for lateral location. At the front a pressed steel cross member housed the coil springs, and provided a mounting for the rack-and-pinion steering gear. There were lower wishbones and the arms of the Girling shock absorbers provided the upper mountings for the swivel pins. The car was fitted with 16-inch (406mm) pressed steel wheels.

By 1947 the TC Midget had been in production for a couple of years and was starting to build up export markets for MG, which would benefit the saloon once it appeared. There were some mechanical similarities between the two cars, although for the most part the new car used more modern components. The Y-Type was powered by a single-carburettor variant of the XPAG engine fitted to the TC. In this form the power output was reduced from the 54.4bhp produced in TC guise to just 46.6bhp.

One of the most appealing aspects of the Y-Type was the interior. Leather seats and polished woodwork were attractively presented, and sufficient creature comforts existed to reassure buyers that they owned a car that was a bit special, and worth the price premium. The new saloon was identifiably an MG. In addition to driving behind that handsome

radiator, drivers were faced with a dashboard layout that used octagonal surrounds to conceal ordinary round instruments.

For the paintwork, there was a wide choice. Some cars were finished in two-tone colour schemes by

The Y-Type quickly gained popularity as a thoroughly modern small MG saloon

employing the simple expedient of fitting wings and running boards painted in one of the other colours. The basic colours were black, light green, dark green, red, cream and grey. The duo-tone cars were usually supplied with the lighter colour for the body and the darker for the wings. To complement the exterior colours there was a choice of maroon, beige or green upholstery that featured an attractive pattern of pleated panels on the seat faces. In 1947 the price of this luxury small saloon was £525, plus £146 11s 8d purchase tax.

The Y-Type quickly gained popularity and acceptance as a thoroughly modern small MG saloon but built in the tradition of the pre-war cars. Initially there were no open versions as the factory was hard pressed to construct sufficient saloons to meet the worldwide demand. However, once things settled down a bit there was more incentive to build what customers wanted, and by 1948 the factory felt that there was a demand for an open version of the Y-Type to give buyers a four-seater alternative to the TC sports car that shared the production lines at Abingdon with the saloon.

The company were obviously limited by cost considerations when designing the open version of the

YA/YB Saloon
1947–53

ENGINE:
Four-cylinder, ohv

Bore x stroke	66.5 x 90mm
Capacity	1,250cc
Power	46.6bhp (tourer 54bhp)

TRANSMISSION:
Four-speed gearbox

Final drive	5.143:1 (YA)
	5.125:1 (YB)

BODY STYLES:
Four-seater, four-door saloon, and four-seater, two-door open tourer

PERFORMANCE:
(from contemporary sources)

Max speed	70mph (113kph)
0–60mph (97kph)	27 seconds

LENGTH:	13ft 5⅙in (4.1m)
WIDTH:	4ft 10¼in (1.48m)
WHEELBASE:	8ft 3in (2.51m)

NUMBERS BUILT:

YA	6,158
YB	1,301
YT	877

The interior is one of the most appealing aspects of the Y-Type saloon. Leather seats and abundant wood make the cabin feel very luxurious and up-market, as if it were a sort of miniature Bentley of the day.

Y-Type and could not consider using a totally new body. However, while sharing the front and rear wings, bonnet and bootlid with the saloon, in other respects the tourer bodies differed considerably. The rear section of the body was identical around the boot and spare wheel compartments, but had longer quarter panels to carry the hinge post for the rear-hung doors. The doors themselves were longer than those on the saloons, to give easy access to the rear seats. In line with sporting car fashion of the time, the top edges of both doors were 'cut away' to give driver and front-seat passenger additional elbow room.

The scuttle area of the body was, again, quite different. To give the car the appeal of a sports car, the traditional double humps and folding windscreen used on the TC were incorporated into the YT body. Also transferred was the dashboard, which looked the same as that on the two-seater: fabric-covered to match the upholstery with a large tachometer in front of the driver and matching speedometer placed in front of the passenger. The minor dials and the switches were all contained in a central panel, like the one used on the TC.

Mechanically the cars differed in detail. The chassis was slightly modified and carried a different part number. The tourer was lighter than the saloon, so different rear springs were fitted and the steering rack and column were changed. The open tourer needed something more sporting than the saloon, so it gained an engine similar to that used in the TC, complete with twin carburettors and modified camshaft. The dynamo had a drive for the tachometer, the saloon having been restricted solely to a speedometer. For the American market the YT was fitted with flashing direction indicators, these being incorporated within the front

sidelights by means of double-filament bulbs and at the rear by interrupting the brake light circuit with relays when the indicators were required. In other export markets the flashing direction indicators were not fitted.

The interior space was identical to that in the saloon, except that the rear-seat passengers had their elbow room slightly reduced by the pockets used to store the hood irons. The front seats could be tipped up to gain access to the rear. When the hood was lowered, the hood and frame were kept in a compartment that extended round each side of and behind the rear seat, where it was concealed by zip-fastened flaps. The rear window could be lowered to provide additional ventilation with the hood erect. The tourer provided accommodation for four in reasonable comfort, but the production run was short – fewer than 800 in total – and survivors are comparatively rare. As the majority of cars were exported, it is in countries like America and Australia that one is most likely to find the cars now. However, interest in Britain and Europe has seen quite a number of cars repatriated in recent years.

By the end of 1951 the Y-Type had been in production for over four years and was now sharing space at Abingdon with a new Midget two-seater sports car. The TD had been introduced in 1949 and, being based on a modified Y-Type chassis, shared many components with the saloon. However, the mechanical specification of some parts had been changed for the sports car and, to harmonise production, a number of alterations to the Y-Type were introduced late in 1951.

Actually, although the revised car looked externally little changed, the modifications were extensive, fully justifying a change of model name to YB. Most importantly, the braking system and running gear were brought up to date and rationalised with the TD. The Lockheed brakes fitted to the

YA were little different from those used on the TA/TB/TC, having just one hydraulic cylinder for each front brake drum. The YB, however, had a twin-leading-shoe system, with two cylinders for each front brake drum, the front brake drums being integral with the hubs.

At the same time, the YB was fitted with the more modern Nuffield hypoid back axle, which was potentially much quieter in use. The steel road wheels were changed from 16 inches (406mm) to 15 inches (381mm) in diameter and the tyres increased in width from 5.00/5.25 to 5.50 section. A front anti-roll bar and heavier-duty rear shock absorbers were introduced to improve roadholding, and the Panhard rod at the rear was deleted. As a result of the mechanical changes some body modifications were required. The smaller wheels took up rather less space under the rear wings, so these were made slightly

The YT is a useful four-seater open car for the family man. Most of the output was exported, mainly to America and Australia. All the tourers were of YA specification.

deeper, something that is quite apparent when viewed from the side of the car. To accommodate the wider tyres the spare wheel stowage compartment was made an inch taller.

On the road both versions of the saloon feel similar to drive, although the observant will notice the better braking and reduced body roll of the YB. Stepping out of a modern saloon and into the driving seat of any Y-Type, one is immediately struck by the apparent lack of room in the cabin. Actually this is not as bad as it at first feels and there is quite good headroom, and enough rearward seat adjustment, to cater for all but the tallest of drivers. The body is quite narrow by modern standards and bulky coats and heavy footwear are best avoided. The attractive leather seats are comfortable, if a little

The YB has smaller wheels and deeper-section wings. The improvements made to the specification when this model was announced make it the preferred choice for many enthusiasts.

upright, but they offer little in the way of side support when cornering.

However, whatever shortcomings there are in the amount of space in the front of the car are more than made up for by the appeal of the interior appointments. There is quite a bit of woodwork inside a Y-Type and the two octagonal instruments look very appealing set in the polished-wood dashboard. The speedometer on the right of the steering column has both a trip reading and an inset electric clock, while on the left is a combined ammeter, oil pressure gauge and petrol gauge. Just above the ignition key is a press button for the starter. It is surprising how satisfying it is to turn on the ignition and hear the frantic ticking of the single SU fuel pump before pressing a button to start the engine – quite

Although the modest output of the 1,250cc engine ensures that really sparkling performance is lacking, a good Y-Type has no difficulty in keeping up with modern traffic on ordinary roads. High-speed motorway travel is not an option for a standard car!

different from a modern car. On the move the 1,250cc engine pulls well, aided by low overall gearing. Some vibration from the engine is transmitted through the gear lever, and you are always aware of just how hard it is working to propel a car that weighs well over a ton when laden. Nevertheless, the 'Y' has no difficulty in keeping up with traffic flows on city and urban roads, although high-speed cruising on motorways is impractical with a standard car. An ideal cruising speed is around 55mph (88kph) when the engine is revolving at 3,370rpm.

The overall gearing of the YB is slightly lower. The gear lever is longer than on the TC but still has a precise action, making pleasurable the frequent gear changes necessary to maintain a reasonable average speed.

Synchromesh on the upper three ratios is good, although fast changes down the gears need some care.

The steering is heavy at parking speeds but lightens nicely on the move. The car steers straight, with very little kick-back through the adjustable steering wheel, and the rack-and-pinion mechanism means that there is no lost motion in the system. Some modern radial tyres suit the car very well; here the YB owners have far greater choice as the smaller wheel sizes are more readily available. Some owners still prefer the feel of the car on the original-type cross-ply tyres. While the ride is firm by modern standards, and bumps and potholes make themselves all too evident, the car rides well and provides comfort for driver and passengers. It bobs up

Competition Y-Types

At first glance the Y-Type does not look a likely competition car – too tall, too slow, too heavy, and far better suited to a trip to the shops than an international rally or production car race. However, Y-Types were driven competitively (and a few still are) and they fared rather better than their paper specification would lead you to expect, their lack of power being compensated for by handling and roadholding that were in advance of much of the competition.

The Monte Carlo Rally was the premier rally in the early post-war years and attracted a sizeable entry from Britain. In 1950 experienced rally driver Betty Haig teamed up with Barbara Marshall to enter a Y-Type in what turned out to be the most difficult Monte Carlo Rally thus far. Only five cars reached the final control without penalty and the MG

was not one of them, having been involved in an accident early in the event. The following year another Y-Type, driven by Major and Mrs. Pownall, was one of the Glasgow starters and this time the car did make the finish, being placed 45th overall.

On the racing circuit the name most associated with the Y-Type is Dick Jacobs. Dick was the proprietor of an MG dealership, Mill Garage, and had become involved in racing MGs. In 1950 Y-Type components were used in the construction of a lightweight, aluminium-bodied special that Dick raced, but it was the YB saloon he entered in the BRDC Production Touring Car race at Silverstone that was to become better known. With the car but two weeks old, and still in standard trim, he won his class against stiff opposition from the Jowett team. In the same car he was

Reg Holt completes the Hastings tests in the 1953 *Daily Express* Rally.

to repeat the trick for the following two years, a pretty remarkable feat. Jacobs also obtained the last Y-Type chassis, which he fitted with a full-width fibreglass coupé body.

The best-known of the British rallies was the RAC event, which, in the 1950s, consisted of long road sections and a series of special driving tests held on race circuits and seaside promenades. In the 1951 event Len Shaw entered the former Haig car and was placed third in class, first in class going to Jim Readings in another Y-Type. For the 1953 event a team of three YBs was entered by the factory. Driven by Len Shaw, Reg Holt and Geoff Holt, the cars took the team award, with the car driven by Len Shaw placed sixth overall against strong opposition.

The spare wheel stows in the compartment below the bootlid. On the YB the locker is deeper to accommodate the wider-section tyres.

and down readily on bumpy roads, and the rear suspension on a laden car can meet the bump stops or thump down on to the underslung chassis over humps in the road.

The Y-Type corners well but will lift a rear wheel and oversteer if provoked. In practice the degree of body roll, and poor location in the seat, encourages the driver to adopt more sedate driving manners. However, the view over the bonnet, with separate wings and vibrating headlamps, evokes cars of an earlier age, making the driver feel that he is in charge of something special.

Rear-seat passengers are provided with plenty of space and there is a central arm rest to stop them sliding about during energetic cornering. A blind for the rear window is operated by a ring pull by the driver's door, and the sun roof gives added ventilation for all the occupants on hot days, while the windscreen can be wound outwards at the bottom to give even more fresh air. A recirculating heater was available as an extra and is worth contemplating if much winter driving is undertaken. However, one of the worst things about cold weather travel in any car of this age is the way the windows mist up, or freeze over, in low temperatures. All manner of helpful devices were on offer in the 1950s – small window heaters, Perspex stick-on panels, etc – when winter travel was certainly more of an adventure.

The open YT has altogether a different character. Performance is certainly improved by having the

The built-in jacking system is operated from under the bonnet and either the front or rear of the car, or both ends together, can be raised off the ground for wheel changing.

Coachbuilt Y-Types

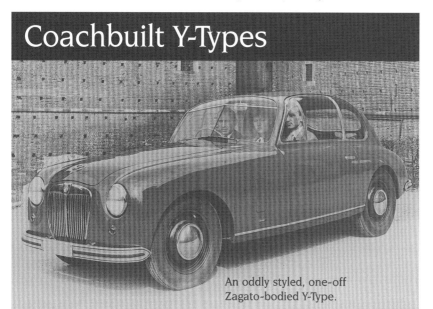

An oddly styled, one-off Zagato-bodied Y-Type.

The Y-Type's separate chassis frame made it a suitable subject for specialist coachwork. Consequently some cars were sold in chassis form, mainly to continental customers because of restrictions in those countries on the import of complete cars. In Switzerland the rules were imposed to protect the local coachbuilding industry and this resulted in the emergence there of some Y-Types with attractive coachwork.

Reinbolt and Christé constructed a number of cars for the Swiss MG importers and distributors J. H. Keller. At the 1949 Geneva Motor Show, a two-door drophead coupé with long, flowing front wings, built-in headlamps and elegant lines appeared on the Keller stand and gained third place in the concours

competition. They also built two- and four-seater tourers, the latter similar to the factory YT but with a fixed windscreen. The two-seater car had cut-away doors and TC-style dashboard, windscreen, seats, hood and sidescreens.

In 1948 American businessman Roger Barlow of International Motors decided to offer the customers of his Californian company re-bodied Y-Types. He visited the MG factory in England and the Milan coachworks of Zagato and a prototype was commissioned. A Y-Type chassis was modified and shipped to Italy where Zagato fitted coupé bodywork of unusual design with sharply curved side windows and windscreen. The styling was not to everyone's taste and the project seems to have gone no further.

twin-carburettor engine and lighter weight. The sports-car-style dashboard and folding windscreen impart a different feel to the car and it can be hurried along minor roads at a pretty fair rate. It still rolls a bit, and the gearing is still too low, but with the roof down it is very pleasant to drive.

The contemporary road tests reveal that a YA took 27 seconds to reach 60mph (97kph) in 1947, and a top speed of around 70mph (113kph) was recorded. A YB tested four years later was no quicker, and modern owners looking for greater performance would do well to consider fitting a cylinder head with larger valves, twin carburettors, 'pancake' air cleaners, and an exhaust system with a slightly larger bore. This will make the car a little noisier but certainly a lot quicker. A popular period tuning aid was supercharging, which improved both the power and the flexibility of the engine. However, tuned or not, a Y-Type makes a pleasant vehicle for those looking for a car with four seats in which to enjoy 1940s-style motoring.

Buying Hints

1. As so many Y-Types have been scrapped, choice is limited. However, with restoration costs for a poor example far exceeding its resale value, it is vital that any car be carefully inspected before purchase – the cheapest may not prove the most economical in the long run.

2. The changes introduced with the YB make this the preferred choice, but as they were less plentiful than the earlier model, to restrict the search to the later cars may prove a mistake.

3. Buying a dismantled car for restoration is the cheapest initially and will suit the person with the necessary skills and facilities to undertake the vast amount of work such a project requires. Always make sure that all the components are with the car and that they are the correct type for the model.

4. Mechanically, given all the original parts, there is little that cannot be repaired or replaced. The basic cylinder block must be in good order, but most of the internal components can be found new or second-hand. Crankshafts must be crack-tested as many originals are now suspect. Batches of pistons, bearings, etc, are made from time to time. Always check that a matched set of con-rods is used and that these are carefully checked.

5. The chassis is strong but can rust badly, especially at the back and around the body-mounting outriggers. Any car with a severely rusted chassis is best ignored. Accident damage is not always easy to spot and can be expensive to repair.

6. Banging noises from the back on a test drive can mean that rust has caused the back of the body to part company with the chassis. The rear of the car is particularly susceptible to corrosion and should be carefully examined from the rear door pillars backwards. Look closely at the floor of the spare wheel compartment and its cover, the bootlid and hinge panel, and the wheel arches, which also provide mounting points for the wings.

7. Check the floor, the lower part of the body and the doors carefully for signs of rust or poor repairs. Repairs are difficult and new panels pressed from the original tooling are not available. Some body sections are available – sills, rear floor, bottoms of doors, etc – and these are helpful, but being largely hand-made some adjustments are usually needed to make them fit.

The uncluttered under-bonnet layout makes working on the car easy. Some Y-Types have been converted to twin carburettors to improve power output, and this is a sensible option for those not too worried by originality. All YT tourers had the higher-performance engine.

8. Interior trim is often in a repairable condition and trim kits for completely new interiors are available. These are expensive and it is all too easy to overlook this when working out how much it will cost to restore a car.

9. Fully restored cars, or perfectly preserved originals, do not come on the market often and when they do they are well worth considering in view of the high cost of restoration work.

The TD *midget*

The last of the MG sports cars to have separate headlights, the TD is a pleasing blend of pre-war styling and post-war comfort and handling. Although it is the cheapest of the T-Series cars, it is by no means second best.

For some reason sports car buyers are often credited with being conservative, preferring tradition over innovation in their choice of car. When the TC was introduced as the new 1945 MG, motoring journalists praised the fact that it was little changed from the pre-war cars that had earned the company such a good reputation. They ignored the drawbacks of its simple beam axle and cart spring suspension, not to mention its archaic steering box. To judge from the majority of contemporary articles, it seemed that the company could go on building them for ever and still find willing buyers. That, however, was far from the truth, as sales would have undoubtedly fallen away as more sophisticated rival sports cars appeared.

Because they sell in smaller volumes than mainstream family cars, it is in the interests of manufacturers to keep specialist cars in production for long periods without major change. A look at many popular sports cars produced over the years reveals that they often lagged far behind more outwardly mundane machinery in terms of technical innovation – a situation that still occurs today. When the Y-Type saloon was introduced in 1947, it immediately made the TC look old-fashioned. The ride and roadholding of the saloon was ahead of the sports car – only its weight, lack of power and perpendicular

FP 5188

TD Midget 1949–53

ENGINE:
Four–cylinder, ohv
Bore x stroke	66.5 x 90mm
Capacity	1,250cc
Power	54.4bhp

TRANSMISSION:
Four–speed gearbox
Final drive	5.125:1

BODY STYLE:
Two–seater open sports

PERFORMANCE:
(from contemporary sources)
Max speed	78mph (126kph)
0–60mph (97kph)	21.3 seconds

LENGTH:	12ft 1in (3.68m)
WIDTH:	4ft 10⅝in (1.49m)
WHEELBASE:	7ft 10in (2.39m)

TD Midget MkII

As TD Midget except:
Power	approx 60bhp
Final drive	usually 4.875:1
Max speed	81mph (130kph)
0–60mph (97kph)	16.5 seconds

NUMBER BUILT:
30,000 (including 1,710 MkIIs)

Although the smaller-sized disc wheels fitted to the TD were not universally popular when the car was announced, they are much easier to clean than the 19-inch (483mm) wire wheels fitted to the TC. This early car has plain wheels, while later TDs had the better-looking pierced wheels.

styling stopped it embarrassing them on the road. It was obvious that a redesign was long overdue and the strength of the overseas sales of the TC, especially in North America, made it imperative that any new car should be available with either right- or left-hand drive.

Poor management, and a lack of clear direction and funding for new models, was rife in the British motor industry at the time. Plans to build a new MG seemed slow to materialise from the Cowley Design Office, and it was the small team at Abingdon who provided the impetus for the TC replacement by constructing their own prototype. Initial experiments at the factory, where a shortened Y-Type chassis was

fitted with a TC body, proved the principle, and the drawings for the production car came from the Design Office at Cowley.

At the front the chassis was similar to the Y-Type, but at the rear the side rails swept over the axle, rather than beneath it. The car was designed to be built with the steering wheel on the left-hand side for some overseas markets, but each version of the chassis differed as the pedal box and pivot shaft mounting bush were welded in place. The Panhard rod used on the YA rear suspension was omitted and the rear axle itself was the modern hypoid unit later fitted to the YB saloon. The brakes also were much improved: twin leading shoes for the front drums provided greater efficiency and a 'fly-off' handbrake mounted on the central tunnel operated the rear brake shoes via twin cables. Like the saloon, pressed steel wheels replaced wire wheels. Then, as now, the TD wheels were controversial. For many, MG sports cars must have wire wheels, but these were never an option on the TD. After about 500 cars had been assembled,

The bulkier wings and extra width of the TD make the car look much more substantial than the TC. The styling is very attractive and wire wheels do nothing to improve the appearance of the car.

the appearance of the disc wheels was improved by having cooling holes punched in them.

The TD body was made roomier than the TC and the incorporation of a steel rear bulkhead behind the seats provided bracing for the rear door pillars. The rear wings bolted to captive nuts on the inner wings, an improvement over the wood screws used on TCs. The wider front and rear wings, the deeper rear fuel tank, and the neat valances covering the front and rear of the chassis, combined to give the TD a far more solid appearance than the previous model. A neat, rigid spare wheel mounting, and the chromed bumpers and overriders essential in overseas markets, also enhanced the appearance of the car. The spare wheel mounting frame was fixed at the lower end to the chassis and at

the top to the body, and incorporated a mounting for the rear numberplate.

The interior of the car would have seemed familiar to TC owners, but the wider cockpit provided more elbow room. The instrumentation and minor controls followed established T-Type practice, but the speedometer and tachometer were placed together in front of the driver and the TD was equipped with a combined choke and mixture control that both richened the mixture and increased the idle speed. The attractive trim was available in either red, green or tan leather, with the dashboard covered to match. A useful addition was the small glove box, which doubled up as the site for a valve radio if this was specified. There was some space behind the seats, but a luggage rack could be ordered when serious touring was contemplated. The sidescreens stowed in a compartment at the back of the luggage area and the hood gave adequate weather protection. Headroom was restricted for taller drivers, but was later improved with the adoption of a revised 'three bow' hood frame.

Initially, cars could be ordered with the exterior paintwork in black, red, ivory, blue and green. In 1951 the range of colours was increased to include a darker red and a bronze metallic. In 1952 the colours changed again, with black, red, ivory and the darker Woodland Green becoming the standard range, and a few cars were painted grey metallic. Green, red and tan upholstery were all available with black paintwork; red and tan with red paintwork; green and tan on the green cars; and red or green on the ivory cars. Bronze and grey cars had red upholstery. All hoods were tan Wigan cloth. Cars sent as kits for assembly overseas often had non-standard colour finishes.

The car was heavier, an increase of about 160lbs (73kg), but the engine

was virtually unchanged, so sporting performance was maintained by a reduction of the rear axle ratio, the miles per hour per 1,000 revs dropping to 14.4 (23.2kph), while the TC did 15.5 (25kph). The low gearing is the only feature of the TD to cause difficulties in modern conditions, and to overcome this many owners fit higher-ratio back axles. For the 1940s TC drivers transferring to a TD, the rack-and-pinion steering must have been the greatest improvement. It ideally suited the TD, giving precise steering and secure handling that is now enhanced by the ability to fit modern radial tyres to the 15-inch (381mm) wheels.

The contemporary motoring magazines bestowed high praise on the new car. The Autocar said, 'The Series TD may be new, but it still looks like an MG and has not gone all futuristic for which many thanks, people will say.' They recorded a time of 23.5 seconds to reach 60mph (97kph), a little slower than the rival The Motor magazine had recorded for the previous model, but when that magazine got their hands on the

All the right fittings for the 1950s sportsman – a folding windscreen, plenty of instruments, and just enough performance and style to enhance his appeal to the local young ladies!

The engine bay of an early TD.

same TD a few weeks later they recorded an improved time of 21.3 seconds.

MG owners have always wanted to use their cars competitively and have needed to extract the maximum performance from them. To cater for this, the factory issued special tuning booklets detailing how to achieve different stages of engine tune. Wanting to enter tuned TDs in competition as standard production cars, they also catalogued a tuned car as a separate model, calling it TD MkII. Previously cars could be ordered with any or all of the tuning modifications, but now most of these were incorporated into the MkII as a complete package.

There has always been some confusion over the MkII, and many ordinary cars fitted with engines carrying a 'TD2' engine prefix have been wrongly identified as MkIIs. The only reliable indication of a genuine car is the chassis number, which carries the prefix 'TD/c'. Externally, little distinguished the MkII from the standard model until late in the production run, when 'Mark II' badges were fitted to both sides of the bonnet and to a plinth on the rear bumper. At the same time, TF-style black and white octagons were fitted to the radiator and the spare wheel hub cap.

The MkII TD/c rolling chassis differed from a standard TD item. At the rear there were brackets fitted to take Andrex adjustable friction-type dampers, these being fitted in addition to the ordinary piston-type shock absorbers; holes in the suspension arms at the front served the same purpose. These units were a throw-back to an earlier age when friction dampers were commonly used. Adjustment of the internal friction discs was achieved by turning a bolt, inwards to tighten them and outwards to loosen them. Mounted on the suspension arms at the front, these dampers both increase the unsprung weight and make adding an anti-roll bar difficult. In competition their use seems to have been to stiffen the car against roll and harden the ride.

Optional rear axle ratios had always been available for the TD, but most MkIIs were delivered with a higher ratio as standard. The normal TD ratio was 5.125:1, but most MkIIs left Abingdon with 4.875:1 gearing. An even higher ratio, 4.55:1, was also an option, and it is this ratio, or 4.3:1

from an MGA, that modern owners prefer. Full advantage was taken of the higher gearing because all MkIIs had tuned engines. The cylinder head was fitted with larger valves and planed to increase the compression ratio. Larger 1½in carburettors replaced the 1¼in SUs, and twin fuel pumps with fully duplicated fuel lines ensured sufficient fuel under high-load/high-speed conditions. These changes raised the power output from 54bhp to around 60, making this, and the TF 1500 introduced later, the fastest of the T-Series cars.

The MkII was built throughout the production run of the TD and can have engines prefixed TD, TD2 or TD3. The TD3 engine was exclusive to the MkII and was only fitted to later versions of this model, the first of these going into chassis TD/c 17030. An external identifying feature of the

The performance MkII model had twin fuel pumps, fed from twin fuel lines. Both pumps supplied petrol to both carburettors, which were larger than those on the ordinary TD.

The later TD had pierced wheels. This is the extra-performance MkII, which had more power and modified suspension. There were no external badges to identify the model until late in the production run.

MkII was the bonnet right-hand side panel, which had a bulge to clear the larger carburettors; these had a larger inlet pipe and a different air cleaner, although some of the earliest MkIIs had no air cleaner.

Unlike many performance versions of other cars, there was little internally or externally to distinguish them from the standard TD. The cockpit was the same and bucket seats were not fitted except as a special order for competition use. Those requiring additional power could have their engine modified to a higher state of tune, and the XPAG engine could be

persuaded to give up to 50 per cent more power without becoming seriously unreliable. The unit often found its way into 1950s racing machinery, Lotus and Cooper being amongst a number to use it in their cars. In all, 1,710 MkIIs were built; just 51 of these were sold in Britain, so until some cars were repatriated in recent years they were comparatively rare.

The engine changes did give the car better performance and those with either of the available higher axle ratios installed are able to maintain higher average speeds than standard

The Arnolt TD

Of all the special-bodied MGs, the Arnolt stands head and shoulders above the others, both for the completeness of the design and for the relatively large numbers built. Although produced solely for the American market, it has since earned worldwide recognition. The Italian coachbuilder Bertone obtained two TD chassis and designed elegant coupé and convertible bodies for them. On display at the 1951 Turin Motor Show they caught the eye of Stanley Harold Arnolt II, who distributed British cars from his Chicago headquarters. He approached

Bertone with an order for a minimum of 100 cars of each type, although only just over half this number were built.

The TD chassis shipped to Bertone had cylinder heads with larger valves fitted, and were delivered from MG in small batches. Building the body on to the TD chassis was not simple. The main steel body frames were welded to the chassis, with the doors hinged on to the frames. Most of the body was steel, the doors, bonnet and boot being aluminium covered. This structure stiffened the TD chassis

considerably, although, surprisingly, the manufacturers quoted a mere 40lb (18kg) increase in weight.

The interior was lavishly trimmed, the rear compartment providing additional accommodation for small children. The engine installation and radiator were unchanged, but the engine compartment had louvred side panels and a different scuttle. The streamlined shape of the body resulted in lower drag, which helped to offset the extra weight.

The open and closed versions of the Arnolt TD.

cars. *Road and Track* compared the models in 1953 and found that the tuned car would reach 60mph (97kph) in 16.5 seconds against 19.4 for an ordinary TD. Top speed was up from 79.6 to 82.9mph (128 to 133kph). From experience, they felt that there would normally have been nearer 5mph (8kph) speed difference between the two models, their test cars not being entirely representative.

TDs are cheap practical and easy to drive even for those unused to older cars

During TD production quite a number of changes were made. The first 100 cars did not have a bracing hoop under the scuttle, almost all of these early cars being exported. Late TDs, that is those built during 1953, were fitted with Armstrong shock absorbers rather than Luvax-Girling, and the front wings had a bulge introduced to clear their greater bulk. After chassis 4251 the brake drums and hubs were combined into a single unit, with the one-piece hub and drum stronger, but difficult to remove without a puller.

With the engine the most significant change came with the 1951 introduction of the TD2 unit at engine 9408. The engine itself was unchanged, but the bell housing was modified to accept the larger 8-inch (203mm) clutch. Both the cylinder head and the block were changed to have round water passage holes at different times (block at 17969 and head at 22735), but the important point to note is that only the later heads accept long-reach plugs. Early cars have the TC oil pump, but from chassis 14224 the type with an integral oil filter was fitted. This later pump was a great improvement as it eliminated the need for external oil

filter pipes. Quite a number of early TDs will have had the later pump fitted and it is a sensible modification. Similarly worthwhile was the substitution of a rod linkage for the clutch, as the previous cable system sometimes failed.

Externally the most noticeable change on later cars is the adoption of circular rear lamps with a corresponding modification to the rear wings. Inside the car the dashboard layout remained basically unchanged, but the centre panel gained a combined oil pressure/water temperature gauge from TD 13914. In 1951 the speedometer and rev counter changed from the chronometric to magnetic instruments, the latter having dished rather than flat dials.

The TDs are easy cars to drive and even those quite unused to older cars quickly learn to handle them with confidence. They are practical, everyday sports cars quite suited to providing entertaining and enjoyable motoring for young and old alike. They are cheap and easy to run and well able to keep up with modern traffic on ordinary urban and rural roads. The MkII model cylinder head modifications with the larger valves are worthwhile for all TDs, but the larger 1½in carburettors less so, as the standard examples have quite large enough intakes at all but the highest engine speeds. Like all T-Types, the TD can suffer from fuel starvation when hot; this occurs when the fuel in the float chambers boils and the pressure created within them blocks the incoming fuel supply. This is less noticeable on cars fitted with the original all-metal needle valves. Keeping the float chambers as far away as possible from the exhaust manifold helps, as does fitting a heat shield.

The original seats are comfortable for most drivers, although the pedal position may not be ideal for those with very long, or very short, legs.

One of the changes introduced on left-hand drive cars was the addition of spacer pieces on the pedals to bring them closer for shorter drivers, but these are easily removed. The large steering wheel is placed close to the driver, even when set as far forward as it will go. However, most find the position ideal, and its size does give good leverage to deal with the weight of the steering at parking speeds. The gear lever is well placed and it has a sweet action, making gear changes a pleasure. The synchromesh on the three upper ratios can be overcome if changes are rushed.

A TD in good mechanical order is a joy to drive. On radial ply tyres run at around 26/28psi (1.9/2 bar), the ride is firm at low speeds but bump absorption good as the speed rises. The car steers beautifully, with some road shocks being felt through the steering wheel. On corners there is a fair amount of roll, particularly on a car without an anti-roll bar. Fitting one, however, increases the tendency for the back to break away first, particularly noticeable as the rear ride height of a TD on original springs in good condition is quite high. Spacer blocks to lower the rear suspension were a popular accessory in the 1950s. At all times, however, the car feels safe and under full control.

Because they were built in reasonable numbers and many survive, a TD is the cheapest route into T-Type motoring. For some reason fewer people are prepared to spend a lot of money on restoring a TD than a TF, which is surprising considering how similar they are. However, price is not the only reason to buy a TD. They are friendly, comfortable cars that give their owners all the advantages of pre-war-style motoring with few of the drawbacks. It is hardly surprising that quite a number have stayed with one family for many years.

Buying Hints

1. The TD is the most plentiful of the T-Series cars and the cheapest on the market today. The majority went to America and there lies the best source of 'restoration projects'.

2. The chassis can rust, vulnerable areas being the body mounting brackets and at the rear around the spring hangers. Being constructed of box-section steel of a relatively thin gauge, serious internal or external rusting will weaken the chassis, but this is rare; more usual is distortion resulting from accident damage. However, only the most neglected car will be beyond economic repair, but one with a really poor chassis should be avoided. Check for the additional rear damper brackets if you are told the car is a MkII.

3. Valve gear rattle is normal, but excessive noise and poor performance can indicate camshaft/follower wear, common on little-used cars. Most engine parts

are available, but engines from other models (Morris, Wolseley 4/44, etc) are not uncommon, so check to see that the correct unit is installed. A tip here is to look for the MG octagon cast into the block. Except on newly rebuilt engines with modern oil seals, some minor oil leaks are to be expected, but beware of serious loss through the bell housing drain as this will probably be from the rear main bearing oil seal.

4. Bodywork has an easier time on the TD than the TC and original bodies are fairly common, especially on imported cars. Rocking the car by the door pillars, and seeing how well the doors fit, will give a good indication of condition, but do remember that there is quite a lot of metal in a TD body so look at the condition of the rear bulkhead, body irons and body mountings. If replacement panels, like wings, are needed, stocks of second-hand parts do turn up from time to time, especially in America.

5. On the road, the car should drive well, the brakes should feel strong and safe, if a little heavy, and the steering should be excellent. If a TD wanders over bumps, or feels at all insecure, suspect worn or badly rebuilt dampers, a stiff or worn steering rack, or worn suspension bushes. Original rear springs last for ages, especially on cars that have spent much time in dry climates, and are often much better stripped, cleaned and fitted with new inter-leaf rubbers, rather than replaced. The fronts likewise often need little more than cleaning and painting.

6. A careful check should be made to ensure that the car has most of its original fittings, as replacements are expensive and some items difficult to find. Never throw away anything that can be cleaned, repainted or replated, and re-used. Often the original factory parts will fit better, and last much longer, than modern substitutes. The only exception is safety-related items, internals of the engine, gearbox and rear axle, and electrical components like plugs, coils and condensers.

The TF *midget*

The TD Midget was certainly a success in the showroom, selling in greater numbers than any previous MG. In 1950, its first full year in production, nearly 5,000 were sold and by 1952 the annual figure had risen to 10,838. By comparison, 3,000 TAs were built during the 1936 to 1939 production period and 10,000 TCs between 1945 and 1949. In 1949 Britain had devalued its currency by 30 per cent, which had given all exports a tremendous boost. However, the market for sports cars was changing all the time and a series of significant events during 1952 made the future prospects for MG sales less certain.

The impact made by MGs on the American market in the late 1940s and early 1950s cannot be overstated. A

whole generation of drivers learned about sports cars and sports car by racing driving TC and TD MGs, and without them the grids at American road races in the 1950s would have looked rather thin. The Sports Car Club of America was formed in 1944, and in 1948 they ran the first road races round the streets of Watkins Glen in New York state. There were two main events, the first determining the starting positions for the second, and in the final, the Grand Prix, a supercharged TC entered by Briggs Cunningham took third place, with MGs finishing in the next seven places.

This pattern was to repeat itself over the next few years with MGs and MG-engined cars dominating their class in road racing in America. Quite a number of the XPAG-engined specials built in Britain by people like Lester, Cooper and Lotus found their way across the Atlantic where they were raced enthusiastically. The sheer

The TF has always been a car where styling has been as important as performance. Although seen at the time as little more than a facelift, the changes made to the car when it replaced the TD have ensured its lasting popularity.

TFs have never been cheap cars. Even in the 1960s they were always more expensive than the TD, and they were even worth more than all but the newest of MGAs. This popularity has ensured a high survival rate.

quantity of TDs sold ensured that they, too, would be used for club racing. Although heavier than the TC, on some circuits the stiffer chassis and better roadholding gave them an advantage, and the Americans became expert at extracting the maximum power from the engine. In California MGs were particularly popular and many were modified for racing. Lowering suspensions, fitting racing windscreens, removing running boards and shortening front wings were popular pastimes, and magazines like *Road and Track* were full of advertisements for 'bolt-on goodies' for MGs.

The sales success enjoyed by the Abingdon cars had not gone unnoticed. Other British manufacturers, as well as some of the Europeans, were casting envious eyes at the American market. Triumph Managing Director Sir John Black was keen to earn dollars for his company but had concluded that their current range of cars was not likely to appeal to the Americans as much as would a new sports car. Budget

TF 1250 Midget
1953–54

ENGINE:
Four-cylinder, ohv
Bore x stroke	66.5 x 90mm
Capacity	1,250cc
Power	57bhp

TRANSMISSION:
Four-speed gearbox
Final drive	4.875:1

BODY STYLE:
Two-seater open sports

PERFORMANCE:
(from contemporary sources)
Max speed	82.5mph (133kph)
0–60mph (97kph)	18.9 seconds

LENGTH:	12ft 3in (3.73m)
WIDTH:	4ft 11¾in (1.52m)
WHEELBASE:	7ft 10in (2.39m)

TF 1500 Midget
1954–55

As TF 1250 except:
Bore x stroke	72 x 90mm
Capacity	1,466cc
Power	63bhp
Max speed	88mph (142kph)
0–60mph (97kph)	16.3 seconds

NUMBERS BUILT:
1250	6,200
1500	3,400

The TF is pleasing from any angle. The sweep of the wings and running boards looks particularly good from a three-quarter rear view. Ivory suits the styling of the car, although brighter whites do not. Ivory cars can correctly have red or green seats, not tan, while black was never an option on Abingdon-assembled TFs.

restrictions precluded the use of many new mechanical components, but Standard Triumph fortunately already built a sturdy four-cylinder engine that could be made sufficiently powerful to give a light sports model good performance. A hastily assembled prototype with a two-seater sports body, cut-away doors, and a stubby tail with an exposed spare wheel, was displayed at the 1952 Motor Show. Reaction to this rather ugly car was sufficient to ensure that the TR2, with properly developed chassis and better coachwork, was launched in 1953.

Triumph were now direct competitors to MG and the TR2 proved a lot faster; with a top speed of over 100mph (161kph) it made the MG look pretty pedestrian. Given this competition from a rival manufacturer, things were made much worse for MG by having another sports car emerge from within their own organisation. The Nuffield Group and Austin had finally merged under the British Motor Corporation banner in March 1952, placing the fate of Abingdon in the hands of Leonard Lord, Deputy Chairman of the group. Lord was keen to have an Austin-badged sports car, and when he saw the new 100mph Healey 100 on the Healey stand at the 1952 Motor Show he decided to produce this as an Austin-Healey.

At Abingdon they had already constructed a prototype of what they thought the next MG sports car should be. Lord rejected this, preferring to spend his money on the new Healey, and MG were instructed to continue building the TD. In spite of 1952 being a good year for sales, word was coming back from dealers that customers felt that the car was looking a bit old-fashioned and the likelihood was that its popularity would wane, especially once the new rivals appeared in the showrooms. In the absence of an entirely new car, it was time to carry out a 'facelift' to freshen up the old model.

In 1953 there was no design office at Abingdon, and this was not

re-established until finally the need for an entirely new car was realised by top management. The construction of a prototype of the revised car was carried out at Abingdon by a small team consisting of Syd Enever, Alec Hounslow and Cecil Cousins, together with the skills of a panel beater. Using a standard TD rolling chassis, and what was basically a TD body frame, reshaped wings, a sloping radiator, and modified fuel tank and chassis fairings, they built a car that looked quite different from the TD.

Service in hot countries had revealed shortcomings in the engine cooling, and these could best be remedied by conversion to a pressurised system, which meant dispensing with the traditional cap atop the radiator shell and replacing it with a pressure cap on the header tank under the bonnet; the external cap on the reshaped radiator surround was just a dummy. The externally mounted headlights on the

The TF was voted best US sports car but performance was below the 1954 Detroit norm

TD were vulnerable and the solution lay in placing them within built-in wing fairings. This was aesthetically very successful and the beautifully sculptured front wings and the lowered, sloping radiator shell produced a car of exceptional elegance.

The bonnet still had a centre hinge, but now only the top panels could be raised; the side panels remained fixed in place unless they were removed for major engine work. Accessibility for routine maintenance was not as good as it had been on the previous models and the lower bonnet line and smaller vents in these side panels meant higher under-bonnet temperatures. At the rear the reshaped and lowered fuel tank,

bucket seats that did not have quite as much adjustment as the TD's seats had offered. Behind these the sidescreen stowage was changed; the TD sidescreens stowed vertically in a compartment at the back of the body, but for the new car the compartment was moved so that they stowed flat in a box beneath the luggage area. A half tonneau cover was supplied with the car, which concealed the stowed hood and covered the luggage compartment.

The instruments were now all grouped in the centre of the dashboard. Although this meant that they were less easily seen, there was something of a fashion at the time for this arrangement, which eased production of both left- and right-hand drive cars on the same line. Like those fitted to the Y-Type saloon, the circular instruments were set beneath chromed, octagonal bezels. The tachometer was placed nearest to the driver, the speedometer on the passenger side, this being the case whether the car was left-hand-drive or right-hand-drive. A central instrument incorporated water temperature and oil pressure gauges and an ammeter.

Storage space within the cockpit was adequate, with two open glove boxes in the dashboard and pockets in the doors; a radio could be fitted in one of the glove boxes with the amplifier mounted under the dashboard. Knobs to park the windscreen wipers were set inside the glove boxes; changing from the unreliable and head-splitting windscreen-mounted unit to one fitted to the firewall under the bonnet was one of the most useful improvements. The horn button was beneath the scuttle on the driver's side of the car, close to the switch for the now standard direction indicators. A map-reading light was provided for the passenger.

Mechanically the TF was little changed, and the pedal positions, 'fly-off' handbrake, adjustable steering wheel and foot-operated dip switch were all carried over from the later TD. The only

The four side screens stow in a compartment behind the seats, although the car looks attractive with them in place and they keep the cockpit warmer on chilly days. A heater was not fitted as standard, but some owners installed a small recirculating unit under the dashboard.

and rear wings with the leading edge curving to meet the running boards, subtly altered the appearance of the car, making it look lower and lighter than the TD. The running board strips were chrome-plated rather than made from aluminium and rubber sections, and these now ran up on to the front wings. The circular rear lights and side lights came from the outgoing TD.

With the bright new exterior came revised trim. Things were moving on in sports car design and the familiar bench seat now looked a bit dated. Its place in the TF was taken by a pair of comfortable, leather-upholstered modifications made for the new car were the standardisation of a higher state of engine tune, similar to that of the TD MkII, and the adoption of the higher-ratio rear axle fitted to that model. The engine changes improved the power output by a modest 4bhp. Because of the restricted space under the bonnet, the TD oil-bath air cleaner was replaced by a pair of pancake filters.

The TF received its debut at the London Motor Show where it shared space on the MG stand with the Z Magnette, a much more up-to-date-looking car. One important feature for those sports car buyers who lamented the lack of wire wheels on the TD was the adoption of these as an optional extra. The TF sold in Britain at £550 plus £230 5s 10d purchase tax, which was £20 more than the TD but £35 less than the mechanically similar TD MkII. The colour choice was similar to earlier cars: black paint with red, green or tan trim; red with red or tan trim; ivory with red or green trim; grey with red trim; and green with green or tan trim.

In the hands of the magazines it received some praise, although little could disguise the fact that the performance was little improved over the previous model. None of the major weekly British magazines carried out full road tests of the TF, but in America *Road and Track* put one through their full test procedure. A top speed of 82.5mph (133kph) was recorded, with acceleration to 60mph (97kph) taking 18.9 seconds. They liked the car, voting it 'America's best sports car buy', but remarked that performance was 'well below the 1954 Detroit norm'. They also experienced poor engine running below 2,000rpm, blaming the carburettors for this as things improved at higher revs. This reinforces the view that with a capacity of just 1,250cc the larger carburettors fitted to the TF are really more for appearance than effect.

In spite of the revisions, sales of the MG were not coming up to expectations, and by 1954 Abingdon had received approval for work to start on an entirely new car. In the interim it was necessary to try to improve public acceptance of the TF, which was not really holding its own in competition with other marques. This led to the development of a larger-capacity engine, which was introduced after some 6,000 TF 1250s had been built. For competition use a number of people had been enlarging the XPAG engine by over-boring.

Engine accessibility is less good than on the TD, although the side panels can easily be removed for serious work.

The round instruments are fitted beneath octagonal bezels, as on the Y-Type. The central dial has instruments indicating water temperature and oil pressure, as well as an ammeter. The knobs in the glove pockets are to move the wiper blades up to the windscreen and switch them on.

This process was not always successful as it reduced the wall thickness around the bores below acceptable limits. To enlarge the capacity without changing the cylinder bore centres, or the head stud positions, the factory produced a new block casting that eliminated the water jacket between 1 and 2, and 3 and 4 cylinders and reduced the size of the jacket between the two pairs of cylinders and at the front and rear of the block.

The effect of increasing the bore size from 66.5 to 72mm was to increase the capacity from 1,250cc to 1,466cc. The cylinder head was unchanged, save for a small increase in thickness, and the compression ratio increased to 8.3:1. The changes resulted in a power output increase of 6bhp and the torque was also improved. To help identify the new version of the TF to potential customers, the factory added 'TF 1500'

badges to the bonnet sides. Advertising agents devised the slogan 'There's a new bee in its bonnet!' to emphasise the improved performance. Prices were reduced and Americans were able to buy one for just $1,995, making the MG the cheapest sports car on the market. Top speed recorded by *Road and Track* was 88mph (142kph), and 2.6 seconds was carved off the earlier model's 0–60mph (97kph) time.

Because of their similar mechanical specification and dimensions, behind the wheel there should be little to choose between driving the TD or the TF. In practice the cars initially feel quite dissimilar, with the separate bucket seats, changed instrumentation and revised coachwork combining to make drivers feel that they are in a completely different car. After a few minutes familiarisation, however, the basic characteristics of the TD chassis

The Naylor TF

The brainchild of Alastair Naylor, an established restorer of original T-Types whose company had really set the standards for such work in the early days of the classic car movement, the TF 1700 was sold as a completely new car that met all current safety requirements. To comply with these a prototype had to undergo the same crash test procedure as any other new car.

Unlike kit car replicas, the basis of the Naylor was a re-created TF chassis, correct in every detail, but mated to modern suspension and running gear. At the front the revised cross member carried co-axial coil spring/damper units while the Austin-Rover Ital rear axle was carried by coil spring damper units, with multi-link location and Panhard rod. The front disc and rear drum braking system also came from the Ital, as did the O-Series alloy-head engine, the radiator, the steering rack, and the handbrake assembly.

The body, wings, running boards and bonnet all came from the original TF, Naylors being established suppliers of these components for restoration work. Rear-hinged doors being taboo, those on the TF 1700 were front-

hinged and had safety-conscious handles. These, and bumpers incorporating the lenses for the flashing indicators, are the main external clues that separate the replica from the original.

Interior trim was luxurious, the leather-covered seats, thick carpets and proper three-point seat belts making the occupants feel comfortable and secure. Certainly the belts, with the mounting points firmly fixed to the chassis, the collapsible steering column, and safer dashboard design gave them a lot more chance of emerging unscathed from an accident. A wood-veneered dashboard carried up-to-date dials and rocker switches, all mounted below a padded crash roll that replicated the one on the TF. Each car was supplied with a full toolkit, including some spare parts, and the handbook was a faithful replica of the one supplied with the 1950s TF, photographs of the 1980s car replacing some drawings where appropriate.

The TF 1700 performed like a slightly more powerful TF. The ride was hard, but not more so than the original, and the car could be provoked into oversteer on tight bends. Some were disappointed that the standards of ride and roadholding were not those of a 1980s car, but that was never on the cards given the chassis specification. However, the cars felt well-sorted and beautifully built, and it is a pity that there were insufficient orders for the £13,000 car to enable the company to survive. The patterns and rights to build the TF 1700 were acquired by Mahcon Group who assembled a few cars in the 1990s as the Hutson TF. The company even sold a few as kit cars with fibreglass wings, to be assembled using second-hand Marina components.

The Naylor TF 1700.

The bench seat on the earlier T-Series cars was replaced on the TF by a pair of bucket seats. For some drivers these proved to be not as comfortable.

only come alive when pressed hard. Treated gently, and pottered along winding country roads, they feel nice to drive, but then so does any open car. However, using all the revs and pushing the car hard through corners soon reveals why T-Types were so highly regarded at the time. The balance between available power and handling is ideal, and there is a great deal of satisfaction to be gained from extracting the maximum from them. There are certainly no worries about breaking anything – just look at how fast the cars are still being driven by the racing fraternity!

The extra power of the 1500 engine makes that model feel livelier, and it comes without affecting the engine's ability to thrive on high revs. Driving the car hard has little effect on reliability, although the nature of modern fuels does cause the engine to run hotter than it should and the temperature gauge needs watching. TF 1500s seem no worse than 1250s, and it is worth remembering that overheating in the TF can be caused by the radiator slats being at too shallow an angle, which restricts air flow.

TFs are all-weather cars with the hood and sidescreens giving good protection. The improved wipers also help here, although visibility in the rain is not up to modern saloon standards. Although the original hood was made of a woven material and those seeking originality will want something similar, there is much to be said for opting for vinyl material for practicality; it does not fade and can be cleaned more easily. There is certainly no reason why a TF cannot have a full tonneau made of vinyl as they were not supplied as original equipment, and some cars would have been fitted with covers made of this sort of material by their first owners. The main thing is to have a car that can be used. T-Types were never meant to be pampered toys kept in a garage – the more you use them, the better they are!

assert themselves and one realises that on the road there is nothing to choose between them. Taller drivers often find that they are able to make themselves more comfortable in a TD seat, the seat backs in the TF being rather too upright and lacking in lumbar support.

Once familiar with a TF, the precise steering, well-chosen gear ratios and the urgent roar from the engine soon encourage drivers to make the most of the limited performance. The thing about cars like these is that they really

Buying Hints

1. Because of their attractive appearance, TFs have always been more expensive than other T-Series cars. Consequently, a greater proportion survive in good condition and there are always quite a number for sale from which to choose.

2. Many TFs seem to have been restored then used infrequently, if at all, and these cars are often in better condition cosmetically than mechanically. However, as it is usually cheaper to make a car go well than look good, do not ignore these cars as long as the price is right.

3. However good the car may look at first glance, it is the basic condition of the chassis frame and body that is important. Both can be repaired, at a price, but require the car to be completely dismantled. The box sections of the chassis rust from the inside out and the body mounting brackets and rear spring mountings can rot. The chassis can also suffer badly from the effects of quite minor accidents. The body must be carefully examined. Look at the fit of the doors and door pillars, make sure that the lower wooden sections are sound (these can be seen from under the car), and look at the rear bulkhead and metal cladding.

4. Because so many cars have been restored to a high standard and are offered for sale at prices well above those asked for other T-Series cars, buyers should be cautious about paying too much money for a car that they are going to put to everyday use. Inevitably, restored cars deteriorate when used heavily, and with the TF a well-worn example can be difficult to sell. The moral here is not to pay too much in the first place!

5. All the remarks made in previous chapters about XPAG engines apply equally to the XPEG unit fitted to the TF 1500. However, both versions of the TF suffer more from fuel starvation caused by heat because there is less air space around the engine, so a heat shield is essential.

6. Gearboxes on both the TD and TF are not as strong as they could be. Look for excessive noise, poor synchromesh, and slipping out of gear. That said, noisy gearboxes can continue to work long after one would expect them to expire! At the time of writing, almost all internal components are available, even close-ratio gear sets.

7. Cars painted in the original colours are more desirable. The factory schemes available are described above, but it is worth stressing that black trim was never an option, and neither was tan with ivory paint, both combinations frequently occurring on restored cars.

8. The majority of restored TFs will have wire wheels. Chromed wires were never an option and their appearance does little for the cars. Beware of cars with bolt-on replacement hubs that convert a disc-wheeled car, as some are of poor quality and a few have failed in service; they also widen the track a little.

The ZA & ZB *magnettes*

The Z Magnette was not only the first MG to employ modern techniques of monocoque body construction, but was also the last MG four-seater saloon to be built at Abingdon. The revival of the Magnette title for a car quite unlike the famous pre-war K3 Magnettes that had brought such glory to the MG name may seem strange. However, one must remember that the majority of Magnettes built in the 1930s were purely touring cars, many four-seater saloons. Using the name was a logical way to associate the new saloon with past MGs, and this succeeded, in spite of some complaints from enthusiasts at the time.

Worthy though the Y-Type saloon was, its styling undoubtedly owed more to the 1930s than the 1950s, and by 1952 it appeared rather staid and old-fashioned. The dawn of the jet age had brought with it a taste for all-enveloping bodywork; features like running boards and externally mounted headlights were looking increasingly anachronistic. With bodywork based on the Morris Eight, at the time the smallest saloon in the range, the interior was rather cramped; to carry a reasonable quantity of luggage the fold-down lid had to be used to extend the capacity of the boot. Any replacement would have to both look more up-to-date and provide greater room and passenger comfort, a tough brief considering the upheaval at the time within the newly merged company.

The Magnette was an attractive car with the Palmer-designed body looking as fresh and stylish now as it did in the early 1950s. This is a ZB, identified by the straight side strips.

In 1949, prior to the merger with Austin, the management of the Nuffield Group were planning replacements for some of their ageing range of cars. Alec Issigonis had been responsible for the Morris Minor, which had just gone into production, but a team needed to be established to design future MG, Riley and Wolseley models. Gerald Palmer, who worked for Jowett, where he designed the innovative and successful Javelin, was approached by Nuffield Technical Director A. V. Oak, and accepted the task of designing a new range of cars.

The Magnette had showroom appeal and a sportier image than the Wolseley 4/44

At Cowley, Palmer's brief was to design saloon cars for the MG and Riley ranges, as well as Wolseley four-seater and six-seater saloons. All the cars were to use standard components, engines, transmissions, etc, from within the Nuffield Group. Given the comparatively short development period envisaged, as well as cost restraints, it was clear that four different body shells, one for each model, was impractical. The solution lay in having just two basic body shells, a smaller one for the MG and small Wolseley models and a larger one for the six-seater Wolseleys and Rileys. Minor panel changes, together with different grilles, badges and trim, would distinguish each marque from the others.

Palmer proposed giving the MG version of the small saloon a lower ride height, with consequent changes to the sills and wings, as well as a floor-mounted gear change, a dashboard layout with an octagonal theme, and, of course, a traditional MG radiator grille. The plans he produced were influenced by current Italian automobile design, and he credits the Pininfarina-bodied Bentley displayed at the 1948 Paris Motor Show as one inspiration.

The merger, long mooted, finally occurred in March 1952 and this was to influence the new saloon cars at a late stage in their design. Initially, faced with the prospect of using existing Nuffield components, the 1,250cc XPAG engine of pre-war parentage from the YB was to power both the MG and Wolseley small saloons. As part of the advantage of establishing the group, the idea was to have common mechanical components across the whole range of cars. Consequently, at a late stage in development the decision was taken to use the 1,489cc B-Series engine in the small saloons and the C-Series unit in the larger. However, the cars were almost ready for release, and redesigning them to take the BMC engines and transmissions would delay their launch.

The rational course of action at the time was to go ahead with the programme to build the Wolseley 4/44, while delaying the release of the MG version until it was ready to accept the bigger engine. With hindsight, this was the correct choice as the smaller engine would have struggled to provide the MG with the sort of performance buyers required, while Wolseleys were not seen as sporting cars. Fitting the XPEG TF 1500 engine would have levelled things up a bit, but it was not available in 1952. The decision must have been helped by the fact that the cars were destined for assembly at different factories. The Wolseley 4/44 was revealed to the public at the 1952 London Motor Show as the smallest-engined car in the Wolseley catalogue, and the MG variant finally arrived at the 1953 show where it shared honours on the MG stand with the TF Midget.

Although a monocoque body was an innovation for an MG, they had been used by other manufacturers for many

ZA Magnette
1953–56

ENGINE:
Four-cylinder, ohv

Bore x stroke	73 x 89mm
Capacity	1,489cc
Power	60bhp

TRANSMISSION:
Four-speed gearbox

Final drive	4.875:1

BODY STYLES:
Four-door, four-seater saloon; Varitone version had larger rear window

PERFORMANCE:
(from contemporary sources)

Max speed	81mph (130kph)
0–60mph (97kph)	23.1 seconds

LENGTH:	14ft 1in (4.29m)
WIDTH:	5ft 3in (1.6m)
WHEELBASE:	8ft 6in (2.59m)

ZB Magnette
1956–58

As ZA Magnette except:

Power	68bhp
Final drive	4.55:1
Max speed	86mph (138kph)
0–60mph (97kph)	20.8 seconds

NUMBERS BUILT:

ZA	17,599
ZB	19,000

The black car is a Wolseley 4/44, closely related to the Magnette, but having the single-carburettor Nuffield engine, like the Y-Type.

years. The ZA body was developed and built by Pressed Steel and consisted of a number of sub-assemblies that were united on an assembly jig during manufacture. The main floor section incorporated a stressed prop-shaft tunnel and strong sill sections at either side. At the front, twin chassis extensions were welded to the front suspension cross member and carried the mounting brackets for the engine. At the rear, the boot floor and inner wheel arches formed the basic structure. The main door and screen pillars, scuttle panels and roof all add to the stiffness and strength of the shell, while the bolt-on

doors, bootlid, bonnet and front wings are the only non-structural sections.

Development of the MG Magnette had not been entirely straightforward. One of the ways that Palmer had wanted to distinguish the Magnette from the 4/44 was to lower the suspension to give the car a more sporting appearance and better handling. He decided to attach the axle casing to the rear springs by means of rubber bushes and to use a torque arm to resist twist under acceleration and braking. However, one of the prototypes exhibited severe axle tramp under heavy braking, so bad as to make the car virtually unmanageable. There was no easy solution, other than to revert to conventional U-bolts for axle attachment and to remove the torque arm. The rear springs had to be given greater camber, making the car sit a bit higher than originally intended, but at least the problem under braking disappeared. The suspension was by coil spring and wishbones at the front, and half-elliptic leaf springs at the rear. As a departure from previous MG practice, telescopic rather than lever arm dampers were fitted.

The Magnette certainly had showroom appeal. Visitors to the MG stand must surely have observed the outward similarity of the MG to the Wolseley that had appeared a year earlier, but anyone examining the two cars more closely would have been left in no doubt as to which was the more desirable. Column gear changes were all the rage at the time as they allowed three people to sit together on the front seats. However, good though they may have been on automatics, or on large-engined American cars, they had some drawbacks, and tortuous linkages made finding the right gear a bit of a lottery. The Wolseley was saddled with one of these gear changes but the Magnette was given a floor-mounted gear lever, which was thought to be more in keeping with a sporting image.

Under the bonnet of the Varitone.

The interior of the car is comfortable and attractive. The all-wood dashboard and dished steering wheel identify this as a ZB.

In common with the Wolseley, the seats were trimmed in leather, but the MG had bucket-shaped seats in the front. The rest of the interior was trimmed to a high standard and well equipped. Unlike the sports cars, it was even fitted with a heater and de-mister at no extra cost. Wooden door cappings complemented the wooden dashboard, which had a metal top panel that was convincingly painted to resemble real wood. Although the car lacked a tachometer, thought by many as essential in any sporting car, the half-octagonal-shaped speedometer was flanked by fuel, water temperature and oil pressure gauges, as well as an ammeter. Above the windscreen there was a neat electric clock alongside the anti-dazzle rear-view mirror.

There was an attractive range of colour schemes to tempt buyers: grey with grey trim; green with green or biscuit trim; black with maroon, biscuit or green upholstery; and maroon with a maroon or biscuit interior. Later the choice was extended; for example, grey cars could have maroon trim. The ZA Magnette was priced at £645, plus £269 17s 6d purchase tax, and represented good value for those looking for a well-appointed car at reasonable cost – the famous badge was a bonus.

Direct competitors were few. The Ford Zodiac was slightly cheaper and performed well, but it lacked the handling, refinement and class of the MG, and was considered 'flashy' by many. Rovers were 30 per cent more expensive, and more suited to business than sporting use, and Sunbeam-Talbots, while possessing a sporting pedigree, were heavy and also expensive. There were, of course, many ordinary family saloon cars available from BMC and other manufacturers, but none offered the performance and style of the MG.

Press cars did not get into the hands of the major magazines until towards the end of 1954 when The Autocar squeezed a maximum speed of 81mph (130kph) out of theirs, with their rivals at The Motor managing 80.7mph! Both magazines timed the dash to 60mph (97kph) at around 23 seconds. The B-Series engine fitted to the ZAs produced 60bhp at 4,600rpm, considered a reasonable output for the time but not really sufficient for a sporting saloon weighing 22cwt (1,119kg). Subsequent engine

A showroom poster advertising the 'airsmoothed' Magnette.

The Farina Magnette MkIII and MkIV

Cars, like clothes, are as much about style as utility. The rounded, all-enveloping designs, considered so modern in the early 1950s, were by the end of the decade giving way to cars of more angular shape with larger window areas. Italian designers were considered fashionable and the British Motor Corporation asked Pininfarina to work on the new range of cars to carry the badges of all the marques in their portfolio.

The first of their designs to reach the public was the A40. This had the now familiar 'two box' shape and, given minor revisions, could have established the 'hatchback' firmly in the market well in advance of cars like the Golf. More important to the company's fortunes was ADO9, the medium-sized car destined to replace the varied assortment of Austin, Morris, Wolseley and MG saloons then on offer. Delays in getting the cars ready saw them miss the October 1958 Motor Show, but the Austin A55, Morris Oxford, Wolseley 15/60 and MkIII Magnette were all launched over the next few months.

Sharing what were basically identical body shells, it was the different grilles, badges, lights and trim that separated the various models. In addition the MG version was given the B-Series engine in twin-carburettor form; this produced about 11bhp more than the single-carburettor engine in the other versions. The car had a roomy body and excellent luggage compartment, but dynamically the chassis design left a lot to be desired. Whereas the ZB Magnette had rack-and-pinion steering and good road manners, its replacement was saddled with a shorter wheelbase and longer overhangs, and a cam-and-lever steering box. In consequence, it had vague steering and excessive roll-oversteer, hardly the characteristics of a sporting saloon.

The new Magnette was, however, well-equipped, having leather-covered seats, walnut dashboard and door cappings, and a well-stocked instrument panel. However, it was no longer built at Abingdon and appeared to be an MG in name only. In 1961 the Magnette was fitted with a 1,622cc engine and the steering and suspension were revised in an attempt to improve the handling and roadholding. The wheelbase was lengthened by 1.2 inches (30mm), the front track widened by 2 inches (51mm), and the rear track by 1¼ inches (32mm). Anti-roll bars were fitted, together with revised dampers and rear spring rates. The car was now called the Magnette MkIV; it was a vast improvement over the MkIII and was to remain in production, selling in small numbers, until 1968.

Although rejected by those seeking real sporting transport, many Farina Magnettes gave good service as family cars with some of the appointments of a luxury saloon. The bodies were over-engineered and resisted terminal rust for longer than some of their peers, and today a good MkIV is an interesting alternative for those looking for a 1960s saloon.

The MkIII Farina Magnette.

A superbly restored ZA engine compartment, correct in every detail.

modifications were to see this rise to 68bhp at 5,200rpm.

One of the reasons why the press cars were delayed may have been the number of last-minute specification changes introduced while the first few cars were being assembled. They also encountered difficulties adapting the Abingdon assembly lines and building techniques to deal with a monocoque car. The most noticeable difference between the first 250 cars off the line and those built later is the lack of swivelling quarter lights on the front windows. The grille slats and surround were also slightly different on early cars. Less noticeable on the later cars was the reduction in the final drive gear ratio from 4.3:1 to 4.875:1, a change made to improve acceleration. In spite of claims in the brochure that the cars had a wooden dashboard, on

the first 6,500 ZAs the top was of woodgrain-painted sheet metal.

Some fairly major changes in specification were introduced in 1956, and by Motor Show time the model name had been changed to ZB. Externally the ZB can be immediately identified by the straight chrome strips on the front wings; on earlier cars the front ends of the strips followed the line of the wheel aperture. The B-Series engine had already been progressively modified, gaining better oil circulation, improved bearings and larger carburettors. The ZB engine produced 68bhp, thanks to an improved cylinder head and raised compression. The majority of the engine changes had been introduced at car ZA 18101, and were allied to a higher-ratio final drive (4.55:1).

The Z-Magnette in competition

MG had always been keen to enter their cars in competitions, seeing it as a cost-effective means of publicising their products. In 1954 the directors of the British Motor Corporation decided to form a Competitions Department at Abingdon, appointing John Thornley of MG as chairman of a new Competitions Committee. Not having the time to supervise the day-to-day operations himself, he gave Marcus Chambers the job of running the department.

A programme of rallies and races had already been agreed before the appointment was made, one of these being the 1955 Monte Carlo Rally, in which a team of three of the new ZA Magnettes had been entered. Gerald Palmer was well aware that the power available from the BMC B-Series engine was insufficient to give the cars rally-winning performance and had already drawn up a design for a twin-cam cylinder head to boost power output. However, the shambolic state of the organisation at

the time meant that it took until 1958 for this to put into production, when it appeared in the MGA Twin Cam in an under-developed form.

Given limited power and some mistakes in car preparation, it is hardly surprising that the Magnettes did not figure well in the final results. The MG team revived a pre-war tradition by running as 'The Three Musketeers', the cars carrying the names 'Aramis', 'Athos' and 'Porthos'. The cars were driven by Reg Holt, Geoff Holt and Len Shaw, all of whom had enjoyed previous success in MG team cars. The same ZAs ran in the 1955 RAC Rally but were once again uncompetitive. For the Tulip Rally that year Pat Moss took over Reg Holt's car, but crashed before the start. The car was repaired but a damaged oil pipe eventually put her out of the running. The other cars in the team were not highly placed.

Marcus Chambers was aware of the car's shortcomings and favoured building sufficient production cars,

lightened and fitted with twin cam engines, to homologate these for competition purposes. The whole idea was a non-starter, but he did commission the production of a batch of aluminium body panels, such as bonnets, to reduce weight. However, fitting these to the car entered by Nancy Mitchell in the 1956 Tulip Rally led to her disqualification as they were outlawed by the rules.

On the track, three ZAs were entered in the 1955 BRDC International Production Car race at Silverstone. Driven by Alan Foster, John Waller and Dick Jacobs, the cars finished in the first three places in their class. The following year a Magnette was entered by Dick Jacobs and driven by Alan Foster who was unlucky to be deprived of a class win by a Borgward in the experienced hands of Reg Parnell. In the 750 Motor Club Six-hour Relay race that year the Magnette team took First Prize.

The factory team of ZA Magnettes for the 1955 Monte Carlo Rally.

The range of colours had already been widened, but buyers were now also given the choice of two-tone colour schemes, which were becoming popular on all makes of car at the time. The Varitone version of the ZB, also introduced at the 1956 Motor Show, was endowed with another 1950s fixation, the wrap-around rear window. Perversely, Varitone models were occasionally finished in a single colour, while still retaining the bigger rear window and the chrome strip that normally divided the two colours. All ZBs had a parcel shelf under the dashboard.

One option introduced then was something called 'Manumatic' transmission, a system that allowed manual gear changing without need of a clutch pedal. Briefly, the mechanism was powered by vacuum from the inlet manifold, which opened and closed throttle servos and pressurised the hydraulically operated clutch. At idle, the clutch was disengaged; when the throttle was opened bob weights within the clutch forced it into engagement and the car moved off. Gripping the gear knob activated a solenoid that allowed vacuum

pressure to disengage the clutch and, once the gear change was accomplished, releasing the knob re-engaged the clutch. It sounds complicated, and very few BMC cars survive with the system intact.

ZA and ZB Magnettes are very attractive cars with styling that has stood the test of time far better than many others of that era. The driving position seems high after a sports car, and the seats do not give as much support as those on most MGs. However, there is sufficient head room and seat adjustment for tall drivers and one very quickly feels comfortable. The familiar B-Series engine pulls well and acceleration is adequate, rather than brisk. Initially, the car feels quite large and ponderous, but a few tight bends and the opportunity to try out the gears and brakes soon reveal just how easy the car is to drive, and how well it copes with modern roads.

The cars are roomy, full four-seaters with an immense amount of luggage space under the counter-balanced bootlid. Mind you, reversing needs care as there is quite a lot of motor

car lurking, unseen, behind that rear window. The steering is excellent and the roadholding good, especially on radial tyres. The brake pedal pressures are high, but the all-drum system is reassuringly efficient. Even a short drive in a Z Magnette reveals just why they were so well regarded by enthusiastic drivers in the 1950s. The combination of a smooth, modern appearance, excellent road manners and good performance lifted them well above the average family saloon of the time. This still holds good now, and there are few nicer 1950s saloons for everyday use. The ZA and ZB Magnettes are true MGs, and well worth searching out and preserving.

The early dashboards had a metal top that was painted to resemble wood. This early ZA has the correct flat, not dished, steering wheel.

Buying Hints

1. It is more difficult to find a good example of a Magnette than of a sports car of the same age as fewer have been preserved and cherished. Patience is needed as a poor car could be very expensive to restore.

2. Rust is a problem, but the thickness of steel used and the over-engineering of the chassis structure means that it is not quite as bad as on some other cars. Unfortunately, the inherent strength of the chassis meant that far too many ZAs and ZBs ended their days as 'banger racers'.

3. The condition of the body is the first consideration. It rusts in all the usual places – sills, doors, door pillars, floors, etc – and a test for filler is essential on a newly restored car. Badly repaired cars are common and remedying defects could cost as much as starting with an unrestored car.

4. Unlike the situation with the later sports cars, no panels pressed from original tools are available new. However, some repair sections – sills, lower doors, floors, etc – are available, as well as hand-made wings. However, fitting these parts does require considerable skill as they often need to be comprehensively re-worked and this is expensive to have carried out professionally.

5. Interiors are often good. A complete retrim could cost almost as much as a car in reasonable condition would fetch on the open market. However, the pleasure to be gained from having a car with pristine leather seats set off against newly polished woodwork may be worth the effort and cost.

6. Mechanically the cars are easily repaired. Their similarity to the sports MGs enables engine swaps, and even overdrive gearboxes and disc brakes, to be contemplated. A word of caution, however – few of these swaps are as easy as they appear, and some body modifications, changed mounting points, etc, will be inevitable. Take advice from specialists.

7. The early ZA engines suffered from weak bearings but most cars will by now have been rebuilt and fitted with bearings made of better materials. The option of fitting a ZA with an engine to ZB specification, and a higher rear axle ratio, could be considered justifiable improvements.

8. There are still some cars around that have been in the hands of early owners for all the intervening years and have covered nominal mileages. These cars will always be more desirable than ones that have been neglected or totally rebuilt from rusty wrecks.

9. Look for and preserve the sort of period accessories, like radios, picnic sets and toolkits, to complement the classic 1950s styling of the Z Magnette.

The ZB model was also available in Varitone guise, two-tone paint being all the rage at the time.

The MGA
1500,1600 & 1600 MkII

The MGA is probably the most important car in the post-war MG story. Although its launch had been delayed for a couple of years by the ineptitude of the BMC top management, it still arrived just in time to revive MG fortunes in the market and ensure the survival of the Abingdon factory for another 25 years. Sales of the T-Series cars had been good, but they were falling fast in America by the time the MGA arrived on the scene. The last full year of TF production was 1954, and the combined total of 1250 and 1500 models built was 6,516 cars, 4,200 of these going to North America. In comparison, 1952 had seen the

company make 10,838 TDs, selling 9,901 of these to North America.

Once the MGA had been announced it was more a case of trying to keep up with the demand than worrying about selling the cars. In 1956 they assembled 13,410 MGAs and of these 10,595 earned North American dollars. By 1957 the annual total had risen to 20,571. Twice as many MGAs left Abingdon that year than the total TC build during its four-year production span, and helped by a competitive price the American market absorbed 17,195 of them. Had the company not been able to bring the MGA into production in a comparatively

The smooth, aerodynamic lines of the MGA were far more in tune with the 'jet age' than had been the traditional styling of its T-Series predecessors. Today, however, it is these wide expanses of curved metal that pose the greatest problems for the restorer. Small imperfections are immediately evident, and poorly fitted doors and wings are difficult and expensive to put right.

short space of time, sales of the TF would probably have dwindled to the extent that the Abingdon plant would have shut altogether; the other MG, the ZA Magnette, could have been assembled alongside the Wolseley 4/44 at Cowley. However, the company's ability to launch one of the most successful sports cars of all time was due to the foresight of a few key MG personnel.

To obtain a worthwhile improvement in performance from any car powered by the 1,250cc XPAG engine the designer

The MGA's fine aerodynamic body was evolved directly from the EX 175 experimental car

had to overcome two main difficulties inherent in the standard T-Series MG – weight and drag. Fitting a lighter body and discarding unnecessary equipment reduced weight, and fitting cycle wings reduced drag a little, but there was still the driver to consider. Intrepid *Autosport* photographer and racing driver George Phillips had a T-Type special constructed for use in the 1951 Le Mans race. A lightened TD chassis was fitted with an all-enveloping body designed by Syd Enever. UMG 400 looked the part with its sleek bodywork, but the driver, sitting atop the chassis, stuck out too far into the air stream. The answer lay in building a new chassis, a route taken by other exponents of the virtues of the XPAG engine in the 1950s.

A young apprentice designer at Abingdon, Roy Brocklehurst, was given the task of drawing plans for an experimental chassis. Incorporating the same suspension as the TD, this had the side rails running alongside the main passenger compartment, rather than underneath, thus providing the space for the occupants to sit between them. Two of the experimental chassis

frames were constructed, one being fitted with coachwork based on a reworked version of the body on the Phillips Le Mans TD. This car, coded EX 175 by the Experimental Department, was fully road-equipped with windscreen, lights, bumpers, etc, and at first glance looked much like any production MGA; the most noticeable differences were a lower windscreen and the bulge in the bonnet to clear the XPAG engine. EX 175 proved capable of 100mph (161kph) performance, fitted with the near-standard T-Type engine. This was the car that had been turned down by Sir Leonard Lord as the TD replacement.

When the MG team were eventually given permission to develop a new car it was to EX 175 that the newly re-established design office at Abingdon turned. At Cowley Gerald Palmer had proposed building a much lighter monocoque car, but although an initial prototype had been constructed, this would have taken longer to develop and probably taken more money from the tight budget. There is little doubt that Abingdon favoured their project, which had the added advantage of being easily built on their production lines in much the same way as they were already assembling T-Types.

When the new MG made its first public appearance at the Frankfurt Motor Show in 1955 it looked thoroughly modern. To drive home the message that the car was thoroughly up-to-date, the advertising slogan used was 'First of a new line, the completely new MG Series MGA'. The chassis frame had been developed from EX 175, the changes being fairly minor, and the front suspension and rack-and-pinion steering from the TD/TF were retained, although the detail design of the components changed. Following traditional pre-war MG practice, twin 6-volt batteries were mounted on cradles fitted just ahead of the rear axle, which was a narrower version of the BMC unit fitted to the Z Magnette, rather than the Nuffield design fitted to the TD/TF. Drum brakes were fitted all round, a tandem

MGA 1500
1955–59

ENGINE:
Four-cylinder, ohv

Bore x stroke	73 x 89mm
Capacity	1,489cc
Power	72bhp
	(initially 68bhp)

TRANSMISSION:
Four-speed gearbox

Final drive	4.3:1

BODY STYLES:
Two-seater sports car and two-seater closed coupé

PERFORMANCE:
(from contemporary sources)

Max speed	99mph (159kph)
0–60mph (97kph)	14.5 seconds

LENGTH:	13ft 0in (3.96m)
WIDTH:	4ft 10in (1.47m)
WHEELBASE:	7ft 10in (2.39m)

MGA 1600
1959–61

As MGA 1500 except:

Bore x stroke	75.41 x 89mm
Capacity	1,588cc
Power	79.5bhp
Max speed	100mph (161kph)
0–60mph (97kph)	13.3 seconds

MGA 1600 MkII
1961–62

As MGA 1500 except:

Bore x stroke	76.2 x 89mm
Capacity	1,622cc
Power	90bhp
Final drive	4.1:1
Max speed	103mph (166kph)
0–60mph (97kph)	12.8 seconds

NUMBERS BUILT:

1500	58,750
1600	31,501
1600 MkII	8,719

The radiator grille blends well with the curvaceous body; some reproductions now available are of poor quality and fitting them is difficult.

master cylinder serving to operate both these and the hydraulic clutch.

The XPAG/XPEG engines used in the TD/TF and in the prototype gave way to the BMC B-Series unit first seen at Abingdon in the ZA Magnette. This had been conceived at Longbridge as one of a series of standardised engines. Of simple and unadventurous design, it lacked features like an overhead camshaft and cross-flow cylinder head. Initial power output in single-carburettor form was a measly 50bhp, but raising the compression and fitting an extra carburettor livened things up a little. However, it did have the virtue of being both simple and

reliable, and capable of being later enlarged, initially to 1,588cc for the MGA Twin Cam and 1600, and later to 1,622cc and 1,798cc for the 1600 MkII and MGB. Engines for the MGA produced 68bhp and these were fitted with a geared drive from the camshaft for a mechanical tachometer. The BMC four-speed gearbox used in the Magnette was retained, but a remote gear lever assembly was fitted.

The most noticeable feature of the MGA, its striking aerodynamic body, was evolved directly from EX 175. It is remarkable how closely the production car followed the shape of the experimental car, and its beauty is a tribute to the small design team at Abingdon. The body comprised a number of steel pressings, with those forming the 'F'-section door pillar and sill assembly providing the only link between the front and rear parts of the body. The wings and front apron were bolted in place. In established Abingdon practice, the chassis, running gear and mechanical components were first assembled before the completed and trimmed bodies were lowered on to them; the bodies arrived at the factory ready painted and with the hoods and sidescreens in place.

Prior to its public announcement, motoring journalists had already driven the MGA. The *Autocar* were impressed by the performance and recorded a best time to 60mph (97kph) of 15.6 seconds

with a full load. The highest speed recorded, 99mph (159kph), was achieved with the hood and sidescreens in place. *The Motor* were rather more critical of some aspects of the MGA in their test report. The low second gear was commented upon, as were the markings on the speedometer and tachometer dials. These were later recalibrated, with speeds in 10mph (16kph) increments rather than 20. *Road and Track* were impressed with the MGA, being surprised by just how much the top speed had increased over the superseded TF 1500. With a similar weight and power output, the MGA was over 10mph faster.

MGA buyers could choose to have their cars painted black with red or green trim; red with red or black trim; white

The MGA coupé is an attractive car. The larger rear plinths for the rear lights and flashing indicators identify this as a 1600 model.

was certainly competitively priced and deserved to succeed, and it did!

In 1956 the factory listed a hard top as an optional extra. This was supplied with aluminium framed sidescreens with sliding Perspex windows. To cater for those wanting all the comforts of a closed saloon, a coupé version was announced a year after the first open MGA appeared. This very pretty car had an integral steel roof incorporating a wrap-around rear window and a larger and more curved windscreen. The lockable doors were completely redesigned and featured winding side windows, swivelling quarter lights, and had neat exterior handles that rested on rubbers set into the window frame. Coupé interiors were more luxuriously trimmed with a covered dashboard, map pocket in the footwell, roof headlining, and full carpeting.

Although the MGA was selling well and dominated the sports car market, other manufacturers were also in the picture. The Triumph TR2 introduced in 1954 was faster than the MGA and had the option of overdrive. It was a tough car and very popular in overseas markets, and in 1957 it was given more power and disc brakes on the front wheels, a first for a mass-market sports car. To compete, MG had been working since the MGA was launched on a higher-performance model and this was offered for sale in 1958. The full story of the Twin Cam is covered later, but its introduction was eventually to lead to changes on the ordinary MGA and the announcement of a new model, the 1600.

By 1959 disc brakes were becoming as desirable as anti-lock brakes are now. Rivals Triumph fitted discs to the TR3, and the new Sunbeam Alpine was to be equipped with them. The Alpine was a new breed of small sports car, with wind-up windows in the doors and saloon-car standards of cockpit comfort. MG could do nothing immediately to counter this challenge from Sunbeam, but they did decide to give their car better brakes and more

The coupé interior is plushly trimmed. The upholstery on the seats is of a different pattern from that on the open cars. The rexine-covered dashboard is of a different shape from the one on the roadster, but the instruments and layout are the same.

with red or black interior; blue with grey or black seats; or green with grey or black interior. Hoods could be in light blue or black. Having learned their lesson with the TD, wire wheels were firmly on the options list and were almost invariably chosen for American market cars. Other factory-fitted extras included a 4.55:1 axle ratio for competition, adjustable steering column, heater or fresh air ventilator, and heavy-duty Dunlop Road-Speed tyres.

The basic price for the MGA in Britain was £595 plus £249 0s 10d purchase tax, and rivals in the market included the Triumph TR2 at a basic price of £650, traditional sports cars like the TR2-engined Morgan Plus 4 at £595 and HRG at £895, and, of course, the Austin-Healey 100 at £750. Foreign sports cars were expensive: the cheapest Porsche was £1,260 plus tax and Alfa Romeo £1,595, as were specialist sports cars like the AC Ace at £1,100 and Aston Martin at £2,200. An XK 140 Jaguar would set you back £1,598 8s 4d including tax. The MGA

The front side lights on the 1600 and 1600 MkII were larger than those on the 1500, and had an orange segment for the flashing direction indicators.

power. Unlike the all-disc system that was fitted to the Twin Cam, Lockheed front discs were used but drums were retained for the rear.

Twin Cam MGAs had a 1,588cc engine, achieved by increasing the bore from 73 to 75mm. This change was now carried over to the pushrod car, raising the power by 7.5bhp and the torque by 12 per cent. The axle and gear ratios were unchanged. Performance was boosted, with *The Autocar* recording a 0–60mph (97kph) time of 14.2 seconds and a maximum speed of just over 100mph (161kph). Externally the 1600 was little different from the 1500 it replaced. Changes in the flashing direction indicators saw the introduction of new, larger front sidelights with amber segments incorporated, and separate amber flashers at the rear, mounted on lengthened plinths on the wings above the brake/side lights. '1600' badges on the bootlid and scuttle identified the new model.

Fresh colour schemes were adopted and hoods could be grey, beige or light blue to tone with the exterior colour. The side screens were changed to incorporate sliding windows, similar to those already offered to buyers of the detachable hard top but fabric-covered to match the hood rather than aluminium. Cars could now be black with beige or red trim; red with red or beige trim; blue with black trim; beige with red trim; grey with red interior; and white with red or black interior.

The dashboard layout on any MGA is very pleasing. The horn is below the speaker grille in the centre, and on the right-hand side of the steering wheel is the self-cancelling switch for the direction indicators. The rexine covering identifies the car as a 1600 MkII; the Twin Cam dashboard was also covered like this but had a different tachometer.

The rear lamp cluster on the 1600 MkII came from the Mini; it was probably cheaper than the previous 1600 twin units.

Even with the spare wheel removed, room in an MGA boot is limited. Luggage rack manufacturers prospered!

The arrival of the 1600 helped sales. In 1959 there were over 23,000 MGAs built, the greatest number for any single year. In 1960 production fell to fewer than 17,000, and to compete with newer rivals it was obvious that a total redesign was needed. As a stop-gap, the final version of the MGA appeared in June 1961. The external changes were to the lights and grille; the rear light clusters were replaced by units from the Mini parts bin, and were mounted on plinths on the rear panel rather than the

wings, and the grille had its vertical slats recessed at the bottom. Inside the car, the top of the scuttle was covered to remove reflections in the windscreen on light-coloured cars. '1600 Mk II' badges were fitted to identify the revised model.

However, the most important changes were mechanical. The engine capacity was increased again, from 1,588cc to 1,622cc, and the unit was redesigned internally. Wider main bearings and a sturdier crankshaft, as well as modified pistons and con-rods, made the bottom end of the engine much stronger. The cylinder head had reshaped combustion chambers and larger valves. Power output was 90bhp at 5,500rpm, which compared favourably with the 79.5bhp produced by the 1600 engine. A higher axle ratio of 4.1:1 was fitted, giving more relaxed cruising at motorway speeds. The MkII was the best of the pushrod MGAs, almost as quick off the mark as a Twin Cam without that model's drawbacks.

The MGA has tremendous appeal. The comfortable leather-covered seats, set low in the cockpit, the large steering wheel and well-placed, stubby gear lever, and the comprehensive array of dashboard dials and switches all combine to heighten the sense of occasion when entering an MGA for the first time. Legroom is adequate for all

but the tallest drivers, and the high cockpit sides give a feeling of security to both driver and passenger. On cars built before chassis number 78249, rearward seat adjustment is slightly restricted by the stowed hood and sidescreens; on later cars the system was modified, with the hood frame set further back under the rear deck and the sidescreens stowed above the rear bulkhead, rather than between it and the seats. Hood stowage is neat, with the collapsed hood frame, hood and windscreen header rail concealed under the rear deck.

An MGA is a blend of the charm of a T-Type and the practicality of an MGB. The separate chassis construction allows for 'body off' rebuilds, and its mechanical simplicity and good parts supply keep costs in check. However, the best part of any MGA is the pleasure it gives the driver. Although the beautifully curved bodywork and small bonnet aperture impose some restrictions on access, the view over the delicately shaped front wings and sensuously rounded bonnet are adequate compensation. Driving a good MGA, any model, is a pleasure. The roadholding and handling are superb and the ride not too harsh, making long journeys a pleasure. The distinctive exhaust note adds immeasurably to the fun of driving the car open, when the close-set windscreen and removable sidescreens give good protection on cold days.

The small boot restricts the amount of luggage carried, and very tall or short drivers could wish that the pedals were moveable, but an MGA is generally a very easy car to use daily. The body is vulnerable, with the aluminium panels, boot, bonnet and doors easily dented, but its relative cheapness and availability make it an ideal car to use all the time rather than just occasionally. The hood gives adequate weather protection and good visibility, particularly as those now fitted to most cars have the larger rear windows introduced for the later models. Pushed hard, the handling is neutral and on

The 1955 Le Mans MGA - EX 182

Unlike many other prototypes in the race, the MG EX 182s closely resembled road cars. Only relatively conservative engine tuning, all-aluminium bodies, a larger fuel tank, and special equipment like racing windscreen and additional instrumentation distinguished the racing cars from production MGAs. The 1,489cc BMC B-Series engine had a novel induction system; the cylinder head had the two pairs of inlet ports extended through to the off-side of the engine, where they were linked by a balance pipe. The idea behind this was to utilise the fuel/air mixture from both carburettors for a greater part of the engine's compression/ignition cycle. With the compression ratio raised and larger valves and a modified camshaft fitted, power output was up from 68bhp to approximately 82bhp at 5,500rpm. Because of the long straights at Le Mans, the car was fitted with a rear axle ratio that gave 115mph (185kph) at 5,500rpm in top gear.

A former Le Mans car in modified form ran in the Tourist Trophy at Dundrod in 1955, as shown here.

In the race the cars performed well, with the maximum speed recorded being 119.5mph (192kph) down the Mulsanne straight. About the same time as one of the Mercedes entries crashed into the spectators in front of the pits, Dick Jacobs was involved in an accident further round the circuit. His injuries were serious enough to end his racing career, but the other cars finished in very creditable 12th and 17th places. Accident apart, it was a successful return to international motor racing for MG.

Converting a left-hand drive MGA to right-hand drive

Of total MGA production, nearly nine out of every ten cars were left-hand drive, and these are now the most plentiful. The many cars repatriated from export markets in recent years are ready candidates for conversion to right-hand drive. One of the reasons why this may be a good idea is that cars from dry climates usually have less body rot.

MGAs are easy to convert as they were designed to be built for either market. The list of parts required is short and most are readily available:

Steering rack: This can be either new or rebuilt, often supplied as an exchange unit for the old rack.

Pedals: The pedal box and blanking plate can be easily changed over, but the clutch and throttle pedals differ. LHD versions of the clutch are a different shape but these can be modified, while for the throttle a new pedal with bush, bracket, bolt, distance tube, pedal stop and stop bracket is required. New brake and clutch hydraulic pipes are needed.

Dashboard: This can be new or second-hand; coupé dashboards are not available new. The roadster dashboard needs to be painted body colour unless it is covered in rexine for a Twin Cam or 1600 MkII.

Rev-counter and speedometer cables.

Electrical fittings, such as the dip-switch and LH dipping headlamps, have to be considered, but on the 1500 the dip-switch can be changed over without modification, while on later cars a new bracket is needed.

Tonneau cover.

Wiper arms (the motor park position needs to be changed).

Carpets will need changing, as only the driver's side had a heel mat.

radial tyres the grip is good. There is quite a lot of roll, and oversteer can be provoked, but the car is basically very safe.

The gearbox ratios are wider than ideal – a close-ratio box was a competition option – but this is masked by the wide torque band of the engine. It is a pity that overdrive was never available, but the gearing is not as low as on the T-Types and most drivers will be happy with the standard set-up, particularly with the 4.1:1 on the MkII. There is a conversion kit available to fit the five-speed gearbox from a Ford Sierra to MGA 1,588cc and 1,622cc engines, while the MGA 1500 can be converted by the use of a 1600 engine backplate; in fifth gear the engine speed is reduced by nearly 20 per cent, giving more relaxed cruising.

MGAs are exceptionally nice cars to drive, although the coupé can get a little warm on sunny days. The rear light fittings identify this car as a 1500.

The MGA shares with most other MGs that indefinable quality of being fun to own and drive. Additionally, it is one of the prettiest sports cars of its time and attracts the sort of attention and admiring glances from onlookers that drivers of more mundane machinery will never experience. Their true value is way above their modest cost, something to take advantage of!

Buying Hints

1. Decide exactly which model to look for – do not be tempted to buy a closed car if a roadster is really the goal. All MGAs are nice to drive, but the more powerful, disc-braked cars have greater appeal and are usually a little more expensive.

2. The design of the MGA – the flat sides and long front wing line – make it easy to spot poorly restored cars or those where there is a lot of chassis and body damage. Looking down the sides of a car, and examining door and panel fits, will reveal most of the problems in this area. Misalignment will take a lot of time and effort to correct, so a poor car is best left with the vendor.

3. The most vulnerable areas for body rot are the door pillars, sills and lower edges of the wings. Repair panels for all these parts are available, but fitting is difficult. A lot of replacement wings, for example, need considerable work to make them align correctly with the doors and the rest of the body. Look carefully at the wing piping – using an over-thick section is a popular way of concealing poor work. Light grey plastic piping was standard on all cars, whatever their paint colour.

4. The chassis can rust badly. The side rails just ahead of the doors, the rear around the spring hangers, and the inside face adjacent to the floorboards are the usual rust traps. Repaired chassis are common on rebuilt cars, but standards of workmanship vary. Remember that a car with a badly aligned chassis will never drive well and will have had many of the body panels modified to make them fit. Cars may be encountered that are shorter on one side than the other.

5. Most suspension components, springs, etc, are available. Dampers are often worn but new ones of a slightly different pattern can be obtained.

6. The mechanical components are simple and repairs inexpensive. However, a high-priced car must have all the correct components. Engine swaps and other changes are common, cars fitted with units from other BMC models being one example, so look for clues like lack of a mechanical drive for the tachometer. At the time of writing, replacement cylinder heads in aluminium are available. Fitting a later B-Series engine does improve the performance of earlier models, but some surgery is necessary,

spoiling originality. Look for excessive oil leaks from the bell housing and noisy gearboxes and back axle.

7. The colour and condition of the trim is important. Many cars from warm climates will have swapped their leather seat facings for plastic. Cars finished to factory specification with original colour combinations, etc, are worth more and often look better. Some of the replacement parts available in recent years – grilles, bumpers and electrical fittings – are poorly made replicas of the originals. Remember that some cars were assembled overseas, in Australia and South Africa for example, and these had different paint colour options.

The MGA 1600 engine bay. The 1500 model has a relay for the flashing indicators on the rear bulkhead.

The MGA
twin cam

The MGA Twin Cam was built in very small numbers, just 2 per cent of total MGA production, but the reputation it gained during the two years it was in the catalogues has ensured it a place in MG history, and has made the model the most sought after of MGAs. Reliability problems with the earlier cars led to a spate of complaints from customers and dealers and, eventually, to the withdrawal of the model from sale. The irony was that by the time the last car left the line sufficient modifications had been incorporated into the engine to make it almost as reliable as the pushrod unit.

The development of the MGA Twin Cam is a fascinating story, and one that is symptomatic of the difficulties inevitable with mergers between groups of companies when competing interests and divided loyalties produce results that are not in the best interests of the enterprise as a whole. As recounted earlier, once the British Motor Corporation was formed one of the first decisions taken by the new management was to design a new range of engines to replace the many and varied power units in use at the time. Gerald Palmer was appointed as the designer in charge of new MG and Wolseley models, and work on the ZA Magnette and Wolseley 4/44 was well advanced by the time he was told to use the B-Series engine in place of the old Nuffield unit. The Wolseley was launched with the old engine but the ZA benefited from having the new B-Series BMC unit, which produced just 60bhp in twin-carburettor form.

Externally, only small badges and the centre-lock steel wheels identify the high-performance Twin Cam from the ordinary pushrod car. Start the engine, however, and the deeper exhaust note soon warns the onlookers to stand clear!

5252 RE

MGA Twin Cam
1958-60

ENGINE:
Four-cylinder, dohc

Bore x stroke	75.41 x 89
Capacity	1,588cc
Power	108bhp with

9.9:1 compression; 100bhp with 8.3:1 compression

TRANSMISSION:
Four-speed gearbox

Final drive	4.3:1

BODY STYLES:
Two-seater sports car and two-seater closed coupé

PERFORMANCE:
(from contemporary sources)

Max speed	115mph (185kph)
0-60mph (97kph)	9.1 seconds

LENGTH:	13ft 0in (3.96m)
WIDTH:	4ft 10in (1.47m)
WHEELBASE:	7ft 10in (2.39m)
NUMBER BUILT:	2,111

The extra performance given by the powerful Twin Cam engine makes these cars the obvious choice for those looking for the ultimate MGA.

Although more involved with designing cars than engines, Palmer was able to persuade his superiors that a more powerful version of the BMC B-Series would be just the thing for a performance version of the Magnette, making the car more suitable for the sort of competitions envisaged by the company to promote sales. He was also working at the time on his replacement for the T-Series Midget, which would have been lighter than the MGA eventually chosen for production and, given his proposed twin-cam engine, would have been very quick.

The brief he was given meant that any engine he designed would have to use the standard block to keep costs to a minimum. The unit he conceived was very close to the one eventually produced, except that the valves were inclined at an included angle of 80°,

rather than the 90° Palmer proposed. In addition, the capacity rose from 1,489cc to 1,588cc. The actual development of the engine was entrusted to James Thompson and Eddie Maher at Morris Engines Branch in Coventry; Palmer had no input at later stages, having left BMC for a job at Vauxhall.

Strangely, possibly out of a desire to keep his old colleagues in the game, Leonard Lord also asked the Austin engine design team at Longbridge to come up with a twin-cam engine, the brief also allowing them to opt for an entirely new cylinder block. By 1955 the MGA was ready to go into production, and John Thornley at MG, having learned of the more powerful engine, was keen to produce some higher-performance MGAs for limited sale to the public.

With prototypes of both engines available in 1,500cc form, it was decided to try them in a couple of cars at the Tourist Trophy race at Dundrod in September 1955. The cars were

The covered dashboard was fitted to all Twin Cams. The 'competition' seats were, however, an option, although today most of the cars have them. The dashboard layout is the same as for the pushrod cars but the tachometer 'red-lined' at 7,000rpm is the give-away. This car has a headlamp flasher switch to the right of the steering wheel, in addition to a non-standard ammeter and 'modern' cigarette lighter.

those prepared for Le Mans; they had lightweight bodies but looked externally identical to production MGAs. However, to improve streamlining, the car with the Palmer-designed engine had the wings modified, with the headlights placed much closer to the ground.

On test the Austin twin-cam engine did not produce any more power than the tuned pushrod unit used for Le Mans, and it was replaced with one of these prior to the race. Last-minute changes to the other engine saw it gaining

Weber carburettors in place of Solexes, but it was fated not to complete the event as piston failure after 34 laps put it out of the running. The Austin engine was abandoned, but work on the Morris unit proceeded spasmodically.

With MG's competition efforts curtailed after the bad publicity that motor racing received as a result of the dreadful 1955 Le Mans crash, record-breaking to publicise the marque was once again to the fore. In 1956 EX 179, which was based around one of the prototype EX 175 chassis, was readied for a fresh record attempt at Utah. Two unsupercharged versions of the twin-cam engine were prepared; both were still 1,489cc but one was more highly tuned than the other. With the more powerful unit in the car it took the flying 10 mile (16km) record at a speed of over 170mph (274kph). With the less highly tuned engine installed, EX 179 took a number of endurance records, including the 12-hour 1,500cc class record at 140.71mph (226kph).

In 1957 MG produced their ultimate record car, EX 181. Unlike the previous car, it was designed stem-to-stern for the job and had a tubular chassis frame and lightweight body of extreme aerodynamic efficiency. For the engine, which was placed behind the driver, a specially strengthened twin-cam unit was used. Boosted by an enormous Shorrock supercharger, the 6.75:1

compression ratio engine produced 290bhp at 7,300rpm. In the hands of Stirling Moss, EX 181 took five new records at speeds of up to 245.64mph (395kph). This was good publicity for MG and, one would have thought, good development for the engine.

However, to maximise the competition potential of any car using the twin-cam engine, a decision was taken at some stage to increase the capacity from 1,489cc to 1,588cc in order to bring it close to the 1,600cc class for International Touring Car events. This change was achieved by increasing the bore, a process that also involved modification of the water jacket within the block casting.

The public were given details of the high-performance MGA on 15 July 1958. At that time only a few cars had been assembled and some of these

Many MGAs, even Twin Cams, have luggage racks to supplement the meagre room in the boot. Although the Brooklands track closed 20 years before this car was built, it looks quite at home on the banking. The 1600-style rear lights identify this as a later car.

The De Luxe models

Fewer Twin Cams were built than had originally been envisaged and some special components – wheels, brakes, etc – remained in stock when production ceased. To utilise these, four-wheel disc brakes and centre-lock steel wheels were offered as options on the 1600 and 1600 MkII. Initially, people ordering these would have had a Twin Cam chassis, with repositioned steering rack, etc, but later the standard chassis was used.

The De Luxe was never a catalogued model and the specification of the cars varied. In South Africa some cars were badged as De Luxe but did not have Twin Cam components, merely wire wheels and other extras. There seem to have been only 82 1600 models built to De Luxe specification, but over 300 1600 MkIIs. With the MGA nearing the end of its production run they possibly needed to finish the remaining stocks of Twin Cam parts, as well as offering a few more lavishly equipped cars to boost sales.

Because quite a number of Twin Cam MGAs were converted to pushrod cars by both owners and dealers, there is often confusion over identity. The answer lies in the number on the log book or chassis plate. All Twin Cams carried a number in the range 501 to 2611 with the prefix starting with the letter 'Y', eg YD1 501 ('D' means that it was a roadster, while coupés were 'M'). The MGA 1600 numbers ran from 68851 to 100351 and the 1600 MkII from 100352 to 109070, and both of these had prefix letters that identified the make, engine size and body type, 'GHN' for open cars and 'GHD' for the coupé.

The 1600 and 1600 MkII De Luxe models have Twin Cam disc brakes all round and Dunlop centre-lock wheels.

There must have been some initial disappointment that the performance version of the now familiar MGA did not look all that different from the standard cars. Although there had been a few detail changes to the metalwork, externally the Twin Cam could only be distinguished from the pushrod car by the 'Twin Cam' badges on the bootlid and alongside the scuttle vents, and by the centre-lock Dunlop steel wheels. These wheels were much stronger than wires and similar to those used by Jaguar on the D-Type, although for the 'D' they had light-alloy centres. Unlike ordinary wire wheels, those on the Twin Cam are driven from the hubs by four pegs bolted to the wheels rather than by splines.

Road tests on the twin cam gave engineers and buyers some cause for concern

Dunlop also supplied the all-disc braking system, which was similar to that fitted by Jaguar to their cars at the time. Separate cable-operated callipers on the rear discs provided the handbrake, although these needed to be well-maintained and carefully adjusted to work well. To complement the mechanical changes, the cockpit received a rexine-covered dashboard and a different speedometer and rev counter. The option of more heavily padded competition de luxe seats was offered, but not all Twin Cams have these; initially very few were equipped with them, but towards the end of the production run a much higher proportion of cars had them fitted. These seats are comfortable, but do reduce legroom for taller drivers. Additional to the usual extras available on the standard cars, the Twin Cam was available with an oil cooler and close-ratio gearbox, as well as the option of the 4.55:1 rear axle ratio also available on the pushrod car.

Wow! Much of the pleasure of owning a Twin Cam comes once the bonnet is open. The design of the rocker covers is a work of art – mind you, reaching some components to work on them is slightly less pleasurable.

were presented to the press at the military test track at Chobham in Surrey. The track was a good place to demonstrate a car whose main purpose was high-speed performance, each driver being permitted three laps of the banked circuit. Of course, the major magazines immediately obtained cars to subject to their full road test procedures, results of which must have been eagerly awaited by the BMC marketing men.

The roadholding and handling of the Twin Cam is much like all MGAs. The extra weight of the engine does not adversely affect the balance of the car.

The Twin Cam body was modified in a number of areas. The duct panel behind the grille is noticeably shorter than on the standard cars as the radiator is mounted further forward to clear the bulkier engine. From chassis 592 (roadster) and 594 (coupé) access panels were provided under the front wheel arches. The shape of the bonnet was changed so that it cleared the taller engine and the bonnet prop was moved to the left-hand side of the car; these bonnets were later used on all 1600 and 1600 MkIIs.

The engine mounting brackets were different from the pushrod cars. The front springs were also modified to compensate for the heavier engine and were slightly longer than the standard units. Initially an extra, an anti-roll bar was made standard on Twin Cams using the later, 1600-style bodies, and the

front chassis extensions were modified to accommodate these. Taper roller bearings of the type later used on MGBs were fitted to the front hubs, and the stub axles differed from those fitted to pushrod cars. The rear axle case was standard, but the ends of the tubes and the hubs were different.

The road test reports appeared immediately after the public unveiling of the car and must have given the engineers some reasons to worry. Both *The Motor* and *The Autocar* were positive about the virtues of the Twin Cam, but the cars tested exhibited faults about which the average buyer would have had every justification to complain. Oil consumption was high, one car using 5 pints (3 litres) of oil during one 800-mile (1,287km) journey, and the engine required 100 octane fuel to perform acceptably.

The performance was good. Top speed did not match the company's claims of it being a 120mph (193kph) car, but both magazines recorded around 114mph (183kph), which was exceptional for a 1,600cc car in 1958. However, they published widely differing results for the 0–60mph (97kph) sprint: *The Autocar* said 13.3 seconds and *The Motor* 9.1. However, both cars took about 41 seconds to reach 100mph (161kph), and one can only speculate that either the car run by *The Autocar* was in a state of tune that only favoured high-speed running, or there was something different in the way the two cars were driven and the figures recorded. Given that an ordinary 1600 MGA with 79.5bhp took 14.2 seconds to reach 60mph, a Twin Cam with 108bhp and only just over 100lb (45kg) of additional weight should have been able to better 13.3 seconds.

In the hands of ordinary car buyers the Twin Cam quickly gained a reputation for unreliability. A combination of insufficient engine development and unsympathetic usage saw a spate of engine failures and soaring warranty claims. This is no place to labour the difficulties suffered by early owners as most cars today have engines that have been modified to overcome their original weaknesses. However, it is as well to understand what caused the trouble in case any have escaped attention.

Many engines failed because of holed pistons; this was usually caused by pre-ignition when using fuel of too low an octane rating, or by incorrect ignition timing. The piston specification was changed four times in an attempt to overcome both this weakness and excessive oil consumption, with the final version introduced at chassis 2251

One of the ex-works Twin Cam cars that ran at Sebring in 1959, now restored and on the track once again.

being the definitive answer. The trouble was that the 9.9:1 compression originally specified, and persevered with for the initial modifications, was just too high for safe use with lower octane fuels, or when the ignition timing was outside the ideal settings. With the compression ratio reduced to 8.3:1, engine reliability improved greatly. The ignition timing was critical and the factory decided to reduce the possibility of pre-ignition by removing the vacuum advance mechanism from the distributor, a new unit being introduced in January 1960; this was intended to be fitted to all earlier cars by the dealers.

Problems were also encountered with the tappet buckets. Early engines had short buckets running directly in the aluminium head and these could jam or turn; the valve then hit the piston crown with expensive results. The design of the tappets was first changed at engine 1087, to stop them jamming in the guides, and from engine 2211 steel liners were introduced; these modifications must be incorporated in all engines. There were initially some problems with the cooling system. To stop water loss, from chassis 652 the pressure cap on the header tank was replaced by a plain cap, with a separate water pressure release valve and drain pipe fitted to the inner wing.

Approached now, at first it is difficult to come to terms with a Twin Cam if you are in awe of its reputation for giving trouble, or think of it as a thinly disguised racing car. In practice, anyone familiar with a standard MGA will feel at home in the Twin Cam cockpit and will not find that the extra power causes any embarrassment. Most cars now run with the lower-compression pistons and these are to be recommended. For some reason quite a number of MGAs suffer from overheating, something rare when the cars were new. The cause can often be traced to a blocked radiator, poor airflow caused by closed-up slats in the grille or omission of the seal between the bonnet and radiator surround, or

incorrect timing. With the Twin Cam the situation is worsened by the restricted space around the engine, so they are not cars that like to spend long periods idling in traffic.

On the open road a good Twin Cam is a joy. There is a far harder edge to the engine note, and increased mechanical noise from under the bonnet, these combining to make the driver well aware that he is at the wheel of something special. The engine must be run at higher revs to be fully appreciated; changing up too early leaves the impression that the car is not as powerful as figures suggest. In many ways the Twin Cam engine behaves much as one has come to expect from modern 16-valve power units, which seem to give of their best at higher engine speeds. Idling is lumpy and it seems to be difficult to combine an even tick-over with a smooth power delivery; this is mainly because it is important not to run the engine too lean, giving too rich a mixture at idle. Some units are better than others, usually where an expert has spent a lot of time running the car on a rolling road and selecting the correct carburettor needles.

The centre-lock Dunlop wheels fitted to all Twin Cam MGAs are peg-driven, unlike the splined wire wheels that were optional on pushrod cars.

A Twin Cam is an exciting car to own. Adding extra engine power to the traditional MGA virtues of a strong chassis, safe handling and a comfortable ride is the icing on the cake. Few enthusiastic drivers could fail to enjoy a fast run in a Twin Cam, top down, on roads where the power and roadholding can be fully exploited. The sounds from the hard-pressed engine combine with the prominent, but not raucous, exhaust note to produce a motoring experience to remember. There is also the visual beauty of the engine. At meetings, see just how many people stop to admire the impressive sight of the well-filled space under the bonnet of a Twin Cam. The polished cam covers are a work of art, and the standard engine looks puny by comparison.

Buying Hints

1. Because Twin Cams are rarer and more expensive it is important to check that any car on offer is a proper Twin Cam and has all the correct components. The Twin Cam Register of the MG Car Club have compiled lists of the remaining cars and details are available to club members.

2. The engine is far more expensive to work on and requires specialist skills for some operations. Cylinder heads have sometimes been planed in an attempt to cure gasket failures and many reduced to scrap because the valve heads have been brought too close to the piston crowns. Because new heads are not available and second-hand ones in good condition are in short supply, over-skimmed heads are sometimes used with over-thick gaskets, but this should be considered merely as a temporary solution.

3. The longer tappet buckets, modified valve springs and shim retainers, as well as the steel inserts in the cylinder head, must have been used when the engine was rebuilt. Buyers should ask for proof of this, or ensure that the work was carried out by a knowledgeable specialist. Given the current situation with fuel supplies, a lower-compression engine is a better bet.

4. It is essential that the cooling system always has the correct anti-freeze solution added to the water to inhibit electrolytic corrosion of the waterways in the aluminium cylinder head.

5. Any car bought as a 'restoration project' must have all the correct engine components and these should be useable; finding replacements could be difficult and costly. Before parting with good money for a non-running engine, have it examined by an expert, as it may be little more than scrap and quite worthless.

6. Because the brakes are similar to those used on the Jaguar MkII, replacement components are available. Check that the handbrake works.

7. All the remarks made in the chapter on the pushrod MGA about the condition of chassis and body components apply equally to the Twin Cam. The only qualification is that, with fewer cars available, buyers cannot afford to be quite so fussy if a Twin Cam is their goal. However, the costs of carrying out repairs should not be underestimated.

8. Coupés are rarer than roadsters and often less expensive; they are attractive cars but the cockpit can get a bit uncomfortable on hot days. It is an expensive operation to convert a coupé to a roadster, with new doors and other body panels required in addition to the windscreen, hood and side screens. A converted car will always be worth less than an original roadster.

Midget/Sprite
948cc & 1,098cc

The 'Midget' title was first used by MG for the 847cc M-Type introduced at the 1928 Olympia Motor Show, and was then applied to a succession of models, the TF being the last of the line. The MGA was seen as a completely new type of MG, and 'Midget' no longer seemed appropriate for a car 13 feet (3.96m) long with an engine capacity of nearly 1,500cc.

Although the MGA was successful, Abingdon were all too aware that it was too expensive for some buyers. One solution was to build a more basic version, and in 1956 some work was done on designing one with a single-carburettor B-Series engine, smaller wheels and cheaper steering gear. Later a car was built using the BMC A-Series engine. Neither was successful, the first because it was

difficult to reduce the specification of the car enough for it to be sold for significantly less than the current MGA, and the second because the 37bhp produced by the A-Series engine available at the time was just not sufficient to power a car as heavy as an MGA. In the end it was to a car conceived elsewhere that MG were to turn for their budget sports car.

The Donald Healey Motor Company were building expensive, low-volume sports cars at their factory in Warwick and although these were selling fairly well in America they really needed something cheaper if they were to survive long term. In 1952 they exhibited a modern two-seater sports car with attractive, streamlined bodywork at the Motor Show, and it was this car that led to the association with BMC and the birth of the

An early 1,098cc, disc-braked MkI Midget. The pierced disc wheels were replaced by stronger wheels without the holes soon after this car was built. Although otherwise very original, this Midget lacks the polished aluminium strip on the front edge of the bonnet.

668 EBL

PUBLICATION No. E. 6134

THE NEW MG MIDGET

Safety fast!

THE CAR THAT *Starts ahead*

The announcement brochure for the first post-war under-1-litre MG sports car.

Austin-Healey marque. In 1956, at a policy meeting attended by Donald Healey and Leonard Lord, the idea of making a smaller and cheaper sports car was proposed. At Warwick, Healeys started working on a car based around the engine, gearbox and front suspension components from the Austin A35 saloon. Designs for the new model were produced very quickly and by January 1957 a prototype car was ready for assessment by the BMC management, who approved production.

The chassis and body for the new Austin-Healey, which was to be called the Sprite, were to be produced as a single unit, an innovation for a BMC sports car. The strength of the chassis was based around a boxed scuttle structure, deep boxed sills, and a rigid prop-shaft tunnel. The chassis was light and rigid, giving the car good performance with an engine of modest power output and a virtual absence of scuttle shake. The body was kept as

simple as possible. The rear section had pleasing, rounded lines, but no external access to the luggage compartment; at the front the wings and bonnet were united as a single, rear-hinged section that gave excellent access to the engine and front suspension.

The styling, as finalised, was a little odd, with the headlights set in pods on top of the bonnet, giving rise to the universal nickname of 'Frogeye Sprite'. Quarter-elliptic rear springs were an unusual feature that produced a firm ride and a degree of 'rear-end steering' caused by axle deflection under weight transfer on corners. However, quick and accurate rack-and-pinion steering from the Morris Minor endowed this small sports car with handling that enabled a well-driven Sprite to show a clean pair of heels to far more powerful machinery.

The Sprite was an immediate sales success with over 21,000 sold in 1959, the first full year of production. However, there were many complaints about access to the luggage compartment, so when sales fell back in 1960 the bosses at BMC decided on

Midget MkI/Sprite MkII
948cc 1961-64

(Note that although Mark designations for the Midget are one behind the Sprite, MkI Midgets and MkII Sprites are basically the same model)

ENGINE:
Four-cylinder, ohv
Bore x stroke   62.9 x 76.2
Capacity   948cc
Power   46.5bhp

TRANSMISSION:
Four-speed gearbox
Final drive   4.22:1

BODY STYLE:
Two-seater sports car

PERFORMANCE:
(from contemporary sources)
Max speed   88mph (142kph)
0-60mph (97kph)   18.3 seconds

LENGTH: 11ft 5½in (3.49m)

WIDTH: 4ft 6in (1.37m)

WHEELBASE: 6ft 8in (2.03m)

Midget MkI/Sprite MkII
1,098cc 1961-64

As MkI/MkII 948cc except:
Bore x stroke   64.6 x 83.7
Capacity   1098cc
Power   55bhp
Max speed   89mph (143kph)
0-60mph (97kph)   17.0 seconds

Midget MkII/Sprite MkIII
1,098cc 1964-66

As MkI/MkII 948cc except:
Bore x stroke   64.6 x 83.7
Capacity   1,098cc
Power   59bhp
Max speed   92mph (148kph)
0-60mph (97kph)   14.5 seconds

NUMBERS BUILT:
(Midget and Sprite combined)
MkI/MkII 948cc   36,530
MkI/MkII 1098cc   20,816
MkII/MkIII 1098cc   52,506

The dashboard of the 948cc MG Midgets was simple but attractive. A full range of instruments kept the 1960s sports car driver happy and the cheap and cheerful Midget certainly did not disappoint in this respect. The seats of the 948cc cars were the same design as those used on the 1,098cc MkI Midget and early MkIIs, but they had less padding and different-style covers.

modifications. Healey at Warwick, and the Abingdon team under Syd Enever, designed new front and rear sections for the car. To keep costs low, the basic structure remained unchanged; the new front wings and front panels were merely bolted in place, and the separate bonnet was hinged at the scuttle using the existing hinge points. The rear wings and rear decking were welded to the body and a separate boot lid was fitted into the rear deck. To give more cockpit space the top of the rear panel behind the seats was cut back.

The chassis and running gear were identical to the earlier cars, but the 948cc A-Series engine received a stronger crankshaft, a raised compression ratio, larger inlet valves with double valve springs, and 1¼in SU carburettors. Power output was up from 42.5 to 46.5bhp. A close-ratio gearbox was standard equipment. For the MkII Sprite, as the new model was to be called, the seats, dashboard and trim were little changed. It was launched in

May 1961 and received a warm welcome. The weight had increased, but the more powerful engine and better gear ratios gave the car better performance than the previous model.

In 1961 there were still separate dealer networks handling sales of Austin-Healeys and MGs; the latter had been anxious to have a lower-priced model and had been casting envious eyes at the Abingdon-built Sprites sold through Austin dealerships. With the redesign it was decided that the car would be sold as both an Austin-Healey and as an MG, the latter being announced shortly after the Austin-Healey Sprite launch.

Although the MkI Midget – the Mark designations were destined to remain one step behind those of the Sprite – was mechanically identical to the Austin-Healey, there were many minor external and trim changes to distinguish the cars. MG owners must have appeared the more affluent as the Midget cost £669 15s 10d in Britain against £631 10s 10d for a basic Sprite. For the extra, they received different covers for the seats, covered cockpit side rails, an ivory-coloured steering wheel, better rubber floor covering and additional carpeting, sidescreens with two sliding panels instead of one, chrome side strips on the body, a bonnet centre strip, and an MG radiator grille. Ace wheel discs were an optional extra and fibreglass hardtops of differing patterns were available for both the Midget and the Sprite.

Midget buyers had an attractive range of colours from which to choose, these differing from the Sprite. The cars were offered in black with red trim; blue with blue trim; grey with red trim; red with red or black trim; and white with red or black trim. Both the Sprite and the Midget could be ordered with a cushion for the rear parcel shelf that matched the front seats. The ivory-coloured steering wheel was dropped in favour of a black one after a few months of production.

The MG was enthusiastically received, and was compared favourably with the under-1,000cc pre-war Midgets by many journalists, who found that the combination of light weight, agility and a real sports car environment for driver and passenger made the new MG a lot of fun at a very reasonable price. *The Autocar* found that top speed was 85mph (137kph) and that 60mph (97kph) was reached in just over 20 seconds. They did criticise the brakes, which they felt were only just adequate for the performance on offer.

This criticism was addressed when the cars were revised in time for the 1962 Motor Show. The 948cc engine was enlarged to 1,098cc, giving a welcome boost in power of 8.5bhp. The clutch was enlarged by an inch and the gearbox gained much-improved baulk-ring synchromesh on the three upper ratios. At the front, the drum brakes were replaced by Lockheed 8.25-inch (210mm) diameter discs, producing an ideal set-up that was retained until the end of Midget

production in 1979. Inside, the trim was much improved, gaining crash rolls above and below the dashboard, padded door trims, full carpeting, and more deeply upholstered seats. The Sprite had all the Midget mechanical and cockpit improvements, but kept the plain grille and lack of exterior chrome that had characterised the model. The revised cars were still called MkI Midgets and MkII Sprites, but the factory designation changed to GAN2 for the Midget and HAN7 for the Sprite.

Although the 1,098cc engine was more powerful, it later gained a reputation

Although wire wheels were initially not available on the Midget, buyers could have these attractive Ace Mercury wheel trims on their cars. Few surviving MkI Midgets retain them.

The Jacobs Midgets

The BMC Competitions Department expended most of their efforts on the big Austin-Healeys, the Minis and the MGB, but some Midgets were prepared for competition. The best known of these were the Midget coupés entered by Dick Jacobs, the owner of the prominent South Woodford MG dealership, Mill Garage.

With the promotional material sent to Jacobs when the Midget was announced was a drawing of its side elevation. Looking at this alongside pictures of an Aston-Martin DB4, he was inspired to build a Midget coupé, and took his idea to John Thornley at Abingdon. It was received with enthusiasm and Syd Enever and the Development

Department were asked to design and build cars based on these proposals. The bumpers were discarded and the nose re-shaped to give better aerodynamics. The bodywork and fixed hardtop were made of aluminium, riveted and bonded to the steel chassis.

The overall weight was reduced to 11cwt (559kg). Standard suspension was retained, although softer rear road springs, Aeon progressive bump rubbers and stiffer dampers were used, and disc brakes were fitted. With the engine bored out to 979cc and fitted with a 45DCOE carburettor, the power output was 75bhp. In spite of this modest state of tune, to ensure reliability in long-distance races, the coupé

Midgets were capable of around 120mph (193kph) with acceleration to match.

Three of these cars were built, two – 770 BJB and 771 BJB – going to Jacobs for him to run as a team. Driven by Andrew Hedges and Alan Foster, they achieved considerable success in national and international events and were later progressively improved by fitting larger-capacity engines.

Of the three Midget Coupés built at Abingdon, two went to Dick Jacobs and the third to John Milne in Scotland, where it remains.

The neat sidescreens are easily attached to the doors and give the occupants some additional weather protection. On these cars the hood frame and cover stow away in the boot. The light blue tonneau cover is the original one supplied with the car new.

for having a weaker bottom end than either the 948cc or the later 1,098cc and 1,275cc units. However, the cockpit improvements made the car feel quieter and more refined and the increased engine power and better brakes were welcome improvements. The Autocar ran a full test of the 1,098cc Midget and recorded a top speed of nearly 90mph (145kph) and reached 60mph (97kph) in just over 17 seconds. Soon after the 1,098cc car went into production, and following some wheel failures on competition cars, the pierced steel wheels gave way to stronger, unventilated ones. Wire wheels were now a popular option.

The colour schemes for the 1,098cc Midget were black with red or brown trim; blue with blue trim; green with black trim; grey with red trim; red with red or black trim; and white with

brown, red or black trim. The Sprite was offered in a similar range of colours with the additional option of yellow with black trim. On both marques the colour of the hood and tonneau cover varied according to body colour, with black, brown, grey, red and blue being available.

Although the quarter-elliptic rear suspension had originally been designed for the MkI Sprite for reasons of simplicity and light weight, in practice it had certain limitations: the springs had to be stiff, which compromised ride comfort, and the deflection of the axle caused a degree of rear-end steering. For drivers used to the car this was of little consequence as they knew that it would tighten up its line as it rounded a bend, and compensated instinctively by straightening the steering wheel a little.

Adding the bulkier windscreen and doors to the car made the MkII Midget look quite different from the starkly simple MkI. This beautiful car, one of the last MkII models built, has been in the hands of one owner from new, covering just 34,000 miles in his hands.

The new rear section introduced for the MkII Sprite was capable of bearing the stresses imposed by a more conventional rear suspension, although the quarter-elliptic springs were retained. With the introduction of the MkII Midget and MkIII Sprite in March 1964, the opportunity was taken to fit half-elliptic rear springs, which made the rear suspension softer and the handling more predictable. There was also a small weight saving as a bonus.

The changes made for this model were far-reaching, encompassing major body engineering revisions and engine modifications in addition to the new rear suspension. When the MkI Sprite

had been conceived it was as a cheap sports car without frills, and items like archaic sidescreens were seen as acceptable. By 1964 things were different. The introduction of cars like the Sunbeam Alpine in 1959 and the MGB in 1962 had changed buyers' perceptions of sports car; they found that the combination of a good hood and winding side windows could make the cars almost as practical as a saloon for winter travel.

A direct rival to the Sprite and Midget was launched at the 1962 Earls Court Motor Show. The Triumph Spitfire used the all-independent Herald chassis, and its Michelotti-designed bodywork had a combined front wings and bonnet unit that lifted to give superb access to the engine and front suspension. Good ride and roadholding was, however, marred by the tendency for the rear swing axles and transverse leaf spring to 'jack up' when cornering, resulting in sudden breakaway. The interior of the Spitfire was fairly basic, but the provision of a good hood and winding side windows set it ahead of the BMC small sports cars.

To remain competitive, the BMC engineers had to come up with similar appointments for the Sprite and Midget. One problem they faced was that of persuading a winding window mechanism, as well as internal and external door handles, to fit in such tiny doors; enlarging these would have entailed far-reaching structural alterations to the main body tub. The solution adopted was to place the internal door handle with the lock at the rear edge of the door, which removed the need to have a mechanism to link the door handle with the lock. The doors were made a little thicker at the top with a section incorporated to accommodate the swivelling quarter lights, window glass and seals.

It was not all gain, however, as the doors lost some vital elbow room for driver and passenger, as well as the map pockets; a small oddment shelf was fitted above the passenger's legs to compensate. The new windscreen looked similar to that used on the MGB and incorporated a bracing strut in the centre that also served as a mounting for the adjustable rear-view mirror. Longer windscreen wiper blades increased the cleaned area of glass.

A redesigned but still detachable hood frame was provided and the hood fabric now had a rigid front rail fitted, which was held to the windscreen frame by a pair of over-centre catches. Inside the car, much had changed. The

Despite their size, Midgets are strongly built and occupants are well protected

revised seats introduced in 1962 were retained, but the dashboard was completely redesigned. A black, crackle-painted steel pressing replaced the leathercloth-covered panel of earlier cars, and the speedometer and electrically driven tachometer sat in an angled housing conveniently placing them on either side of the steering column. The fuel gauge and combined water temperature/oil pressure gauge sat on either side of the centrally mounted ignition key/starter switch with the other minor controls. The flashing direction indicators now had a self-cancelling stalk on the steering column, and a pair of arrows by the steering column illuminated when they were operating. A new steering wheel carried a central horn push, marked with either Austin or MG badges.

Under the bonnet there were also a number of important changes. Because the first 1,098cc engine was felt to be weak, the crankshaft was stiffened and the main bearing journal diameters increased from 1.75 to 2 inches (44 to 51mm) for the MkII unit. The MG 1100 cylinder head, which had enlarged inlet

valves and improved gas flow, was fitted, along with an improved exhaust manifold. The engine now produced 59bhp, an increase of 4bhp. More important, it was now a much more robust unit and better able to cope with further tuning. A rear-mounted SU electric fuel pump replaced the mechanical unit used previously. Road testers praised the revised suspension and reported a maximum of speed 92mph (148kph) and a time of 14.5 seconds to 60mph (97kph). Increased sales resulted: over 22,000 Midgets and Sprites were built in 1964, and their improved comfort led to many being purchased as second cars.

Sadly, very few MkI Midgets and MkII Sprites survive in first-class condition, the position with the winding-window MkII/MkIII being much better. For some reason a great many people are prepared to spend a lot of money restoring MGAs and early MGBs while the early Midget is regarded as something of a poor relation. The body of the Midget and Sprite is, in any guise, a lot more difficult to repair than an MGB, door fits and sill/door pillar replacement defeating many amateur restorers. The early cars also suffer badly from rot around the rear spring mountings and this, too, is difficult to remedy.

For the MkII the dashboard was totally revised. Metal pressings were used with the speedometer and tachometer housed in angled pods on either side of the steering column. The gear lever knob on this car is not original.

The 1,098cc A-Series engine fitted to the MkII Midgets is a sweet, free-revving unit. Although less powerful than the 1,275cc engine, it gives the cars sufficient performance to make driving a pleasure. The circular housing above the inlet manifold is the valve for the closed-circuit breather.

However, getting behind the wheel of one of these early cars is to re-live the essence of basic sports car motoring enjoyed by those of us lucky enough to have run these cars new. The seats are upright but comfortable; taller drivers often re-drilled the side holes in the back rests to gain a little more rake. The steering wheel is quite large and placed close to the chest. In spite of the restricted size of the cockpit, taller drivers have no difficulty in making themselves comfortable once they adopt a knees-wide-apart driving position. The foot-operated dip switch makes a comfortable rest for the left foot, while the closely set brake and throttle pedals are ideally placed.

The instrument layout is good, although it can take a while to remember to cancel the turn indicators as the switch for these is in the centre of the

dashboard and the warning light can be missed in bright sunlight. The rear-view mirror is too low for many drivers and vibrates badly; a stick-on replacement is a better alternative. The side screens are fixed to the tops of the doors by knurled screws, an old one penny piece being the ideal tightening tool! The hood fits well, with the rigid bar sewn into the front edge clipping tightly into the slot in the windscreen frame, but it vibrates at speed. With the hood and sidescreens packed away in the boot, these early cars look attractive and feel a lot smaller somehow than the later versions with their bulkier doors, windscreen and side windows.

Performance with the 948cc engine is adequate rather than good, but the drum brakes feel better than some reports would lead one to expect. However, they do need a good push on the pedal and will never feel quite as reassuring as the later discs. The 1,098cc cars are noticeably quicker, the disc brakes and better trim making these the best of the quarter-elliptic-sprung cars. These springs do give a harder ride than half-elliptics, but this is by no means bad and the rear-end steering is only noticed occasionally. The overriding impression is of just how much fun these cars are to drive.

The crackle-black paint on the dashboard of the winding-window 1,098cc cars places them firmly in the 1960s. The dashes may look less attractive than the earlier cloth-covered ones, but they are well laid out with the angled pods placing the main instruments exactly where they are most visible. The steering wheel is comfortable to hold and the self-cancelling indicators a great improvement. As an extra, the steering-column-mounted indicator stalk also doubles to flash the headlamps. The seats on early MkIIs are the same as those on the previous model, changing in August 1965 to the variety fitted to early 1,275cc cars.

When erected, the hood and winding side windows give the MkII a saloon car feel with fewer draughts and less hood vibration. However, the fixed front rail makes the hood itself more difficult to stow in the boot, and the removable frame is time-consuming to assemble. The extra power of the revised engine makes the 1,098cc MkII almost as quick as the 1,275cc cars, and this power unit is one of the smoothest and most robust of the A-Series engines. The suspension changes give a more comfortable ride, but steering still needs a light touch. Drivers find themselves carrying out minor corrections as small bumps upset the car's composure, but this is no chore and is soon forgotten in the delight of handling such a nimble and entertaining machine.

In current traffic conditions the small size of the car can be an advantage once it has been accepted that every other car looks large, and that lorries and buses look enormous! It is certainly advisable to fit and wear seat belts in view of the rigid steering column and toggle switches; the static variety are best suited to the car. However, despite its small size, the body structure is strong and the occupants well protected in accidents. Super little cars!

For Buying hints and Specifications, see the end of the following chapter.

MG 1100 and MG 1300 saloons

The announcement of the MG 1100 in October 1962 was overshadowed by the concurrent arrival of the new MGB, but the MG saloon was the more advanced car, having a transverse engine layout, front-wheel drive, and a truly revolutionary suspension system. 'Hydrolastic' spring units were developed by Dr Alex Moulton in an attempt to reduce bounce, pitch and roll. The front and rear suspensions were interconnected, sharing the effect of hitting irregularities in the road more equally between both ends of the car. When the front wheel was raised by hitting a bump, it lifted both the front and rear of the car, keeping it level and reducing pitch. When the back wheel reached the same bump the shock was, in turn, partly shared by the front wheel. The MG 1100 system worked well, aided by a rear anti-roll bar and anti-pitch bars within the rear subframe.

The MG 1100 was distinguished from its Austin and Morris stablemates by having a 55bhp, twin-carburettor engine, two-tone paintwork, and plush interior. It sold fairly well but never captured the sort of attention from sporting enthusiasts enjoyed by the Mini Cooper. In America a two-door version was marketed as 'The MG Sports Sedan', backed by a vigorous marketing campaign and even the entry of a racing car with hydrolastic springs at Indianapolis.

There was also an up-market 1100 with heavily padded leather seats, loads of walnut-veneered woodwork, picnic tables, and the MG version of the 1,098cc engine. This car was sold elsewhere as the Vanden Plas Princess 1100, but for the American market a catalogue was produced showing it badged as the 'MG Princess 1100', although few cars found their way over the Atlantic.

BMC had developed a 1,275cc version of the A-Series engine for the Mini Cooper 'S', and a larger-capacity engine would obviously give the 1100 range a welcome boost in performance. In 1967 some cars were sold fitted with a single-carburettor 1,275cc engine. From October 1967 the whole range of 1100s had a revised bodyshell with less prominent rear fins and new rear light clusters. The MG version was available both as an 1100 MkII and as the MG 1300, which had the single-carburettor 1,275cc engine producing 58bhp. Early in 1968 the 1100 model was dropped and the 1300 gained a twin-carburettor 65bhp engine. All-synchromesh transmission arrived a few months later.

For the 1968 Motor Show the car received further revisions and gained the title 'MG 1300 MkII'. With improved seats, better instruments and a more powerful 70bhp engine, the superb roadholding made the car as quick on cross-country journeys as the contemporary Midget. This model was available solely in two-door form and production ceased in 1971. The years have not treated the MG 1100/1300 models well, the majority being scrapped due to terminal rust problems.

The MG 1100 was a more powerful and better trimmed version of the Morris/Austin 1100 designed by Issigonis. The transverse power unit and front-wheel drive produced a combination of good roadholding and spacious cabin that made the 1100 range popular with buyers.

Midget/Sprite
1,275cc & 1,500cc

Sales of the revised Sprites and Midgets held up well following the major revisions in 1964 that had seen the introduction of winding windows and a better rear suspension for BMC's small sports car. In 1963 16,477 of the 1,098cc quarter-elliptic-sprung cars were sold, with 1,227 fewer Midgets produced than Sprites. In 1964 all but 1,246 of the cars built were the revised model, and combined sales for the year leapt to 22,607 cars. That year was the high point in the production of the Midgets and Sprites, and thereafter it fell to just over 18,000 in 1965 and 13,866 in 1966. It is interesting to see that the Triumph Spitfire sales for those years were 19,966 and 17,077 respectively, and that they too had a bumper 1964 with 23,387 cars sold.

The rivalry between the BMC small sports cars and those from Triumph obviously influenced the way the cars developed, with each organisation progressively increasing performance and equipment levels to match the other. One has to say that Triumph gained the upper hand in the battle with their sales always exceeding the combined totals for the BMC twins. Eventually, as we know, the culmination of this rivalry was the merger of the two companies under the British Leyland banner. Of course, these models were not the only small sporting cars on the market. Italy had a long tradition of building exciting machinery and for a time even added their touch of flair to the Sprite with the re-bodied Innocenti 950 Spider. These cars had attractive coachwork married to Sprite underpinnings and included such luxuries as winding

When the 1,275cc Midget was introduced the rear deck behind the cockpit was completely redesigned so that a revised, fold-down hood could be fitted. This design was to remain in use until production ceased in 1979, and is one of the easiest to use of all MG hoods. A neat cover for the stowed hood was standard equipment.

One of the colours that particularly suits the Midget is Pale Primrose. This attractive 1969 model year car was built early enough to have retained the central bonnet strip. Wire wheels were a popular option.

windows and a lockable luggage compartment well in advance of their introduction on the MkII Sprite. The doors were wider, making entry easier, later cars gained the 1,098cc engine, and there was even a coupé version introduced in 1967. Over 17,000 cars were built between their introduction in 1961 and 1970, when assembly ceased; unfortunately none were produced with right-hand steering.

The 1,275cc Cooper S was one of the breed of tuned saloon cars that

Midget MkIII 1275 1966–74

Sprite MkIV 1275 1966–71

ENGINE:
Four–cylinder, ohv
Bore x stroke	70.6 x 81.3
Capacity	1,275cc
Power	65bhp

TRANSMISSION:
Four-speed gearbox
Final drive	4.22:1, later 3.9:1

BODY STYLE:
Two-seater sports car

PERFORMANCE:
(from contemporary sources)
Max speed	94mph (151kph)
0–60mph (97kph)	13.8 seconds

LENGTH:	11ft 5½in (3.49m)

WIDTH:	4ft 6in (1.37m)

WHEELBASE:	6ft 8in (2.03m)

Midget 1500 1974–79

As MkIII/MkIV 1275cc except:
Bore x stroke	73.7 x 87.5
Capacity	1,493cc
Power	66bhp
Final drive	3.9:1, later 3.7:1
Max speed	101mph (163kph)
0–60mph (97kph)	12 seconds
Length	11ft 9in (3.58m)

NUMBERS BUILT:
(Midget and Sprite combined)
1275	123,026
Midget 1500	72,289

For the 1969 model year cars the closed-circuit breathing system was revised and the crankcase fumes were drawn directly into the carburettors without the need for a valve on the inlet manifold. This car is non-standard, as the pipe to extract the engine fumes should come from a canister on the timing cover, not from the rocker cover.

emerged in the 1960s to challenge the established sports cars in the performance market. The agile Cooper may have been able to run rings round the Midget, but its arrival was to provide the means of giving the latter welcome extra performance. Once the 1,275cc A-Series engine was available, it was obvious that a number of current BMC cars would benefit from its use, the Morris/Austin/MG 1100 and the Midget/Sprite being prime candidates. When the bigger engines finally made it into production for the Midget and Sprite, they differed somewhat from the Cooper S unit. To keep the overall price reasonable, the specification of some of the components was reduced, the cylinder head carried smaller valves, the

compression ratio was reduced from 9.5:1 to 8.8:1, and the crankshaft was of lower specification. The power output was 65bhp, 11bhp less than the Cooper but 6bhp up on the 1,098cc engine. Torque increased by 16 per cent, but the rear axle ratio remained unchanged.

In addition to having the larger engine, the 1,275cc Midget/Sprite had a diaphragm-spring clutch, which was both more powerful and lighter in use. Separate brake and clutch master cylinders were fitted, which were later to become essential in markets where dual-circuit brakes were required. Visually, the most apparent change was to the hood. A totally new hood frame was designed, which was permanently bolted to the rear door pillars. At the back of the cockpit the rear deck of the body was cut back and a raised lip placed around the edge of the compartment to provide a mounting point for the hood fabric. The hood frame and front rail were

In the late 1960s MG's belt tightening prevented any plans for a brand new model

united, and the whole lot folded neatly down into the space behind the seats. Raising or lowering the hood was now easy, with just two clips to the windscreen frame and a few side fasteners to cope with. A neat cover to conceal the furled hood was standard, and a full tonneau cover was available at extra cost.

The revised hood with an additional hoop to support the fabric better complemented the lines of the car than the previous effort, which looked a bit tall in outline. The alterations to the rear deck blended neatly with the

vertical section at the top of the doors, making this part of the car look much neater. Inside the cockpit there were few changes. The bulkhead panel between the cockpit and the boot now sloped backwards at the top to provide room for hood stowage. However, little usable space was lost in the luggage compartment and owners no longer had to find room for the hood frame and cover.

The MGB-style seats introduced during the production run of the earlier model continued in use, these having a modicum of rake adjustment provided by means of moving a couple of bolts under the back rest. Rearward seat travel was still restricted by the bulkhead, but tall drivers had sufficient headroom. Colour schemes for the 1,275cc cars were similar to those of the superseded model: blue, green, red, white and black. Pale Primrose joined the list late in 1967, and for the 1968 model year the shade of blue was changed and the white made brighter. All cars had black trim with light-coloured piping, except for a few early red, black and white cars, which could have red trim as an alternative. Hoods and tonneau covers were black.

The Austin-Healey Sprite MkIV was in most respects identical to the Midget; only the simple, aluminium grille, lack of chrome side strips, and different badges separate the models.

Red or blue interior trim had been available on the MkII cars, and red remained an option for early 1,275cc cars with black paintwork.

The cars were considered to be sufficiently changed to warrant new Mark designations and factory code numbers. The Sprite was now the MkIV and the Midget the MkIII, coded by the factory as HAN9 and GAN4 models respectively. Cars were soon in the hands of the motoring press who, on the whole, were happy about the increased power and the new hood, but were starting to criticise aspects of the overall design of cars that they saw as being increasingly outdated. *Autocar* persuaded their car to reach a maximum speed of 93.5mph (150kph) and reached 60mph (97kph) in 14.6 seconds. This was not a lot better than the figures for the earlier model, but a test of a similar car a couple of years later produced an acceleration time to 60mph of 13.8 seconds, achieved in a car with the 3.9:1 rear axle fitted to all those built after December 1968.

The 1969 model year cars were fitted with fully reclining seats that had a

different pattern of pleats in the covers, and black, rather than light-coloured, piping. The door panels were also all black. The reclining mechanism was operated by chromed handles on the inner edges of the seat backs. The bonnet lost the central chrome strip, and from chassis number GAN4 66226 (HAN9 77591) the side lights in the front wings were lowered.

The late 1960s was a period of change for the motor industry. Jaguar/Daimler merged with BMC in 1966, and in early 1968 the Leyland Group, which by then had control of MG's great rivals, Triumph, combined with these companies to form the British Leyland Motor Corporation. The effect of this on the MG factory was to scotch any chances of an entirely new MG. The Spitfire was now built within the same group and there was a reluctance to spend any more money than was absolutely necessary on ageing MGs. In 1970 money was found to revise the

Triumph Spitfire, which in MkIV guise was a much improved car.

However, for MG the first real changes appeared on 1970 model year cars. These were cosmetic, amounting to little more than a facelift. The Midget lost the chrome side strips never worn by the Sprite, and both models gained a chrome strip at the top edge of the sills, which were now painted satin black with either 'Midget' or 'Sprite' in chrome lettering arranged along them. The radiator grilles for both cars were based on the Sprite grille; it was painted satin black with a chromed strip set about an inch in from the edge and MG or Sprite badges in the centre. The polished aluminium sections around the grille were also now painted satin black, with a narrow strip on the front edges left polished to match the strip on the grille.

Initially, the windscreen surrounds and wiper arms were also given a coat of matt black anti-dazzle paint, but this was soon dropped.

Neat new bumpers were fitted; at the back the former full-width example was replaced by a pair of thinner section that flanked a squarer numberplate. At the front a thinner full-width bumper mated well with the lowered side lights. Pairs of overriders with rubber inserts were fitted front and rear. The rear light lenses were squared off to give a larger lit area. Reversing lights had already been introduced after the 1,275cc cars had been in production for about a year, and around the same time the electrical system was changed from positive to negative earth. To complement the styling changes, the Sprite and Midget were fitted with

1969 model year cars had all-black trim with reclining seats. This upholstery pattern was only used for that year.

A 1972 'round wheel arch' Midget with a factory hardtop. These were made of fibreglass and look good when painted to match the rest of the car.

steel Rostyle wheels, with wire wheels still an option. These models were given the factory codes GAN5 and HAN10, but were still officially MkIII and MkIV models, although the Mark designation was slowly dropped from the literature.

Bright colours were popular at the time and a stronger red replaced the more traditional Tartan Red, with Bronze Yellow and Blaze (orange) joining the range. Dark green was still available for the more sober buyer! The interior trim featured a revised seat upholstery pattern and new door trims, as well as the introduction of the Autumn Leaf trim (a sort of tan colour) on some cars. The steering wheel had a leather rim and pierced alloy spokes, later modified because of fears that fingers could be trapped in the holes. The dip-switch moved from the floor to a steering column

stalk. Both models carried British Leyland badges on the front wings.

Unfortunately there were no mechanical changes introduced with the new model and the Sprite was now nearing the end of its separate existence. The company paid royalties to the Healey family for each car they sold and when the agreement to use their name expired in 1970 it was not renewed, and the 1,022 Sprites built in 1971 were badged simply as 'Austin Sprites', with the factory chassis prefix changed from HAN10 to AAN10.

In all, 31,977 of the facelift cars were sold before there were further changes at the end of 1971. The rear wheel arches were rounded off to match the style of the front wings, resulting in a more attractive car, with the consequence that 'round wheel arch' models are now the most sought-after

Spridgets. Rostyle wheels of a similar pattern to those used on the MGB replaced those used previously, although wire wheels were still an option. The fuel tank capacity was raised from 6 to 7 gallons (27 to 32 litres) to improve range. The gear lever knob was larger and the dashboard had rocker switches.

Cars built for overseas markets differed from those for the home market, with North America cars seeing a number of changes around this time. For example, as early as November 1967 they received padded dashboards of an entirely different design, dual-circuit brakes, and collapsible steering columns. Exhaust emission controls meant that engine

specifications also varied. Externally triple windscreen wipers, side marker lamps and different colours for lamp lenses distinguished these cars. The 1973 model year cars were blessed with bumpers fitted with huge, black, energy-absorbing overriders as the first stage of an attempt by the company to comply with minor impact regulations.

For the 1975 model year the rules called for there to be absolutely no damage from low-speed collisions, even to items like side lamps, and this was worsened by the need for the bumpers to meet a height requirement that meant raising the Midget ride height by 1½ inches (38mm). The Midget bodyshells had to be

A rubber-bumper 1500 Midget. Introduced in September 1974, these heavy bumpers transformed the appearance of the cars. The rear wheel arch returned to the original shape as the round arch was not felt to be strong enough.

The Lenham-bodied Midgets & Sprites

No sooner had the MkI Sprite appeared on the scene than companies emerged to supply parts to make them look different. Hard tops were an obvious choice, as were lightweight fibreglass bonnets to replace the one-piece front. Prominent in the field was the Lenham Motor Company, which made fibreglass hard tops. Prompted by a customer, it produced a fixed-head coupé version of the MkI Sprite, selling these both as kits and as complete cars. The full conversion included a one-piece fibreglass bonnet and a rear body section with a steeply raked back window and flat

Fitting the bodywork involved cutting off the entire rear deck and rear wings, leaving merely the door pillars and lips around the rear wheel arches. The door pillars had to be braced, then the complete fibreglass rear section was bonded to the remaining metalwork and the edges blended with filler. The front of the roof was fixed to the windscreen using the hood clips. If a lightweight front was specified, the bonnet, front wings and front panels were discarded, and the fibreglass moulding was hinged to the front chassis rails and secured at the rear by Triumph Herald clips.

considerably strengthened to absorb the additional loads. Boxed extensions to the chassis rails carried heavy, rubber-faced bumpers mounted front and rear, shaped to align with the existing bonnet and wings. Adding such large extensions to a small car like the Midget was never going to be entirely successful and in spite of the best efforts of the designers few would say that the revised cars were an improvement.

The front box section stiffeners were welded to the main chassis structure, as was the front panel section. The rear panel was modified to accommodate the new bumper fixings and the front wings no longer had sidelight mountings as these were now incorporated in the headlamps, the flashing indicators being fitted within the rubber bumpers. The front suspension cross member was altered to increase the ride height and different springs were fitted front and rear. The rear wings returned to their original shape as the round wheel arch was not felt to be strong enough to resist minor accident damage.

tail panel. These also fitted the MkI Midget and MkII Sprite.

The later Le Mans coupé for the winding-windows MkII Midget had a fixed roof and rear section with additional side windows. Having these, and the standard door windows and quarter lights, made the interior feel very pleasant. There was also a considerable weight saving, and some converted cars were used in competition.

Fitting the Lenham fibreglass fixed roof and rear section to a Sprite or Midget transformed the appearance of the car. As the original steel rear wings and rear body panels were discarded and the replacement section bonded in place, the modification was permanent and the car could no longer be used open. With some other manufacturers, the 'fastback' roof sections were merely bolted in place and the car could easily be returned to standard.

These changes increased the overall weight considerably and to provide sufficient urge to maintain a reasonable level of performance the A-Series power unit was replaced by the Triumph 1,493cc engine and gearbox used in the Spitfire. It was felt that the existing engine was incapable of being taken out to a larger size, and for the American market the power obtainable from the existing A-Series engine would have dropped drastically if modified to meet the US emission regulations. There was the added advantage that the company would only have to get one engine through US tests and maintain one set of spare parts with overseas distributors. The fortunate Triumph Spitfire 1500 owner could opt to have an overdrive unit, but Midget drivers had to be content with a standard Marina-based four-speed gearbox. At first the 3.9:1 rear axle ratio used on the 1,275cc cars was retained, but later a 3.7:1 ratio was fitted.

Despite the drastically altered looks, for the driver and passenger little changed. The all-synchromesh gearbox had reverse alongside third gear instead of top, so the gear knob carried the revised gate pattern. The carburettors were on the opposite side on the Triumph engine so the choke and heater controls swapped sides on the dash. Otherwise, the cockpit would have been all too familiar to owners of the previous model; seats, trim, steering wheel, switches, etc, were all unchanged, with only the accelerator pedal differing. The launch price of the 1500 was £1,351.35p. The high inflation rates of the 1970s saw dramatic rises in car prices. The 1970 model Midget cost a total of £818 5s 3d, but the April 1980 price for the last few cars built was £3,820.97p. Wow!

A car tested by *Autocar* recorded a top speed of 101mph (163kph) and reached 60mph (97kph) in 12 seconds. Although the car now weighed 142lbs (64kg) more than its predecessor, this was more than offset by the greater power and torque of the larger engine. With 100mph (161kph) performance now available for the first time from a Midget, the 1500 should have been a better car. However, adding so much extra weight at each end, and increasing both the overhangs and ride height, had seriously compromised the handling. Testers thought the steering still good, but found that the rear end could break away quite suddenly if the throttle was closed mid-corner.

Today Midgets are one of the cheapest routes into ownership of a classic sports car. They are also great fun. The 1,275cc cars are really the pick of the bunch with a strong engine, a gearbox with well-chosen gear ratios, and all the creature comforts one could wish for in this sort of car. The engine pulls well and benefits from having either the 3.9:1 gearing fitted from 1970 or, better still, the 3.7:1 of the later 1500 models. Those used to high-revving 16-valve engines will be surprised by the amount of torque delivered at low engine speeds. Although cockpit space is limited, most drivers can get comfortable provided they are prepared to compromise a little. The seats are comfortable although it is essential that the rubber diaphragm in the seat base is in good enough condition to absorb some of the road bumps transmitted by the hard suspension.

At its best top down on meandering back roads, the Midget is a capable everyday car. A plentiful supply of cheap spares is assured by the considerable number of cars still in use that have A-Series engines. Running expenses are low, helped by cheap insurance deals and miserly petrol consumption. Their small size makes them easy to park and there is always enough room for them in even the smallest of garages.

There are still plenty of 1500 Midgets in everyday use, and the strong bumpers are invaluable protection in supermarket car parks. Although many see these cars as flawed, they are still

The interior of a very original, low-mileage 1500. The Triumph Spitfire dials with graduations every 20mph show this to be one of the later cars. From August 1977 the Midget had the 3.7:1 axle ratio, which reduced the stress on the engine at higher speeds.

The Triumph engine has the carburettors on the opposite side of the engine from the earlier cars. The heater inlet pipe has swapped sides, as has the choke control on the dashboard. Dual-circuit brakes were now fitted.

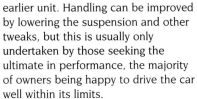

Boot space on all Midgets is limited. This 1500 has the original plastic tool bag and the fabric bag containing the optional tonneau cover.

great fun to drive and give their owners all the advantages of fresh-air motoring enjoyed by those running the earlier cars. The performance is adequate and the gearbox is both quieter and more robust than the earlier unit. Handling can be improved by lowering the suspension and other tweaks, but this is usually only undertaken by those seeking the ultimate in performance, the majority of owners being happy to drive the car well within its limits.

It remains surprising that far fewer enthusiasts consider buying a Midget than an MGB. Although Midget production never reached the levels attained by the larger MG, there were quite a number made and there should be many survivors. However, earning a name as a cheap and cheerful sports car seems to have harmed their long-term survival, with very few of the MkI models still on the road and the position of the later models jeopardised by the reluctance of owners to spend much on their restoration. Considering how nice they are to own, this is strange.

Buying Hints

1. The first thing to consider is whether a Midget or Sprite is suitable. A short test drive may not be convincing – it may be better to try to persuade an owner to demonstrate their car or try to arrange a long test before the search starts.

2. Beware of buying an outwardly reasonable-looking Midget that still needs a lot of money spent to make it sound and reliable; either pay more for a really good car or look for a restoration project that makes a cheap basis for a full rebuild or Heritage shell; remember that it will cost more to produce a near-perfect car than it will be worth on the open market.

3. Many cars offered for sale are concocted from parts taken from a number of different versions and these have often been given non-original interiors, wheels, etc. This may not matter too much, but should be reflected in the price paid, as original cars are more valuable.

4. The Midget/Sprite body shell goes rusty, and it is the condition of this above all else that should concern buyers. Examine any potential purchase carefully as many cars will have been run and restored on a budget, often extending to an over-liberal use of filler to conceal the need for more permanent repairs.

5. Rust is easily spotted. Vulnerable areas like the front door pillars and sills are obvious. Look at the shut-lines round the door openings and make sure that the door hinges are firmly attached. Poorly fitting doors are common as repairs to the door pillars and sills are difficult on very rusty cars and supporting the car incorrectly can distort the whole body.

6. Front wings bolt in place and are easily replaced, but look for rust on the inner wings and make sure that the gap between the wing and sills has not been covered. A delve beneath the trim panel in the footwells can reveal rust on the inner wings.

7. Floors rust badly, especially when the car is kept outside, as few hoods are completely weatherproof. Look under the carpets and particularly along the edge by the sills. When rust has really taken hold the entire floor and inner sills may need to be replaced, not a job for the faint-hearted as it is difficult to maintain the correct alignment of panels.

8. It is particularly important to look carefully at the rear bulkhead and at the spring mountings. On quarter-elliptic cars in particular, severe damage here calls for wholesale surgery and considerable skill. On the later cars the condition of the mountings for the rear spring hangers is also important. Boot floors rust, as do the lower sections of the rear wings.

7. The good news is that Heritage shells are available, as are all the necessary panels, such as doors, bonnet, wings, etc. The bad news is that not every model is catered for and owners of early cars in particular will have to repair the original shell if the originality of their car is to be maintained. Some of the tooling used for new panels is past its best and these sometimes differ dimensionally from the originals.

8. On the mechanical front there is little to worry about as parts are plentiful and repairs fairly cheap. However, the real weak area is the front suspension, which must be greased every 1,000 miles, in spite of advice to the contrary in the factory service schedules. Unless the car has been very well maintained, or has had a recent suspension overhaul, budget for one in the purchase price. While in this area, examine the shock absorbers for signs of weakness or leaks - rebuilt units usually fail after a short time in service and new ones are a better proposition.

9. The A-Series engine will betray wear with low oil pressure and a smoky exhaust, but rebuilt engines are reasonably priced and the cylinder head can easily be converted to run on unleaded fuel. The 1500 engine has a weak bottom end, not helped by an oil pump arrangement that allows all the oil to return to the sump when the engine stops; bearing wear on starting is inevitable. However, the engine is more powerful than the A-Series unit and is still just as cheap to repair.

10. To overcome the lack of overdrive, there are conversions available to fit five-speed gearboxes to the earlier cars and Triumph overdrive units to the 1500. These do require a certain amount of body surgery, in addition to the mechanical work, and this must be competently executed.

The MGB
& MGB GT

Developing a new car is a long process and work on a replacement for the successful MGA started soon after the first of them had rolled off the Abingdon production lines. The hurdles faced by the design team at MG included the usual shortage of sufficient money for the sort of development work undertaken by other manufacturers, and the difficulties imposed by management and sales organisations that were out of their direct control. An example was the strange accounting methods within BMC that allowed a system of allocating group profits that differed from plant to plant, and gave American distributors greater discount on MGs than on Austin-Healeys. As a result, top management could respond to a

request for more development money for new models by saying that the MG factory made little or no profit in spite of record sales. Similar arguments were to lead to the final closure of the plant by the Leyland management in 1980.

In spite of this, right from the outset proposals for updating and improving the MGA were advanced. The idea of a cut-price model has already been mentioned, but there were also schemes for enlarging the luggage compartment and for building a stretched MGA with occasional rear seats. Frua, an Italian stylist, was sent an MGA 1500 chassis in 1957 and he designed and had built a striking new body for the car. It bore more than a passing resemblance to other 1950s Italian sports cars, having been given plenty of chrome trim and a fashionable 'wrap-around' windscreen. The prototype was sent to Abingdon for assessment and drawings were taken from the car,

The simple, uncluttered lines of the early MGBs were never improved by later revisions. The painted wire wheels were an optional extra, as were whitewall tyres.

MGB & MGB GT
1962–80

ENGINE:
Four–cylinder, ohv
Bore x stroke   80.26 x 89
Capacity   1,798cc
Power   84bhp
(varied with specification changes)

TRANSMISSION:
Four–speed gearbox plus overdrive on
third and top gears as an optional extra
Final drive   3.9:1

BODY STYLES:
Two–seater sports car and two–door
2+2 closed coupé

PERFORMANCE:
(from contemporary sources)
Max speed:
early cars   108mph (174kph)
later cars   100mph (161kph)
0–60mph (97kph):
early cars   12.1 seconds
later cars   14 seconds

LENGTH:
chrome bumper cars 12ft 9in (3.89m)
rubber bumper cars 13ft 2in (4.01m)

WIDTH: 5ft 0in (1.52m)

WHEELBASE: 7ft 7in (2.31m)

NUMBERS BUILT:
Roadsters   386,961
GTs   125,282

The shape of the completely removable hood fitted to this car complements the classic body lines. On early examples like this, a red-painted car could have either red or black hoods, while in later years black was the only option.

with both hardtop and GT versions being considered. However, the car was too heavy and costly to build to be a real contender.

Both John Thornley and Don Hayter, who had worked at Aston Martin for a time, were influenced by the Aston DB2/4 and Thornley often expressed a wish to build an MG closed coupé along similar lines. Hayter did some work on a fixed-head car with a sloping rear window that had echoes of the Frua design along the sides and at the rear, but incorporating a more rounded nose and also the slightly recessed headlights eventually seen on the MGB. However, the industry was moving towards monocoque bodies for sports cars, with the Sprite destined to be the first such car from the BMC stable, and it was decided that the MGA replacement should follow the same route.

As well as working on the fixed-head car, Don Hayter had also produced designs for a roadster body for the MGA chassis, and taking this as a basis work was commenced on a monocoque car. With the general styling given approval, full-size drawings were done and the project allocated the BMC number ADO 23. A full-size mock-up was built and the overall design concept received agreement from the management to proceed to prototype stage.

Working under the control and direction of Chief Engineer Syd Enever, the team at Abingdon crafted a car that was to become the best-selling MG of all, a design that still looks fresh many years after it was first conceived.

The decision to construct the car as a monocoque, rather than around the MGA chassis, involved far higher tooling costs, and it probably would not have been built but for an ingenious deal worked out between arch-negotiator John Thornley and Pressed Steel, who were anxious to have the MGB project to build at their new plant in Swindon. Under this

The amount of room in the MGB's boot was a vast improvement over the space available in the MGA. The straps are for securing the stowed hood and frame, while the block of foam rubber was fitted to prevent the hood frame from rattling.

deal, the bill for tooling was considerably reduced and the cost of each body produced was increased, which made the car viable within current budgets.

There was initially some doubt as to what power unit the new car would use. One proposal favoured the MGA Twin Cam engine, but this was dropped when it encountered reliability problems, while consideration was also given to both a new V4 engine and a four-cylinder unit, produced by removing two cylinders from the six-cylinder C-Series engine. In the end it was the faithful B-Series unit from the MGA that was to be used in the new

model. The first prototype MGB had the rear axle coil-spring-mounted, with trailing arms and a Panhard rod providing location. However, there were handling problems during testing and the cheapest way to solve these was to revert to the half-elliptic spring arrangement tried and tested by MG over the years. This meant a slight increase in the length of the car, which nonetheless still turned out to be nearly 3 inches (76mm) shorter than the MGA.

When the new MGB was announced in September its appearance bore a strong family resemblance to the new Midget that had started in production the previous year. The rear of the car had similar styling details such as the rear lights and the shape of the luggage compartment. This was no bad thing and was probably one of the reasons for the ready acceptance of the MGA replacement and the few voices mourning the passing of one of the prettiest cars ever to come from Abingdon. There was no denying the appeal of the MGB. In almost all respects – performance, comfort, space and convenience – it was an improvement on its predecessor. Some said it was now more tourer than sports car, but it was none the worse for that and sales figures were to prove the point.

Towards the end of the development period the existence of a plan to enlarge the capacity of the B-Series engine for use in the proposed Austin 1800 reached Abingdon. This must have answered some prayers, as the existing 1,622cc MGA engine was proving short on power for use in the new car. Enlarging the bore to 80.3mm increased the capacity to 1,798cc, raising both torque and power output. The engine initially retained the three-bearing layout inherited from the MGA, but the

five-bearing crankshaft developed for the saloon was fitted to the MGB engine after the car had been in production for a couple of years.

One of the most appealing features of the MGB was the cockpit, where modern construction had allowed the designers to give the occupants far

Early cars had handles that were pulled to open the doors. These were replaced in 1965 by handles with push buttons.

The engine compartment on a very early three-bearing car. It does not have an oil cooler, an option on home market cars at the time.

The attractive cockpit of an early MGB. The blue seats with light blue piping were fitted to Iris Blue cars.

more space than had been available in the MGA. The tallest drivers now had sufficient legroom and headroom and the area behind the seats could even be utilised for carrying young children, a cushion being an optional extra for a while. Comfort was given a higher priority and no longer were there separate side screens to fit in wet weather. The winding side windows and swivelling front windows fitted to the doors brought the MGB in line with competition from the Triumph TR4 and the Sunbeam Alpine.

The MGB was displayed at the 1962 London Motor Show where press and public alike praised the new MG. The interior space, especially the wider cockpit and larger luggage compartment, meant that the car was now far more practical everyday transport. The extra room had been achieved without making the car much bigger – it was shorter overall and barely 2 inches (51mm) wider. The wheelbase had been reduced by

3 inches (76mm), but moving the pedals and scuttle forward liberated sufficient space ahead of the rear bulkhead to give ample seat adjustment. The seats themselves were set lower. The basic price for the car was a very reasonable £690, purchase tax taking this to £949 15s 3d on the home market. By comparison, the basic price of the Austin-Healey 3000 was £865, the Sunbeam Alpine £695, and the Triumph TR4 £750.

The ride was better than on the MGA. Although the car weighed a little more, softer springs with longer travel were fitted, making the car less taut and nervous over bumps. There was a greater degree of body roll on corners, and an anti-roll bar was an optional extra, as were items like a heater, oil cooler, wire wheels, and folding hood. An overdrive unit became available the following year, much improving the car's cruising ability on the expanding network of motorways. With the folding hood

The GT was introduced in September 1965, adding greatly to the practical appeal of the MGB. Steel wheels with chromed hub caps were standard, but today most restored cars have wire wheels.

option, the frame and fabric cover remained attached to the car and could be hidden away under either the standard short tonneau cover or optional full cover. With the ordinary hood, the frame and cover were stowed in the luggage compartment.

Full road tests were published soon after the public announcement, and *The Motor* report said that the enlarged B-Series engine was found to pull cleanly from as low as 10mph (16kph) in top gear, while giving a maximum speed of over 108mph (174kph). Acceleration to 60mph (97kph) took 12.1 seconds. There was no overdrive on their car; this was not available during the first few months of production. *Autocar* saw the MGB as 'an altogether superior car to its predecessor' and recorded a maximum speed of 103.2mph (166kph), with their example taking 12.2 seconds to reach 60mph.

The five-bearing engine was introduced in October 1964, and in February 1965 *Autocar* tested a car fitted with this engine and an overdrive gearbox. They found the new unit to be more refined at low speeds, but also less free-revving. They recorded average maximum speeds of 103.5mph (167kph) in overdrive top and 99.3mph (160kph) in direct top, 60mph (97kph) being reached in 12.9 seconds. These figures were slightly inferior to those recorded for a car with the three-bearing engine, endorsing the oft-stated opinion that the earlier engine is more powerful despite having the same quoted power output.

There were continual small changes made to the specification, with a larger-capacity fuel tank coming in March 1965 and push-button door handles and anti-burst door locks in

With the 'facelift' in late 1969 came this recessed grille. At the same time the standard steel wheels were replaced by Rostyles, which on this car are fitted with polished rim embellishers.

April that year, but the real news was the introduction of a GT version of the MGB in time for the 1965 London Motor Show. Abingdon had given the job of designing the conversion from open sports car to closed coupé to Pininfarina, and there is no doubt that they did a good job, producing a car of timeless elegance. One improvement was the incorporation of a taller windscreen and door windows as part of the modifications. The cost of a GT in basic specification was £143 more than the open car, but with cars like the Ford Capri, Triumph GT6 and Reliant Scimitar still some way off, it really had few rivals.

The genius of the whole MGB GT concept was the incorporation of a lifting tailgate and a small but useful rear seat. Here at last was an MG sports car that was quite at home in the supermarket car park. Almost immediately it became a popular 'second car', opening up a much wider market for the Abingdon product. The GT shared the general mechanical specification of the roadster, but used a quieter Salisbury rear axle and had uprated seven-leaf rear springs. A front anti-roll bar was standard equipment on the GT from launch, and on the roadster from November 1966. The extra weight of the closed car – about 150lb (68kg) – reduced the performance slightly, but the one tested by *Autocar* reached a maximum speed of 102mph (164kph) and attained 60mph (97kph) in 13.6 seconds.

At the end of 1967 there was a major mechanical revision for both open and closed MGBs, and they gained MkII designation, although they were never badged as such except in Australia. The engine had a pre-engaged starter, a gearbox with synchromesh on all gears and a new radiator, and an alternator with separate regulator replaced the dynamo. Cars were now wired negative earth and gained two-speed wipers. The body had to be modified

to accept both the new gearbox and also automatic transmission, now an option. Inside the cockpit, there were recessed door handles and plastic window winders, the beginnings of a succession of safety-related modifications forced on MG by changes in legislation in most markets. Cars destined for sale in the United States were fitted with an energy-absorbing steering column, a completely different, padded fascia without a glove box, and the transfer to steering column stalks of the operation of the lights, indicators, washers and overdrive switches.

Jubilee MGB GTs had head rests, tinted glass and overdrive that later became standard

The next major revision came for the 1969 model year when the interior trim was simplified by removing the colour choice; the seats were all now black with black piping. However, the adoption of proper reclining frames was a welcome improvement.

Mechanical changes were limited to the adoption of an alternator with integral regulator and the 18GG engine. The axle ratio for automatic cars was changed from 3.909:1 to 3.7:1 to improve acceleration. The only external change was to the front side lights, which moved closer to the radiator grille – an important point to remember when fitting new wings!

More drastic external changes came the following year when, influenced by the Leyland take-over of the company, an attempt was made to 'modernise' the appearance of the car at minimum expense. In the cockpit vinyl replaced leather for the seat facings and there was a new

The recessed grille is not popular now and many restored cars, like this 1972 automatic, have been fitted with the earlier version. Another popular alteration is to fit replacement seats, like the leather-covered ones used here, in place of well-worn vinyl-covered originals. Bolt-on alloy wheels are a practical alternative to Rostyles.

steering wheel with aluminium spokes and simulated leather rim. The indicators, dip-switch, headlamp flasher and horn were operated from a steering column stalk. A new, brighter range of colours was offered and Rostyle wheels were standard equipment – but with wires still on the options list. Most controversial, however, was the change made to the front of the car. The attractive radiator grille, with its neat row of vertical bars maintaining the link with earlier MGs, was replaced by polished aluminium trim strips around the opening of the intake and a recessed, black-painted grille. The MG badge moved to the centre of this recessed

grille, surrounded by another strip of chrome, but nobody thought to remove the bulge on the bonnet that aligned with the badge in its original position. Larger lenses for the rear lights, and a plastic MG badge for the boot or tailgate, completed the picture.

The 'facelift' did little for the appearance of the car, although buyers did not seem to be deterred and sales held up well. A year later there were a number of minor revisions for the 1971 model year cars. The horn push returned to the centre of the steering wheel and door switches operated the map light, while a modified design of hood was introduced, and the option of a totally removable soft-top was dropped. At long last a telescopic bonnet prop was introduced, together with one for the boot on the roadster. The overriders had rubber inserts.

With the finances of the parent company in poor shape and industrial unrest rife in the UK, there was little chance of drastic changes to the MGB, save those necessary to keep the specification of the car in line with changes in legislation. Thus for the 1972 model year improvements were restricted to the addition of fresh air vents in the dashboard radio aperture, a new console for the radio and courtesy light, a padded armrest with cubby hole, and brushed nylon panels in the seat facings for the GT. The inclusion of a courtesy light meant that the special light to illuminate the gear selector on automatics was no longer needed. A safety-related change was the inclusion of an energy-absorbing steering column and rocker switches on the home market cars.

By the time the 1973 model MGBs were announced it must have dawned on the stylists within British Leyland that the grille change introduced three years earlier had been less than successful. Visitors to the MG stand at the London Motor Show must have welcomed the introduction of a grille similar in shape to the original one. The vertical bars were replaced by ABS injection-moulded inserts of 'egg-box' pattern, but the MG badge once again aligned with the bonnet bulge. The interior trim was revised again; the seats had covers with a different pattern of pleating and those on the GT now had full-width nylon facings. The series of holes in the spokes of the steering wheel introduced in 1969 were thought to encourage trapped fingers, so for 1973 these were replaced with slots. A new gear lever knob and gaiter, arm-rest door pulls, matt black wiper arms and blades, and better carpeting completed the up-dating of what was becoming an ageing design.

The last of the annual revisions for the chrome-bumper cars was carried out in the autumn of 1973, with the deletion of the automatic versions of the MGB from the range and the incorporation of hazard warning lights on home market cars. A brake servo was now standard, as were radial-ply tyres and inertia-reel seat belts for the GT. The American market cars were fitted with modified bumpers and huge energy-absorbing overriders early in 1974, while home market cars had a short-lived change to the back bumper that saw the numberplate lights moving from the overriders to the bumper blade. The large overriders on the American cars were a short-term response to legislation calling for there to be no damage to the car in low-speed collisions. However, far more drastic measures were needed to make the cars comply fully with the rules and these resulted in the poor old MGB having to undergo major surgery.

MGBs are effective cars in historic rallies, and a well-prepared example is a match for far more powerful machinery on the twisting mountain roads used for many of these events.

The Coune Berlinette MGB

The factory GT was not the first fixed-head MGB; this honour goes to the Berlinette MGB built by Belgian coachbuilder Jacques Coune, who took MGB roadsters and converted them into attractive closed cars. The modifications were extensive. All the rear section of the body was removed and replaced by restyled rear wings and a fixed, full-length fibreglass roof that was neatly blended into a restyled tail. The front wings also received attention from the panel beaters, the headlights were recessed into the wings and fitted with Perspex covers, and the wheel arches were reshaped. The scuttle was reworked to provide a fixed frame for taller windscreen glass.

The glass in the doors was changed, as were the quarter lights. At the back there was a steeply raked rear window and a pair of front-hinged opening side windows. The interior was retrimmed with access to the enlarged luggage area being both from within the car and through a small lid behind the rear window. The flat rear panel and integral spoiler were reminiscent of the 1960s GTO Ferrari. More than 50 examples were built before the factory MGB GT arrived at a much lower price, stopping production of this attractive car.

Faced with the job of meeting the impact requirements, and matching a ruling that the bumpers had to be a standard height for all cars, involved a substantial redesign of the MGB. Large and heavy 'rubber'-faced bumpers were mounted front and rear on extensions to the chassis rails, and the front bumpers had the flashing indicator lamps recessed within them. Attempting to blend these large bumpers with the MGB body, the designers shaped them to line up with the existing bonnet and wings. On the MGB this was reasonably acceptable, especially on cars painted in the darker colours, but even the most ardent enthusiast could hardly call the result an improvement.

The extra metalwork on the chassis, plus the heavy bumpers, increased the weight considerably. Performance was inferior and the increase in ride height badly compromised the handling. The suspension mounting points and spring heights were changed to give a 1.5-inch (38mm) increase in ride height, with the result that the cars rolled more when cornering and the handling was less predictable. For some reason, probably a lack of time or money, the cars were put into production without sufficient thought having been given to the effect on the handling of the suspension changes. The roadster lost the front anti-roll bar because retaining it caused severe roll-induced oversteer. The answer would have been to fit a rear anti-roll bar in addition to stiffening up the one at the front, a solution adopted later for the 1977 model year cars.

In addition to the major revisions to the bumpers and body, there were some other changes. The fuel pump was moved from underneath the car to a position within the boot, a single 12-volt battery replaced the previous twin 6-volt ones, and to simplify matters the 80mm instruments and panel from the V8, as well as the column stalk from that model, were used on the four-cylinder car. The GT had a revised front anti-roll bar while the roadster adopted the seven-leaf GT rear springs; they reverted to six-leaf ones a year later.

Road testers driving the revised MGBs were none too keen on the suspension while still praising some aspects of the car's design. The roadster tested by *Autocar* surprised by being as quick as earlier cars, in spite of the extra weight, but its performance may not have been typical of the model.

It was decided that 1975 should be the year to celebrate 50 years of MG, and in commemoration all the cars built in that year were fitted with a gold-coloured background to the external badges and the MG octagon on the steering wheel. Additionally, a special run of 750 MGB GTs were built for the home market, which had a number of unique features to separate them from standard cars. The body was painted in Dark Racing Green, as were the chrome waistline strips. The door mirrors were painted black, and gold side stripes incorporating the jubilee logo ran down each side of the car. As with other 1975 cars, all the badges were gold, but these cars also had a separate, numbered dash plaque to be fixed to the car by the dealer. All the Jubilee MGB GTs were fitted with V8 alloy/steel wheels painted in gold and black to complement the dark green paintwork. To make them even more attractive, they were also fitted with head rests, tinted glass, carpets in place of rubber mats, and overdrive; these were all later to become standard on GTs.

The MGBs were not revised in any great detail until the 1977 model was announced in August 1976. The large bumpers were retained, although the appearance of these on light-coloured cars had been

improved from September 1975 by painting the front and rear panels below the bumper line with satin black paint. The handling was improved by fitting the front and rear anti-roll bars mentioned earlier, while the interior of the cars received a lot of attention. There was a new dashboard and console incorporating the heater controls and a clock, and there was also lower-geared steering with a smaller four-spoke steering wheel, new control stalks on the steering column, a gearlever-mounted

In 1975 a limited run of MGB GTs was finished in dark green paintwork and given gold badges and side stripes. The occasion was the celebration, a bit late, of 50 years of MG sports cars.

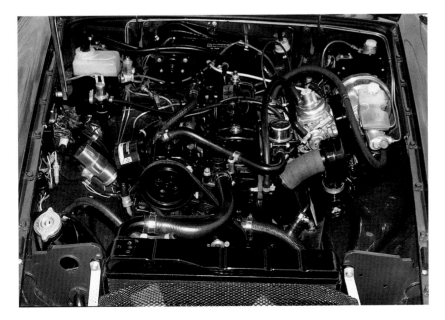

The crowded engine bay of a late MGB built for the American market. Note the single carburettor and exhaust emission equipment.

The Limited Edition GTs were equipped similarly to the open cars, although the grey striped interior was better looking.

switch for the standard overdrive, and new seat fabrics.

Whoever chose the so-called 'deckchair' fabrics to complement a rather poor choice of exterior colours produced some strange combinations. Of the two fabrics, the two-tone grey was less objectionable than the bright orange and brown, but neither looked as good as the plain 'Ambla' seat covers retained for American market roadsters; the GT was no longer exported to that country. There was a definite attempt to justify the higher prices charged for the cars by including more luxurious fittings, better carpets, sun visors, and a glove box that could at last be

opened without using the key, as well as tinted glass on the GTs.

The changes made under the bonnet when the interior was revised did nothing to improve performance. The radiator was moved forwards, an electric fan installed, and the carburettor specification was altered. Power output for the home market cars remained at 84bhp, while in America pollution laws saw power from the B-Series engine reduced to 63bhp, giving performance that *Road and Track* reported as being no better than the 1,250cc TF they had tested 24 years earlier! Home market cars fared better; a GT tested by *Autocar* in 1977 just about reached 100mph

(161kph) and took 14 seconds to reach 60mph (97kph).

Those were the last major changes made to the MGB, and when the final few cars left the production line in 1980 most people thought that they had seen the last new MG sports car. To celebrate the end of production, 1,000 Limited Edition MGBs were built for the home market. A Limited Edition MGB roadster had been built especially for America, and this was launched at the 1979 Auto Expo in New York. These black-painted cars had silver stripes down each side that featured the British flag, and each was fitted with attractive alloy wheels. The home market Limited Edition consisted of 420 roadsters and 580 GTs. Mechanically the cars were identical to the standard production vehicles, but the GTs were all painted Pewter Metallic, with silver side stripes of the same design as those fitted to the American Limited Edition cars, and the roadsters were painted Bronze Metallic with similar gold-coloured stripes. Some of the roadsters were fitted with wire wheels in place of the alloy wheels.

Having recounted at length the rise and fall of the MGB, just what are these popular sports cars like to own and drive? First, anyone getting into an MGB after spending most of their time driving current saloon cars has to readjust their ideas. Modern as the car looks, it is still a 1960s design that was outdated in some respects even when first launched. The recent development of more stylish interiors, walnut dashboards, and transplanting more powerful engines into new bodyshells, has led many to regard the result as a modern car. This is not the case, and many of these expensively built machines prove a disappointment to owners who would probably have been better served by buying an up-to-date sports car. The joy of an MGB is that it is not modern, but it is more than capable of providing satisfactory and inexpensive daily transportation.

Getting into an MGB through the wide doors is a lot easier than an MGA or Midget. Legroom is generous, but tall people sometimes find that the top rail of the windscreen is in their line of sight, this being particularly

noticeable if a pair of the more deeply upholstered replacement seats have been fitted. The steering wheel of the earlier cars in particular feels large, and those short in the leg sometimes find that they are placed too close to the wheel, and also sitting rather lower, than they would like. However, given how easy it is to remove the seat and place packing pieces under the runners, the driving position can be improved. In practice a far greater range of heights and leg lengths can be accommodated in the MGB than in almost any other sports car ever built.

Anyone used to power steering will immediately appreciate why the MGB steering wheel is large! The steering is heavy and does not lighten up all that much at speed. However, it is actually

The open MGB LEs were all painted this colour and had orange and brown striped seats.

standards to the full, accepting that they apply at much lower speeds than in most modern sports cars.

The early rubber-bumper cars have peculiar handling and can become quite exciting to drive at speed on twisting, bumpy roads. The quick steering does allow easy recovery in most situations, but the addition of some form of handling kit can improve matters for this model if not for others. However, whichever MGB is chosen, open or closed, early or late, they all have an enduring appeal that has kept them at the top of the list of sports cars, and ensured that there will always be a good supply of spares to keep them running. Their position as the most popular classic sports car is well-deserved.

Major revisions were made to the 1977 model year cars, one of which was a new fascia. At long last, the glove box could be opened without a key and a clock was standard equipment. As one of the last MGBs built, this car has the revised fascia and all the other minor trim changes, like sun visors on open cars.

an almost ideal compromise for the type of car, giving a far greater feeling of stability and safety on first acquaintance than does the much lighter steering on the Midget. Noise levels with the top up are reasonable, especially with the later version of hood. The zip-out rear window fitted to cars from 1977 is often now specified by owners of earlier models. The best hood is one made of vinyl, being easier to clean and more durable than replacements in mohair or similar materials. The GT drives exactly like the open cars, but the odd rattles, together with the wind noise from the windows, are somehow a lot more intrusive in a closed car.

The roadster is at its best with the hood lowered. The windscreen and winding side windows give good protection, and the head rests fitted to later cars stop some of the buffeting from the rear that occurs on most open cars. A crisp exhaust note and a pleasant sound from the engine add to the enjoyment. Used in this

manner the performance is more than adequate; one just ignores the odd 'boy racer' in his modern saloon who roars past, taking corners at speeds that would see the MGB in the ditch. It is in the field of ride quality and grip that there have been the greatest advances in recent years. No amount of handling kits, wider tyres or modern dampers can compensate for the decades of careful chassis development undertaken by most car manufacturers. The best way to enjoy an MGB is to use the superb handling and roadholding it had by 1960s

Home market cars retained twin-carburettor engines, and these, although less powerful than the first MGB units, gave the cars 100mph (161kph) performance.

Buying Hints

1. With so many cars built, and always a good number for sale at any one time, buying an MGB is easy. The difficult part is finding the right car at the right price. As has been said previously for other models, it is better either to buy a wreck for very little money and rebuild it, or look for a really sound car that needs no work and pay more for it.

2. The advent of Heritage shells has saved a lot of cars from being totally scrapped. However, they have also allowed a lot of people to create cars that never existed. GTs are cheaper to buy and fewer people want them as purely fun cars, so many have reappeared as roadsters. This may not matter too much, but buyers should be aware of exactly what it is they are buying.

3. The excellent service provided by the British Motor Industry Heritage Trust at Gaydon in Warwickshire enables anyone to obtain full build details of their car and its original colour, trim, engine number, etc. The presence of one of their certificates with a car will help verification of its authenticity, but check the details with the log book and remember that new chassis plates are readily available and easily stamped!

4. A rubber-bumper GT is the cheapest route into MGB ownership and provides practical everyday transport. The most expensive MGBs are usually fully restored early pull-handle roadsters, but the MkII cars (those built up to the introduction of the recessed grille) enjoy all the advantages of the early MGBs – leather seats, attractive appearance, etc – as well as having the all-synchromesh gearbox.

5. As with all the other cars in this book, it is the condition of the body that is of most importance. Rust was always a problem with these cars, and the sills, door bottoms and the joints between the wings and top panels gave trouble on most cars once they were a few years old. Many MGBs have by now had more than one set of sills, replacement wings, and other body repairs. The quality of any such repairs is of vital importance to the structural integrity of the car and any signs of badly fitting doors and poor panel gaps should give the buyer cause for concern.

6. The condition of the sills, floors, bottoms of the wings, doors, bonnet and bootlid should be carefully examined. Any external sign of rusting means that the hidden areas like the inner sills are also likely to be bad. Remember that replacing all the sill sections means removing the front wings and the lower part of the rear wings; bodgers often try to avoid the latter and compromise structural strength.

7. The good news is that panels are readily available to repair any part of the MGB body, but unless the buyer has the necessary skills to undertake their own repair work, this can be costly. Get some idea of the price of such repairs before buying a car and build in a percentage to cover unforeseen problems.

8. The MGB engine, gearbox and rear axle are simple and reliable, and rebuilt units are readily available and cheap. That said, the early gearboxes do suffer from weak synchromesh at higher mileages, and the later units will not fit the early cars without major alterations to the transmission tunnel. Cylinder heads are prone to crack and consequently are in short supply second-hand. At the time of writing, new aluminium heads with valve seat inserts for use with unleaded fuel are available. Original heads can easily be converted to run on unleaded.

9. Many cars have been fitted with modified suspension components, uprated dampers, and even completely re-engineered front suspension. The benefits of some changes may be questionable, and, if in doubt, advice should be sought from a competent specialist.

10. The abundant supply of non-standard interior trim, seats, hoods, etc, has led to many cars on offer being quite different from any Abingdon-built MGB. This may not matter to the buyer, but could affect the value of the car when it is eventually re-sold.

11. Common problems encountered with MGBs centre around the electrical system. Wiring has often been tampered with by successive owners when fitting accessories, and stray wires under the dashboard and a poor standard of workmanship are a good indication of possible trouble.

12. Fuel leaks from rusty petrol tanks are common on older cars, as are troubles with fuel pumps. Reliability comes from having a sound, well-installed and shielded petrol pump, a good fuel tank, and an accessible in-line filter in the fuel line.

Major changes in specification (from parts list)

Mk I Models GHN3 first announced September 1962, chassis numbers run from 101.

First style radiator grille, pull-type door handles, leather seats with piping of contrasting colour, steel disc wheels with hub caps or optional wire wheels, cable-driven tachometer. Overdrive available from January 1963.

Jan 1964 (28264) Fillers between rear bumper and body chrome plated not painted.

Feb 1964 18GA engine with closed-circuit breathing introduced for all cars.

Oct 1964 18GB engine with five-bearing crankshaft and modifications to gearbox casing and input shaft. Electric tachometer (from 48767 for all cars plus some earlier chassis).

Mar 1965 12gal (55lit) fuel tank introduced.

Apr 1965 Exterior door handles changed to push-button type and anti-burst door locks fitted.

Sep 1965 Introduction of GT model (71933 RHD 73163 LHD).

Nov 1966 (108039) Anti-roll bar now standard on roadster.

Jul 1967 (approx) Salisbury tube-type axle fitted to roadster.

Mk II Model GHN4/GHD4 introduced October 1967 (138401 roadster 139471 GT) 18GD engine, modified body with wider transmission tunnel, new radiator, all-synchromesh gearbox, overdrive type LH instead of D, 16AC alternator instead of dynamo, recessed internal door handles and safety window winders, quarter-light handles straight not curved, automatic gearbox option. USA cars had energy-absorbing steering column, stalk to control lights, indicators, and horn on left of steering wheel and wipers, washers, and overdrive on the right. Fascia had rocker switches.

Roadster 158371 (Sep. 1968) GT 158231 (Nov. 1968) 1969 model year cars. 18GG engine with pipes direct from breather into carburettors, 16ACR alternator with integral regulator, front sidelights closer to radiator grille, revised pattern of interior trim with reclining seats in black covers and with black piping. Heater was standard from Nov. 1968.

GHN5/GHD5 Recessed grille (187211 Roadster, 187841 GT) 1970 model year cars had steel bonnets, recessed radiator grille, plastic rear badges, new rear lamps, steering wheel with simulated leather rim, 'Ambla' seat covers, stalk for indicators, lights, horn, and Rostyle wheels with wires as an option. North American cars had steering locks, revised switch-gear, side marker lights instead of merely reflectors, and rear quarter bumpers.

Apr. 1970 Head rests now optional on home-market cars.

Aug. 1970 (21901) 1971 model year. Changes included horn push moved from column stalk to centre of steering wheel, map light now operated by door switches on roadster, overriders with rubber inserts, new design of folding hood, telescopic props for bonnet and boot. North American cars fitted with 18GK engine and reverted to a one-piece rear bumper.

Aug. 1971 (258001) 1972 model year cars had the 18V engine, painted black, fresh air vents in fascia and radio position moved to new console, centre arm rest/cubby hole, courtesy light replaces map light, chrome Rostyles optional in all markets, automatic cars lose special light to illuminate selector, GT had brushed nylon panels in seat covers.

Dec. 1971 (266635) Home market cars had new air cleaners.

April 1972 (279340) Quarter-light assemblies stainless steel instead of chromed brass.

Plastic-mesh Grille Aug. 1972 (294251 Roadster 296001 GT) 1973 model year cars reverted to a chromed grille with plastic mesh inserts. The steering wheel had slotted spokes, gear lever knob was of simulated leather, arm-rest door pulls, new pattern on seats with the GT having nylon seat facings, two rectangular air-intakes were cut in the front panel behind the number plate. North American cars have modified anti-burst door locks, door beams, and illuminated rocker switches.

Dec. 1972 North American cars and all automatics get 7-bladed plastic cooling fan.

Mar. 1973 All GTs fitted with V8-type anti-roll bar.

Jun. 1973 (320197) Solid spoke steering wheel fitted.

Aug. 1973 (328101) 1974 model year. Automatic option discontinued, brake servo and radial tyres standard, hazard warning lights on home market cars, inertia reel seat belts on GTs.

Jan. 1974 North American cars fitted with large energy-absorbing overriders.

Jan. 1974 number plate lamps move from overriders to rear bumper.

Mar. 1974 7-bladed plastic fan fitted to all models.

'Rubber' Bumper Cars introduced Sep. 1974 with modified body shells, raised ride-height, impact-resistant bumpers with indicator lamps in front unit, sidelights within headlamps, single 12v battery, collapsible steering column, anti-roll bar deleted on roadster which now had 7-leaf rear springs, V8-type 80mm speedometer and tachometer in revised panel, V8-type column stalks for wipers, flashing indicators and overdrive.

Jan. 1975 To celebrate 'MG Golden Jubilee', the front bumper badge, badge in steering wheel, and boot lid or tail gate badges were gold, not silver.

Apr. 1975 (GT 374858) A special anniversary edition of 750 (751 built but one destroyed in a newspaper publicity stunt) GTs were finished in dark racing green with the side mouldings also painted body colour, side stripe, gold-painted V8 wheels and other extras.

Jun. 1975 Overdrive standard on home market cars.

Sep. 1975 (386601 Roadster 391501 GT) 1976 model year cars had the sections of the front and rear valences below the bumpers painted black and the roadster reverted to 6-leaf rear springs.

Dec. 1975 gearlever gaiter retainer painted black not chrome plated.

Jun. 1976 (410001 Roadster 410351 GT) 1977 model year. Radiator moved forward, electric cooling fan, new steering wheel, front and rear anti-roll bars on both models, revised dashboard and instruments, overdrive switch in gearlever knob, lower-geared steering and new 4-spoke steering wheel, 'deck chair' seats on RHD cars, LHD cars had 'Ambla' seat covers and built-in radio speakers in the doors.

Nov. 1976 The rear numberplate lamp covers changed from chrome to black.

May 1977 Dual-circuit brakes and direct-acting servo fitted.

Jun. 1978 1979 model year. RHD cars had door speakers and radio aerials as standard.

Oct. 1978 (481116 Roadster 480297 GT) Lettering on dials changed with speedometer calibrated in 20mph increments.

'Rubber' Bumper Cars introduced Sep. 1974 with modified body shells.

Mar. 1979 Front and rear hubs changed to make them suitable to take the optional alloy wheels.

Mar. 1979 USA Limited Edition cars featured black paint, side stripes, cast alloy wheels, and various extras fitted by importers.

Jun. 1979 Cast alloy wheels optional on RHD cars.

Aug. 1980 Home market Limited Edition cars built alongside production of standard specification cars.

Oct. 1980 Production ceased.

The MGC & MGC GT

The MGC was one of those cars that was criticised by many when new, but which has gone on to earn cult status within MG circles. The current band of enthusiastic owners are intensely loyal to the model, many having run the cars for long periods. Right from the outset the main disadvantage suffered by the MGC was that it looked too much like an MGB while being really a car with a quite different set of virtues.

Originally the MGC was proposed as an economical way of replacing the ageing but popular Austin-Healey 3000 with a car that could be sold in both Austin-Healey and MG guise. The cost of developing the MGB was

absorbing most of the available funds, so it made economic sense to try to utilise as many of that car's basic components as possible for any new, larger-engined sports car.

The Austin-Healey 3000 used the C-Series BMC engine, which was considered to be both too large and too heavy for a car based around the MGB body structure, and initial plans visualised fitting the 2,433cc six-cylinder version of the B-Series engine developed for some Australian-built BMC saloon cars. However, the Healey family were none too keen on seeing their name used on a car that to all intents and purposes was little different from the MG

Although an MGC can easily be mistaken for an MGB at first glance, the bigger wheels and extra bulges on the bonnet do alter its appearance significantly. MGC wheels and hub caps, as well as being larger than those used on the MGB, are of a different pattern; 72-spoke wire wheels were an option.

MGCs are superb long-distance touring cars, being high geared and powerful enough to make long journeys a pleasure.

MGC & MGC GT 1967–69

ENGINE:
Six-cylinder, ohv
Bore x stroke	83.36 x 88.9
Capacity	2,912cc
Power	150bhp

TRANSMISSION:
Four-speed gearbox plus overdrive on third and top gears as an optional extra. Three speed automatic transmission optional.
Final drive   3.07:1 (non-overdrive cars to chassis 4235); 3.7:1 (overdrive cars from chassis 4236); 3.307:1 all other cars

BODY STYLES:
Two-seater sports car and two-door 2+2 closed coupé

PERFORMANCE:
(from contemporary sources)
Max speed	123.8mph (199kph)
0–60mph (97kph)	10 seconds

LENGTH:	12ft 9in (3.89m)
WIDTH:	5ft 0in (1.52m)
WHEELBASE:	7ft 7in (2.31m)

NUMBERS BUILT:
Roadsters	4,544
GTs	4,458

version, so they pursued the route of updating the existing car by widening it and fitting the 4 litre Rolls-Royce power unit used by BMC for the Vanden Plas Princess R. After the construction of some prototypes the project was, however, cancelled, and in December 1967 production of the Big Healey ceased.

Little work was carried out on the six-cylinder car until the MGB was fully in production. The Australian engine idea had been abandoned and the search for a suitable power plant continued. At Longbridge, a new engine had been mooted for installation in a replacement for the large Austin saloon car range, which previously used the same 3-litre engine as the Healey 3000. The Morris Engines designers at Coventry were commissioned to produce an engine that was to be lighter, more powerful and less bulky than the old unit, ideal perhaps for use in the proposed sports car.

In the event, however, those working on the new unit lost the plot somewhere along the way and when a prototype of the replacement 3 litre engine arrived in the Development Department at Abingdon it turned out to be very little smaller, or lighter, than the old C-Series unit that they had already rejected as being too big to fit in the MGB engine bay. Installing this new engine was a tight squeeze and a considerable amount of work on the bodyshell would be needed to persuade it to fit. The alterations eventually made to the MGB structure were extensive, with virtually a brand new floor pan being required to accommodate the revisions to the front suspension. The MGB arrangement used coil springs and lower wishbones, and the front dampers provided the upper location for the king pins. This relied on a substantial cross member that was too bulky to fit under the sump of the larger engine, so torsion bars were specified for the MGC, rather than coil springs, and the floor pressings under the seats were revised to accommodate the rear mountings for these.

The cockpit of the MGC is the same as the MGB except for the steering wheel, which has a sewn-on leather cover on the rim, and the 140mph (225kph) speedometer. The pattern of seat upholstery, and the non-reclining frames, identify this as an earlier car. The 1969 model year cars had black leather reclining seats and all-black trim.

The MGB lever-arm dampers and wishbones were replaced by two-piece upper and lower forged wishbones and telescopic dampers. A U-shaped cross member was fitted under the sump and this provided the wishbone pivots and mounting pads for the front of the engine. The torsion bars were splined at each end; the front ends fitted into the rear pivots of the lower wishbones and the rear ends to adjustable pivots under the floor. At the rear, conventional leaf springs and lever-arm hydraulic dampers were retained, along with a standard rear axle fitted with a higher-ratio crown wheel and pinion.

Keeping the costs as low as possible meant that there was no possibility of changing the styling of the car any more than was necessary to accommodate the mechanical modifications. Like the MGB, an

aluminium bonnet was used; this had bulges to give clearance for the radiator and the front carburettor. Apart from the substitution of the letter 'C' for the 'B' in the badging, only these bulges, and wheels 1 inch (25mm) larger, identified the new cars from the existing MGBs. Given the choice, Abingdon engineers would have preferred the engine to fit beneath the bonnet without the need for any bulges, but the new six-cylinder unit was just too big. It was less than 2 inches (51mm) shorter, around 20lb (9kg) lighter and produced 5bhp less power than the Healey 3000 engine.

The new engine was a strong unit with the potential to produce a good power output with considerable refinement. However, a lack of sufficient development meant that production engines were disappointing, being less free-revving and developing less power than the specification would suggest. Subsequent work on the engine by tuning firms proved the latent potential of the design as they were able to extract considerably more power with comparatively minor changes to the manifolds and cylinder head. Just why the shortcomings of the engine were not recognised and rectified before the car was launched is one of the many mysteries that surround the activities of British car manufacturers in the 1960s.

With the engine development out of their control, Abingdon had to do the best they could with what they were given. The heavier engine, together with all the chassis modifications, increased the weight of the car by over 340lb (154kg). The majority of this bore on the front wheels, and to keep the steering effort within bounds the rack-and-pinion steering was lower geared and the castor angle was reduced. In spite of their efforts, the greater weight and the lower-geared steering was to make the MGC feel less nimble around corners than the MGB.

The MGC was almost identical to the MGB inside, and only re-calibrated instrument dials identified that you were in the new car. The steering wheel was the same, although on the MGC it had a leather-covered rim. No effort was made to give the cabin the sort of luxury touches that usually distinguish the more expensive model in a range. For the first time on an MG sports car, the cars were available with an automatic gearbox, the popular Borg-Warner model 35 three-speed unit. This gearbox was also available for the home market MGB and was fitted to the MkIV Magnette. The standard MGC gearbox had synchromesh on all four forward gears, overdrive being available as an extra.

Late delivery of engines delayed the launch of the MGC until the October 1967 London Motor Show. Full descriptions of the cars appeared in

the major weekly motoring magazines, and they also included driving impressions, reserving most of their criticism for the full road tests they were to carry in later issues. The prices for the MGC were £1,101 16s 6d for the roadster and £1,249 6s 6d for the GT, including taxes, plus £98 6s 8d for automatic transmission or £61 9s 2d for overdrive.

The press reaction to the car at the time has been the subject of discussion and debate amongst enthusiasts ever since. The launch was badly handled by the BMC Publicity Department, who were already on the defensive having had poor recent coverage for other models. There are stories that the cars given to

This is the standard MGC wheel with elongated slots and a hub cap with a bevelled edge round the rim.

journalists had the wrong tyre pressures, and that magazines failed to receive on time the cars that they had been promised. Still, for whatever reason, most of the reports printed were not calculated to encourage buyers to fork out the extra to buy an MGC instead of an MGB.

Published performance figures revealed that the MGC was quick. The *Motor* test car reached 123.8mph (199kph), reaching 60mph (97kph) in

An early MGC engine. The 1968 model year cars had a valve above the inlet manifold for the closed-circuit breather, the water tap on the heater box, and a separate control box for the alternator.

10 seconds. Autocar recorded 121mph (195kph) in their car, which took the same time to reach 60mph. However, the test teams were very critical of the heavy and unresponsive steering, and of the engine, which they felt lacked low-speed torque and did not feel like a sports car unit. Comparisons with the Healey 3000 found the MGC to be slower, more thirsty, and less fun to drive. Car and Driver in America said that, 'Engine response is very, very slow – almost as if someone found a good deal on a lot of unused millstones and bought them to tack on the end of MGC crankshafts.'

The poor press reaction must have hurt sales, but more damaging in the long run was the way the car was perceived in the market. The higher price, added to larger fuel and insurance bills, meant that it was

always going to appeal to a different sort of customer from the MGB. However, the car lacked the extra equipment and comfort that may have been required by the sort of people prepared to find the higher purchase price. There were some MGB owners who moved on to the MGC in search of extra performance, but most of the customers could have been expected to come from those who otherwise would have looked at rival large-engined performance cars. Those who did take the plunge found that the model's shortcomings were nowhere near as bad as they may have been led to believe, and that they were amply compensated for by a surprising ability to cover long distances without apparent effort.

High overall gearing, and the option of overdrive, made the MGC the ideal

The Lightweight MGS

The story of the development of the lightweight MGCs is an interesting one, particularly as they were the last of a succession of MG race-prepared cars to come from the BMC Competition Department. Stuart Turner, who managed the department at that time, decided in 1966 to build cars that looked like MGCs to race in the prototype category, as it was unlikely that modified road cars would prove competitive against current racing machinery. Six lightweight MGC GT bodyshells were constructed using pressed steel chassis sections with aluminium panels for the doors, roof, wings, etc. The wings were flared to accommodate wide racing wheels and tyres. Because of the delay in getting the standard cars into production, the lightweight bodies were completed well before the MGC was announced and the first car to be built, MBL 546E, had a bored-out four-cylinder MGB engine, enabling it to run in the over-2-litre prototype class in the 1967 Targa Florio. Driven by Paddy Hopkirk and Timo Makinen, the car was delayed by a number of long pit stops, finishing at the back of the field and in third place in class.

The car ran in the 1968 Sebring race in America and, as the MGC had been announced by this time, it was fitted with a 3 litre engine and was entered as an MGS GT in the under-3-litre class. Driven by Paddy Hopkirk and Andrew Hedges, it was placed tenth overall, third in the prototype category and first in class. In the 84-hour-long Marathon de la Route at the Nurburgring in Germany later the same year, the car was placed sixth overall, driven by Julian Vernaeve, Andrew Hedges and Tony Fall. A second lightweight MGC, RMO 699F, had been built by then and this was fitted with an aluminium-block engine. Driven by Roger Enever, Alec Poole and Clive Baker, it retired after running out of water. The first car would have been better placed had it not worn out the brake pads, running a couple of laps without any brakes at all!

The swan song of the two MGS GTs as works cars came in the 1969 Sebring in Florida where neither featured high in the results. After the race both cars were sold to American customers, but happily they both survived and are once again seen on the race track. Motor dealer and racing driver John Chatham bought the remaining four lightweight shells from Abingdon and in due course these too were built up into complete cars.

Two lightweight MGS GTs were built by the Abingdon Competition Department. This is the second; driven by Paddy Hopkirk and Andrew Hedges, the car finished 15th at Sebring in 1969.

The GT version of the MGC shares with the four-cylinder cars all the practical advantages of this type of body, with the added bonus of more power. The 72-spoke wire wheels were an optional extra.

long-distance touring car. In overdrive top the car achieved 27mph (43kph) per 1,000rpm, so the engine was only turning over at 3,700rpm at 100mph (161kph). Although this meant relaxed high-speed cruising, it was one of the reasons why the road testers found that it accelerated less quickly than they wanted. The engineers decided to address this and, except for the cars fitted with automatic transmission, it was decided to lower the overall gearing so that a little more acceleration could be provided at the expense of some of that high-speed cruising ability. At first there had been two different sets of internal ratios for the gearbox, as non-overdrive MGCs, which had a higher-ratio final drive, were given lower intermediate gear ratios to compensate. In the autumn of 1968 the final drive ratio of all manual transmission cars was lowered from 3.071:1 to 3.307:1 for the non-overdrive cars, and from 3.307:1 to 3.7:1 for the cars with overdrive. MGCs with automatic transmission all had 3.307:1 final drive ratios. Given the lower final drive gearing, the non-overdrive cars no longer needed a gearbox with widely spaced intermediate ratios. These changes gave the 1969 model year cars better acceleration, while the overall gearing in overdrive top meant that at 100mph (161kph) the engine was still only doing just over 4,000rpm.

The introduction of safety and anti-pollution regulations in America meant that the MGCs sold there differed from home market cars. For example, the North American cars were fitted with a dual-circuit braking system with twin servos while those for other markets made do with a single-circuit system. As with the MGB, the dashboards on the six-cylinder

cars sent to America were of a totally different design, heavily padded and fitted with safer switches, and accommodating this entailed modifications to the shape of the scuttle. Later tourers had triple windscreen wipers. Safety was also a consideration for cars sold elsewhere, and on all the 1969 models the interior rear view mirror was changed to a plastic-rimmed type and the curved quarter light handles were replaced with straight ones.

The basic engine specification stayed the same throughout the whole production run, but some auxiliary items were modified. The breather on earlier cars had a valve assembly connected to the inlet manifold to feed the fumes from the crankcase back into the combustion chambers. For the 1969 cars different carburettors were fitted and pipes ran directly from these to the crankcase oil separator. North American cars had a complicated closed-circuit breather system that fed compressed air into the exhaust ports to complete the combustion of any unburned fuel. The alternator was changed from type 16AC, with a separate regulator box mounted on an inner wing, to type 16ACR, with an integral regulator. The wiring loom was now plastic-covered, not braided.

Like the MGB, the MGC benefited from a programme of cosmetic alterations for the 1969 model year. The 1968 year cars had leather seats and matching trim panels in black, blue or red, with contrasting piping, but for 1969 the seats were fitted with reclining back rests and all were finished in black with black piping. The carpets were of improved quality. Externally there was a small change to the front wings, with the side lamps moving closer to the grille. On the dashboard the Smiths temperature gauge had centigrade or fahrenheit graduations on cars prior to chassis number 4126 and cold/normal/hot on the later cars.

The effect of the changes to the gearing and improved seats was to give the later cars slightly better acceleration and more comfort, but little was made of this by the company as sales flagged. There seemed to be no efforts being made to address the understeer or to try to liberate more power from the engine for the production cars, although work by the Competition Department and outside tuning companies should have indicated that it was entirely feasible to make considerable improvements in both areas.

Following the Leyland merger, the company seemed to lose all interest in the MGC and it was dropped from the

Enjoy the MGC as a long-distance tourer and forget chasing MGBs round twisty lanes

price lists, perhaps because it competed directly with other cars built within the group. Production stopped with just 4,544 roadsters and 4,458 GTs having been built. Poor sales meant that there were stocks of unsold cars and some of these were purchased in bulk by London MG agents University Motors. They produced a number of 'University Motors Special MGCs' to varying specifications, and the best of these cars exhibited just how good the MGC could have been.

Engine tuning conversions by Downton Engineering Works were available for the MGC and some of the University Motors cars were fitted with these. Buyers had the choice of three states of tune, with the Stage 2 conversion having a gas-flowed cylinder head with larger valves, polished and re-profiled inlet manifolds, twin tubular exhaust manifolds, and a dual exhaust system; the power output was claimed to be

On the 1969 model year MGC engine the fumes from the crankcase were fed directly into the carburettors, the water valve was mounted on the cylinder head, and the alternator had an integral control box.

149bhp at 5,500rpm. The Stage 3 package added triple SU carburettors and raised the power output to 174bhp. Note that the power for Stage 2 was quoted as just 4bhp more than was claimed for the standard engine, but judged by the extra performance reported by testers, the system of measurement must have differed.

There may only be small visual differences between an MGB and an MGC, but the raised ride height produced by the larger wheels, together with those bonnet bulges, gives the car a more muscular appearance. Getting behind the wheel and firing up the engine gives an immediate reminder that in spite of having the same cockpit layout this is no MGB. The noise produced by any six-cylinder engine is something special, and the much-maligned MGC unit is no exception. The engine takes a bit longer than the four-cylinder unit to warm up fully, and in cool weather the choke needs to be used for the first few miles. The steering is heavy at lower speeds, and does not feel as light as one would expect when the speed rises, but the car feels very stable, even when travelling at over 100mph (161kph). In some ways the MGC is better suited to modern

journeys, which often involve long distances on high-speed roads, than it would have been in the 1960s when travel on minor roads was more practical; greater congestion, traffic calming and speed restrictions have now removed much of the pleasure from those sort of journeys.

Understeer is very noticeable on winding roads, and the effort required to work the steering wheel can be tiring. However, pull on to a motorway, engage overdrive, and hour after hour an MGC is happy to cruise at more than 80mph (129kph). In these conditions the car is at its best and will return over 25mpg; around town expect nearer to 20mpg. The automatic gearbox was fitted to quite a number of MGCs, especially GTs, and it suits the characteristics of the engine very well. The gear selector is neat and using the lower two gears gives good control and engine braking in hilly country. The understeer does not seem quite so pronounced on GTs; perhaps the greater weight at the back helps, but that big engine does produce quite a lot of heat, which can make the cabin uncomfortable on warm days.

Overdrive is a desirable option but an MGC without this extra is still a very pleasant car. The earlier cars had higher gearing and wider-spaced gear ratios, giving 24mph (39kph) per 1,000rpm in top gear. Later this was reduced to 22mph (35mph) per 1,000rpm, which is still the same as an MGB with overdrive. Cars with triple-carburettor engines and chassis modifications, such as higher-geared steering racks, wider tyres and up-rated torsion bars, are a delight to drive, but most owners of standard cars will be satisfied with the cars just as they are. The secret is to enjoy the MGC as a long-distance touring car and forget about trying to compete with MGB owners round the twisty bits!

Buying Hints

1. MGCs are nice cars to drive provided the heavier steering is acceptable. Before committing to a purchase, it is important to go for a reasonably long drive in an MGC, just to make sure that it is the right choice.

2. There were far fewer MGCs built than MGBs, and owners tend to keep them longer, so choice is always going to be limited. Prices are a bit higher, but cheaper cars are around, especially GTs.

3. Body rot is just as much of a problem with the MGC as it is with an MGB. Unfortunately, at the time of writing Heritage shells are not available, but there is a plentiful supply of all those separate panels that are common to both models.

4. The main difference between the body shells of the two models centres around the front suspension. The rear mountings for the front torsion bars are under the seat area and here the floor and cross member are quite different. Replacement parts are available but they are expensive and quite tricky to fit. Under the bonnet, the inner wings and front slam panel are different. Replacement aluminium bonnets have been produced.

5. Rust is usually hidden, and the inner wings, and the flange where the front wings bolt to the inner wings, are common problem areas. Mud thrown up by the wheels gathers here, retaining moisture and eventually rotting the metalwork. Examine any proposed purchase carefully and budget for repairs.

6. The sill sections are the same as on the MGB, although a piece must be removed from the inner sill to accommodate the higher floor on the MGC. Like the MGB, the front wings, and the lower portion of the rear wings, must be removed to gain access to replace the sill sections.

7. Front-end shaking at higher speeds is usually caused by poor wheel balance or out-of-true wheels or tyres. Balancing of wire wheels must be undertaken by a specialist, as the average tyre-fitting bay will not carry this out correctly. Wear in the front suspension exacerbates the problem.

8. The majority of MGCs have wire wheels, which are difficult to clean. Knock-on alloy wheels make a popular alternative, but owners of cars with disc wheels will find that the bolt-on variety are much cheaper.

9. The engine has few inherent weaknesses and crankshaft wear is generally minimal. However, it is a lot more costly to rebuild than the four-cylinder unit; parts are more expensive and there are more pistons to deal with! The good news is that a rebuilt engine will run for a high mileage before needing further attention. At the time of writing, new cylinder heads in aluminium are being produced and these are half the weight of an iron head.

10. Oil pressure is generally lower than on an MGB – expect 10/20lb at idle and 45/55lb over 2,000rpm. Oil consumption should be low.

11. The cost of gearbox and rear axle rebuilds is much the same as for the MGB, but some parts are unobtainable new.

The MGB GT V8

MGs are sports cars and should by definition possess performance and roadholding that is superior to the average run-of-the-mill family saloon. However, as the cost of development inexorably rose with each successive new model, manufacturers tended to spend far more money on improving their mainstream cars and less on changes to slower-selling sports cars, often resulting in the average family saloon performing as well as the sports cars in the range.

When the MGB was launched in 1962 it possessed a sufficient performance advantage over the current saloon cars to justify a sports car badge. For a total price of £930 buyers had a 108mph (174kph) top speed and acceleration to 60mph (97kph) in 12.1 seconds, which compared well with 80mph (129mph) and 19.8 seconds for the contemporary Ford Cortina 1500 at £700, and 88mph (142kph) and 17.6 seconds for the £837 Triumph Vitesse. However, by 1972 things had changed. Ford had introduced the Capri, which gave stylish, four-seater motoring at modest cost. Engines from 1,300cc to 3 litres could be specified, with the higher-powered models giving sporting performance.

The price of the MGB with overdrive had risen to over £1,400 but the performance had remained much the same. The most powerful Capri was, at £1,700, more expensive than the MG, but did have a 120mph (193kph) top speed and reached 60mph (97kph) in 8.6 seconds. The 1600GT version of the Capri cost about the same as an MGB, and had a similar top speed but reached 60mph in just over 11 seconds. Saloon cars were becoming quicker and better all the time and the MGB was fast becoming outclassed.

The MGB GT V8 sits on larger-section tyres than the smaller-engined MGB. The appeal of these cars is the effortless performance available in any gear, making the car easy to drive fast.

MGB GT V8
1973-76

ENGINE:
V8, ohv
Bore x stroke   88.9 x 71.1
Capacity   3,528cc
Power   137bhp

TRANSMISSION:
Four-speed gearbox plus
overdrive on top gear
Final drive   3.07:1

BODY STYLE:
Two-door 2+2 closed coupé

PERFORMANCE:
(from contemporary sources)
Max speed   125mph (201kph)
0-60mph (97kph)   7.7 seconds

LENGTH:
Chrome-bumper cars 12ft 9in (3.89m)
Rubber-bumper cars 13ft 2in (4.01m)

WIDTH: 5ft 0in (1.52m)

WHEELBASE: 7ft 7in (2.31m)

NUMBERS BUILT:
Chrome bumper   1,856
Rubber bumper   735

With only the small V8 badges to give the game away, many a driver of a modern 'hot hatch' is surprised to find just how quickly these old MGs move!

The company had been well aware of the need to try to give the sports-car-buying public more performance and the MGC had been their first move in this direction. However, that car had not been as successful as the makers had hoped and the idea of having a more powerful MGB seemed to have been shelved. Individual owners interested in competing had always been able to improve the performance of the B-Series engine, either by working from the advice given in the factory tuning booklets or by approaching one of the independent tuning companies, like Downton or Speedwell.

However, few customers were ever likely to arrange for their road cars to be tuned to improve performance – the attitude of most insurance companies to 'converted' cars saw to that – so it was really up to the company to produce something suitable to satisfy the demand. The main difficulty that Abingdon faced was the usual one of getting sufficient funds to improve the car. The management of British Leyland were not well disposed towards Abingdon and did not want to invest large sums to develop an MG that would directly compete with other cars produced within the organisation. The Abingdon engineers had examined various options that had involved fitting different engines, but most of these needed considerable re-engineering of the car and were ruled out on cost grounds. One engine that would have fitted, the lightweight, Buick-derived V8 fitted to the Rover P6 saloons and Range-Rover, was initially disregarded because it was in short supply – or at least that was what MG were told.

Although the V8 engine is a tight fit in the engine bay, the Abingdon engineers managed to squeeze it in without resorting to having bonnet bulges.

However, it was this engine that was eventually to be used to build one of the best cars ever to emerge from Abingdon.

The impetus behind the eventual adoption of the Rover V8 for use in the MGB was the efforts of an independent engineer whose name will forever be linked to his creation. Ken Costello had established himself as a person who could make Mini saloons go faster round the race track than almost anyone else. However, he did not confine himself to working on these cars and one experiment was the fitting of an Oldsmobile V8 engine in an open MGB roadster. The result was so successful that he started

building similar cars for customers. The small-block aluminium V8 engines were ideally suited for use in British sports cars. The Sunbeam Tiger had been an official factory effort by Rootes, who used a Ford engine and gearbox to transform the performance of their pretty but sedate Sunbeam Alpine. Only the sale of the company to a competitor, Chrysler, stopped them selling in larger numbers.

Ken Costello next turned to the British-built Rover version of the Buick V8 for use in his MGB conversions, using the engine in its standard 150bhp form, mated to the MGB gearbox via a larger, 9.5-inch

(241mm) diameter clutch. He retained the standard MGB rear axle but fitted this with MGC gears that gave an overall ratio of 3.07:1. The engine was too tall to fit under the standard MGB bonnet, the carburettors sitting above the central 'V' of the engine, so Costello designed a fibreglass one that incorporated an ugly bulge. He also fitted a black aluminium 'egg-crate' grille and special 'V-eight' Costello badges to distinguish his cars from the four-cylinder models. Suspension, brakes and steering were unmodified, but harder pads were used to cope with braking from higher speeds.

Overall, the car actually weighed slightly less than an ordinary MGB, so handling was not adversely affected and full use could be made of the extra power. The effect of fitting an engine of similar weight but with twice the capacity can be judged from the road test figures recorded by *Autocar* magazine. Their car reached 60mph (97kph) in 7.8 seconds and was timed at a maximum speed of 128mph (206kph). With engine torque increased by over 80 per cent, the Costello V8 was an exceptionally easy car to drive fast, performance being available from low engine speeds in any gear. The only real drawback was the cost. A completely converted new car cost £975 more than a standard MGB or MGB GT, and was more expensive than other cars of similar performance.

Some police forces used this V8 to evaluate their suitability for patrol work. Although space was too limited for the car to carry the full set of equipment necessary for motorway duties, some of these vehicles did have a role as unmarked pursuit cars.

The rear hatch can carry a fair amount of luggage, making it a useful touring car.

In spite of having very limited development facilities, Ken Costello had built a good, well-engineered road car. Journalists found few faults with those that they drove and most of their complaints owed more to equipment shortcomings in the original MGB than in any problems with the Costello conversions. In spite of the relatively high price of the cars, quite a number were built using new engines supplied direct from British Leyland, who must have been well aware of what he was doing with the units they sold him. In the end the company must have decided that there was a small market here that they could exploit themselves, and the Abingdon engineers were authorised to develop their own car using the Rover engine.

Given their head, the factory engineers had a prototype V8 MGB running in a few weeks, and after a short period of development this was passed to go into production. The car they eventually built used the Range-Rover version of the aluminium V8 engine, which had a lower compression ratio and produced 137bhp at 5,000rpm. The idea of having an unnecessary bonnet bulge obviously offended the factory development team, who worked out a neat alternative inlet arrangement that placed the carburettors at the back of the engine and kept the whole installation low enough to fit beneath a standard bonnet. The distinctive V8 air cleaners incorporated bi-metal valves that allowed warm air from around the exhaust manifolds to be drawn into the engine when it was cold, and cool air when the engine warmed up.

Some sheet-metal modifications to the inner wings were required to enable the bulkier V8 engine to fit in the standard engine bay. Although Costello deemed that little needed to be changed on his cars when the V8 engine was installed, the MG engineers

BL charged too much for the unchanged V8 MGB and sales suffered accordingly

decided to modify the gearbox, suspension and brakes of their version. The gearbox was mated to a different clutch and bell housing (with a modified clutch withdrawal bearing) and was altered to restrict overdrive solely to top gear after testing had revealed that the greater engine torque could cause difficulties with overdrive on third gear. Stiffer springs of similar specification to those used on police MGBs were fitted, and the brakes uprated by using thicker front discs and different front brake callipers. Dunlop D4 wheels shod with wider 175-section tyres were specified, which increased the rolling radius of the wheels slightly and raised the ride height a small amount. These wheels had alloy centres fitted to steel rims and were immensely strong, something wire wheels never were – which is why they did not join the V8 option list.

The MGB GT V8, as the new model was rather clumsily called, was launched on 15 August 1973, at just about the most difficult time to sell a large-engined high-performance car. In October that year Egypt and Syria attacked Israel and this resulted in the five-week Yom Kippur War. The Arab producers retaliated by stopping oil supplies to the West, with consequent

Converting an MGB to V8 specification

The ease with which a V8 engine can be fitted into a four-cylinder body depends largely on which model is chosen. The shells of all the rubber-bumper cars have the inner wings modified to accept the V8 engine, while those built after the 1977 model year changes also have the radiator mounting far enough forward to fit the V8 without modification.

Chrome-bumper MkI shells need to have the gearbox tunnels widened and the inner wings and bulkhead modified before the V8 engine fitted with either the SD1 gearbox or the later MGB box can be accommodated. MkII shells have wider transmission tunnels, but the inner wings and bulkhead will still need to be modified.

The easiest cars to convert are therefore those with the later rubber-bumper shells. Heritage shells to this specification to take chrome bumpers are available on special order but some work will need to be done if a rubber-bumper shell is converted to chrome-bumper specification; the front wings and front valance are different and the cut-away area below the rear lights will have to be replaced.

The ride height of the later cars is also different. The front suspension cross member was lowered, as were the pick-up points for the rear suspension. Fitting lower springs is one solution, but careful thought should be given and advice sought before any major changes are contemplated, as steering geometry, ride and handling can suffer. To control the rear axle without resorting to very stiff springs, some cars are fitted with anti-tramp bars.

The pre-rubber-bumper cars will

require considerable modifications to the steering column, which will otherwise be in the way of the exhaust manifold. The steering gear on the later cars clears the V8 engine.

Any of the Rover V8 engines can be used for the MGB, although some will require different front covers and water pumps to enable them to fit. The later engines have the attraction of being available in larger capacities. There is a wide choice of different carburettor installations to choose from, or even fuel injection, with the original MG V8 arrangement the easiest to accommodate. Using the Rover fuel injection and modern engine management system is an attractive choice for those competent to tackle its complexities, but the bonnet will have to be re-shaped to accommodate it.

There are up-rated braking systems available for fitting to the more powerful conversions. The standard factory V8 brakes were good and sufficient for most conversions, but fitting a servo to any car not equipped should be considered essential. This will not increase the power of the brakes but will significantly reduce braking effort, allowing harder pads to be fitted.

Most conversions use the Rover SD1 gearbox, which requires some modification to gearbox mountings and speedometer drive, or the standard MGB gearbox, which will fit provided an adaptor plate is used. Using the standard gearbox is an economical solution, but really it is not quite strong enough.

The standard MGB steel wheels can be retained but slightly wider alloy wheels are a better alternative. Wire wheels are not strong enough for V8 power.

The interior is much like the ordinary MGB, although the instruments differed from those used in the four-cylinder cars at the time.

shortages and huge price rises that were to frighten people from buying cars that used more fuel. Actually the fuel economy of the V8 MGB was very good, but most people act more on feelings than facts and the common perception of large-engined cars was that they were bound to use more fuel than small-engined ones.

The motoring press praised the performance of the V8 but commented adversely on the lack of any interior or exterior changes to the car to justify its far higher price tag. Once again here was the criticism that had haunted the MGC five years earlier. It seemed that although the company assumed that it was really extra performance that buyers craved, journalists felt that the provision of additional performance alone was insufficient to justify the extra prices charged for higher-performance models. They apparently felt that buyers would like everyone to see that the faster cars were also brighter, bolder and had more comfort than their slower rivals. Perhaps here was

one of the greatest shortcomings of the MG philosophy laid bare: the company obviously thought that the MG enthusiast was willing to trade additional comfort for more performance, while the journalists and the customers felt otherwise.

The truth was that, given the chance, MG would have been happy to incorporate more changes in the cars to justify the higher cost, or to reduce price premium, but these decisions were out of their control. Leyland seemed happy to overcharge for the outwardly unchanged V8 models and to suffer poor sales in consequence. As some justification for the higher price, the MGB GT V8 did have tinted windows, a heated rear window and overdrive as standard, which were extras on the four-cylinder cars. At launch the car cost £2,293.96p, while the current price for the ordinary GT equipped with overdrive and tinted windows was £1,627.71, so the premium charged for the V8 engine was over £600, no less than 40 per cent more!

Pricing the car the way they did, the company could hardly have been surprised to find that the motoring magazines compared it with other cars in the same price bracket and found it wanting. *Autocar* pointed out that the 3-litre Ford Capri with similar performance cost just £1,824 and that the much-acclaimed Datsun 240Z was priced at only a couple of hundred pounds more than the MG. However, there were no complaints about the performance that the big engine gave the car: in spite of its modest state of tune, top speed was 124mph (200kph) and 60mph (97kph) was reached in just 8.6 seconds.

The main sources of complaint were the heavy steering, poor ride, high wind noise, and the lack of some of the appointments they felt a GT car costing over £2,000 really should have enjoyed. The dated dashboard was particularly disliked. As well as from

the high price, another of the main reasons why the basic shortcomings of the MGB GT design were so obvious was that the engine was so quiet and refined. At the high speeds the V8 was capable of maintaining hour after hour, the excessive wind noise from the frameless side windows became far more obvious, while at higher speeds in the ordinary GT the sounds produced by the hard-working engine tended to cancel out the extra wind noise. Had the car they used been a roadster, rather than a GT, the conclusions of the test team may well have differed. However, as the company had decided not to build roadster versions of the V8, this was not an option.

In truth, given the sort of development money available, there was little that could have been done about the wind noise. The GT had been developed

The ride was harder than on the smaller-engined cars, and the large doses of torque available could be an embarrassment on icy roads.

The V8 wheels, also used for the 1975 Jubilee GTs, were made with alloy centres and steel rims. Renovating them is difficult.

originally from an open car, and to save cost at that time the door windows were changed very little. If the car had been designed from the outset as a saloon, the doors would have undoubtedly had fixed frames around the windows, which would have eased the task of reducing air leakage around them.

The complaints about inferior ride and flawed handling were also a feature of the basic design. It seems that the engineers were not able to carry out any major modifications, alterations being limited to changing springs, etc. Stiffer rear springs had been fitted to help control axle tramp on acceleration, produced by large doses of torque from the V8 engine. The stronger rear springs and wider-section tyres raised the ride height a little, and to compensate stiffer front springs were used as well. The effect of these changes was to make the ride harder, and to introduce some instability if power was cut mid-corner. Neither of these

characteristics enhanced the appeal of the car.

So that was the bad news in 1973, but what about the V8 today? Strange as it may seem, some of the things that testers complained of then seem less important now. Modern cars are all quiet, with well-suppressed wind noise and high cruising speeds, and one hardly expects an ageing sports car to match them in refinement. In fact, it is that very lack of modern refinement that is part of the appeal of older cars, and anyone who buys one looking for the sort of motoring they get from their ordinary saloon will be disappointed. Actually, one of the nicest things about driving an MGB GT V8 is the way the ready access to ample power transforms the car. Driven gently, the torque of the engine makes it very easy to live with. On smooth roads the lack of suspension refinement is no handicap and you are always aware that dropping down a gear and flooring the throttle will dispose of most other cars on the road without really trying.

Mere acceleration figures do not convey the full measure of the performance available. There are many sporting versions of modern cars that

on paper appear much quicker than the V8, but on the road they require high engine revs and a lot of effort to beat the MG, which seems to be capable of gaining speed quickly without drama. The ride deteriorates badly on the sort of ill-maintained side roads now so common, and here is where the age of the design shows up most; the answer seems to be not to try too hard, just wind down the windows and enjoy the distinctive sounds emanating from the V8 engine as they are reflected from walls and hedges.

Tyre choice seems to be important. The tyres supplied with the cars when they were new seem to have been of a particularly hard rubber, as they wore out very slowly. The downside of this was that they gave poor grip on slippery roads and the car was best left in the garage if there was ice or snow around, as the engine torque soon caused the rear wheels to lose grip. There seems to be little advantage in fitting wider tyres with the standard suspension. These may give some extra grip but if and when they do break away it is likely to be at speeds where the driver will have some difficulty collecting things together again.

The nicest of all the V8s are the cars that Leyland never built. An MGB roadster is transformed by fitting a V8 engine, and the best of these conversions rivals the factory-built GTs in terms of refinement and tidy installation. The ultimate open V8 is probably the Rover RV8 covered in the next chapter, but some of the converted cars are very nearly as good, and a lot cheaper. There is no substitute for sheer displacement with sports car engines, and fitting an engine that is twice as big produces the sort of MGB to please most keen drivers. The pity is that there are so few around.

Buying Hints

1. With the small number of MGB GT V8s built – 1,856 chrome-bumper cars and 735 with rubber bumpers – choice of original cars will always be very limited. Most V8s when new seemed to get into the hands of people who enjoyed driving them, and mileages quickly built up. The chances of finding a genuine low-mileage example are remote.

2. There are many V8s around that have been converted from ordinary MGBs or built up using a Heritage shell. There is a temptation for vendors to sometimes describe these as 'Costello V8s' in order to inflate the price; the best advice is to ignore such descriptions without documentary proof.

3. There is no standard specification for a Costello-converted car, as it was very much up to the buyer exactly what state of tune and which carburettors, etc, were chosen. Because supplies from Leyland were patchy, some cars had hybrid engines built from imported components. Originally Costello used the Rover 3500S engine, which was more powerful than the MG version.

4. When looking at a V8 roadster, which by definition must be either a conversion or a new creation, the most important consideration is the standard of the workmanship. Some DIY conversions are well-engineered and totally roadworthy, while others are amateurishly converted and possibly dangerous. If in doubt have a full survey by a qualified engineer.

5. Any V8, roadster or GT, has the same potential bodywork problems as the four-cylinder cars. It is quite likely that most cars on offer will have undergone more than one 'full restoration' in their life and should be treated with caution. It is very difficult to find all the rust in a shell on cursory examination, but a close look at the condition of the sills, door pillars and lower wing sections will give clues. Remember that if there is any rust showing externally it will be a lot worse in hidden sections. If in doubt, budget for some repair work.

6. Meticulously maintained, the V8 engine is capable of covering high mileages, but does have some weaknesses. On the original V8 engine the hydraulic cam followers wore after 50,000 miles or so and any rattling at idle is a cause for concern; conversions using later engines do not have this problem. Quite early in their life most factory V8s suffered from cracked exhaust manifolds, but most cars will have been fitted with stronger replacements by now.

7. The MGB GT V8 gearbox was similar to the standard MGB unit and was not really strong enough to withstand much abuse. Most modern conversions use either the Rover five-speed gearbox or the specially developed Costello five-speed unit – both are strong and reliable.

8. Check the overall gearing of any converted car. The original V8 ratio was 3.07:1 and this gives 28.5mph (45.9kph) per 1,000rpm. Using the standard MGB ratio of 3.9:1 gives prodigious acceleration but makes the car far too fussy, and limits too much the speeds available in the intermediate gear ratios.

9. Keep an eye on the oil pressure gauge during any test drive. Pressures are lower than on the four-cylinder cars, 40–50lb at cruising speeds being usual, but readings should be steady and not fluctuate. At idle the reading can be as low as 10lb, but again must be steady.

The RV8

The designers cleverly revised the shape of the 1960s MGB to make it look more modern, while retaining its essential character. The wide alloy wheels fitted with 205/65 tyres would not fit within the MGB wheel arches so the front and rear wings were elegantly reshaped and linked by a modified sill section. Ventilated front discs were fitted, but anti-lock brakes were not available.

W hen the Abingdon factory closed in 1980 many thought that it was the end of the MG marque. A number of other famous British makes like Riley and Wolseley had already been consigned to the history books, and there seemed no reason to suppose that the Abingdon marque would not join them. Later, some comfort could be drawn from the arrival of the MG Metro 1300 – at least the name was to remain even if it was used merely to bolster sales of tuned versions of family saloons. However, speculation about a possible new MG sports car continued to appear in the press from time to time and any editor of a motoring magazine with a space to fill talked about possible successors and 'missed opportunities'.

Speculation intensified in 1985 when Austin Rover exhibited a beautiful styling project at the motor shows that year. The MG EX-E was a

superbly proportioned closed coupé constructed around a revolutionary, adhesive-bonded aluminium alloy frame clad with lightweight plastic panels. A rear-mounted Metro 6R4 V6 engine, which developed 250bhp, would have been capable of giving the car considerable performance had it gone into production.

Much of the credit for the eventual return of MG to sports car production must actually be given to a rival manufacturer, and a Japanese one at that! The launch of the Mazda MX-5 in the late 1980s showed just how large a market there was for the traditional two-seater sports car, the sort of car that used to be the preserve of British manufacturers. Mazda had unashamedly based their pretty little car on past British roadsters, like the MGB and Lotus Elan. By giving it what is now termed 'retro' styling, and keeping the simple front-engine and rear-wheel-drive layout that had proved successful in the past, they were on to a winner. The MX-5 was no mere pastiche, however, being

The wide spare wheel takes up a lot of space in the RV8 boot, but at least it is fully carpeted, as one would expect in a £25,000 motor car.

MG RV8
1993–96

ENGINE:
V8, ohv
Bore x stroke   94 x 71.12
Capacity   3,946cc
Power   190bhp

TRANSMISSION:
Five-speed gearbox
Final drive   3.31:1

BODY STYLE:
Two-seater open sports

PERFORMANCE:
(from contemporary sources)
Max speed   136mph (219kph)
0–60mph (97kph)   6.9 seconds

LENGTH: 13ft 2in (4.01m)

WIDTH: 5ft 6.7in (1.69m)

WHEELBASE: 7ft 7.7in (2.33m)

NUMBERS BUILT:
MG RV8   1,983

endowed with performance, ride and roadholding far in advance of that possessed by the 1960s cars it sought to emulate. Added to this it was reliable, well-built and had a good hood. It has been selling well ever since and updated versions were launched in 1998, 2005 and 2009.

As has been said before in this book, funds to develop sports cars are difficult to find. Even the largest of manufacturers, like Ford and General Motors, prefer to confine their efforts to making sporting coupé versions of their popular cars, where the expensive-to-build floorpan can be carried over from one model to the other. It is far cheaper to re-skin a car, giving it a sporting look, than it is to build a sports two-seater from scratch. Even established sports car builders like Porsche seldom change their models, relying instead on the occasional update to keep customers loyal. In Britain the smaller constructors cashed in on the shortage of volume sports cars, usually by selling cars designed decades earlier to customers not

concerned about having the latest technical innovations. Performance was certainly there in abundance from firms like TVR and Caterham, but their cars lacked the sophistication that could only come from having a large budget to develop new models.

The success of the Mazda in America and Britain caused the Rover Group, who were the privatised successors to the British Leyland empire, to look again at the possibility of a new MG sports car. Various projects were being considered all through the 1980s but none received final sanction as the majority of development effort continued to be directed towards the saloon cars that were the company's bread and butter. However, almost by chance, an opportunity arose to produce a new MG sports car to both keep the marque identity alive and to test public reaction to a possible new volume-produced MG.

The idea of building a 1990s development of the 30-year-old MGB arose only because of the availability of new MGB bodies from British Motor Heritage, a subsidiary of the Rover Group. Demand for repair panels produced from the original MGB tooling had been increasing in the 1980s. There had always been a

steady demand for wings, doors, etc, and these had been almost continuously available as ordinary spares through the usual parts network. However, as more and more cars were restored, some unobtainable parts were in demand and this led to the search for the tooling to make them. It was discovered that most of the 750 press tools needed to make complete MGB bodies existed, and in 1988 the first of many thousands of new bodyshells were offered for sale to enthusiasts.

The logical extension of the bodyshell project was to build complete cars and, under the direction of their Managing Director, David Bishop, British Motor Heritage started to look at the feasibility of such a project. They proposed building MGB V8 roadsters using mainly new parts, but it soon became clear that this would be too complicated an undertaking for their resources. The project was then taken up by Rover Cars themselves and a development team at Rover Special Projects, a small division of the company specially created in 1990 to work on low-volume vehicles and specialist development work, was given the task of updating the MGB design to make it suitable for sale as a new car.

Once work started it became obvious that a great many new or modified components would be needed. Many of the parts originally used for the MGB were either no longer available, or were unsuitable bearing in mind the sort of performance envisaged for the RV8. Like other builders of

low-volume sports cars, TVR and Morgan in particular, it was to the Buick-derived, light-alloy, eight-cylinder Rover engine that the development team turned for a power unit for the RV8. This engine had been considerably developed since it was used in the 1970s MGB GT V8 and was capable of giving the new car even more performance.

In spite of handing the project over to Rover, Heritage were still much involved in building the new MG. The RV8 bodyshells were assembled by British Motor Heritage at Faringdon at the rate of 15 a week. These had to be finished to a higher standard than the MGB shells they had been used to building as the modern paint finishing

The front and rear of the car were completely redesigned. The front fog lamps and indicator lights are recessed into a bumper moulding that has echoes of the shape of the rubber bumper fitted to the 1970s MGB.

process at Cowley did not allow for any rectification of blemishes in the surface of the bodies. Rover quality inspectors were based at Faringdon to examine the completed shells before they went to Cowley for painting and assembly. Although the basic body frame from the MGB was used for the RV8, the wings, bonnet and front and rear bumpers were extensively remodelled to produce a design that looked more up-to-date. The decision to fit the car with 15-inch (381mm) wheels shod with 205/65-profile tyres meant that the wings needed widening to cover them. New front and rear energy-absorbing bumpers were designed and these were finished in the same colour as the rest of the body. The bigger wheels, wider wings, and the bonnet bulge to cover the fuel injection system gave the car a more aggressive appearance than previously.

Most of the smaller components used on the RV8 differed from those fitted to the original MGB. These were either specially made for the RV8, or taken from other models in the Rover range.

RV8s were traditionally built and fully road tested before delivery

In keeping with a car designed to sell at a far higher price than previous MGBs, the interior trim and equipment levels matched those of a luxury car. The very comfortable seats were trimmed in stone-coloured leather, there was a polished elm dashboard, a mohair hood, and a modern stereo system.

Under the modified bonnet, the engine was a tuned 3.9 litre Rover V8 unit mated to a five-speed gearbox. The power available from the larger-capacity engine was 190bhp, and to

cope with this the rear axle had a limited-slip differential and the redesigned rear suspension had torque control arms between the axle and the front spring mounts, to resist axle tramp during hard acceleration. Modern telescopic shock absorbers replaced the MGB lever-arm dampers, and the front suspension cross member from the MGB was modified. Ventilated front disc brakes were fitted, although drums were retained for the rear brakes.

The RV8 was assembled at Cowley by hand, with the production floor arranged so that the small team could build up the cars by traditional methods. The assembly line workers each spent as long as 2½ hours to complete their allotted tasks on each RV8, ensuring that the work was carried out to a very high standard. Each car had a full road test before being delivered to dealers.

To properly enjoy an RV8 it has to be approached as a modernised MGB rather than as a 1990s car. In spite of its up-to-date appearance, it is still a traditional British sports car with all the advantages and drawbacks of the breed. Just how well the plush cabin

The light-alloy V8 engine has Lucas multi-point fuel injection, which provides a power output of 190bhp from the 3,946cc engine.

works will depend more on the build of the driver than anything else. Fitting more deeply upholstered seats removed some of the previously available head and legroom, making it more difficult for taller drivers to get comfortable. Unfortunately, although the windscreen frame was comprehensively redesigned, it was made no higher. The top rail and sun visors are thus right in the line of sight of taller drivers, although matters improve once the seats compress with age. Room in the footwell around the pedals is also rather restricted.

Once a comfortable driving position has been found, the plush cockpit can be enjoyed. The dashboard layout is pleasing, although traditional MG drivers have to accept the absence of an oil pressure gauge. Anyone used to MGBs will immediately notice that there are no quarter lights on the doors, internally adjustable door mirrors taking their place, but the feel of the leather-covered gear lever knob for the five-speed gearbox and the

The dashboard, instruments and controls owe nothing to the original MGB. The cockpit of the RV8 has comfortable, deeply upholstered seats that are covered in soft leather, and the dashboard and door cappings are veneered in polished elm.

satisfyingly chunky steering wheel are very pleasing. This steering wheel is not adjustable and is offset slightly towards the centre of the car.

At idle, engine noise is muted, although one is always aware of the presence of the powerful V8 engine under the bonnet. Under way, the availability of huge doses of torque immediately impresses. The urgent acceleration has the driver reaching to select the next gear as the speed builds rapidly. On smooth, straight roads this power can be used to the full, disposing of all but the fastest of supercars. However, give the RV8 a

The RV8 was hand-assembled at the Rover Cowley factory. Production numbers were low and cars have remained highly priced in the second-hand market.

series of bumpy curves to negotiate and the deficiencies of the dated suspension layout become apparent. The rear will quickly step out of line and the jarring imposed on driver and passenger by bumps in the road call for a rapid speed reduction. That said, the car handles better and feels far more secure than the 1970s V8, and with such a lot of power available it is satisfying to drive. Given the low numbers produced, the RV8 has become a sort of 'instant classic' with low initial depreciation and many of the cars going to owners who use them sparingly.

Inevitably, given the motor sporting history of the MGB, thoughts were given to a similar role for the RV8. The Le Mans 24 Hours race was an obvious candidate and in addition to an official internal study, two other projects came under discussion from independent organisations. Although the idea of a production-based car competing at La Sarthe was not completely dead, Marcos, Morgan and TVR being examples of small British

manufacturers still prepared to tackle the event, the problems of weight and aerodynamics would have been against the MG and the idea was stillborn.

However, a works-supported MG RV8 ran in various British hillclimb championships, and individual cars have been raced at club level, while Team Cowley MG, a group of employees at the then Rover Group plant, campaigned three cars in races and sprints, and one of the two press cars formed part of the Rover team on the 1993 Orient Express Trophy, run between London and Milan.

Total MG RV8 production was to be limited to 2,000 production cars and in the event 1,983 examples were built, in addition to pre-production and development versions. Of these, a little over 300 were purchased in the UK, the balance being exported, mostly to Japan, where the car's retro image and modern mechanicals had similarly strong appeal to the revived Mini Cooper.

One peculiarity of the Japanese market is the very stringent vehicle-testing regime. When the RV8 became old enough to fall victim to this, increasing numbers found their way to auction, with several UK specialists bringing back previously exported cars. They have found a ready market, despite the Japanese-spec air-conditioning system that intrudes into the passenger footwell. In spite of their generally low mileages, these cars frequently return with tyres that have hardened in storage, damage to the hood and rear screen, and splitting of the elm veneers. At least one specialist importer addresses all these issues, including fully servicing the cars and supplying an mph speedometer, along with UK registration and an MoT. Purchased carefully, an export-model MG RV8 can be an exceptional buy, providing what Rover Group had always promised, namely classic motoring without tears.

The MG 6R4 Rally Car

The MG name was given a boost by the 1984 announcement of the MG Metro 6R4 rally car. With four-wheel drive and power from a V6 aluminium engine mounted behind the driver, it was designed to compete in international competition at the highest level. Development was in the joint hands of Austin Rover Motorsport and Williams Grand Prix Engineering of Didcot. After initial testing, 200 cars were built to homologate the car for competition, some of these being sold to the public at £35,000 each. The engine was tuned to give around 250bhp in 'Clubman' form, this being increased to around 400bhp for those built to full international rally specification.

Although based on the standard MG Metro, most of the body and mechanical components were specially made. The wheel arches were extended, and a huge spoiler was incorporated in the cover over the rear-mounted engine to increase downforce on the rear wheels. Unfortunately, specially developed cars like the 6R4 were perceived to be just too quick for use on public road events and they were banned by FISA, the body that governs motorsport, before the 6R4 could show its full potential. In spite of this the car did bring some welcome publicity for the marque at a time when the MG name was in danger of being forgotten in motorsport circles. Quite a number of cars remained unsold when the ban was imposed and these have subsequently found buyers amongst Rallycross competitors where the cars are run under closed-circuit conditions.

The MG Metro 6R4 gave the company a short-lived chance to compete in international rallies before the use of such highly modified cars was banned.

The MGF *and* TF

The MG RV8 was never intended to be more than a celebration of the 30th anniversary of the MGB. That was the official Rover Group line, but the sub-plot was much more significant, namely to warm-up the sports car market with the return of MG to the arena it had once dominated. With the last MGB having been manufactured in 1980 and the MG badge having subsequently been used only on performance saloons, bringing the octagon back on a headline-grabbing sports car was seen as essential, even if the car in question was strictly a limited edition, if sales of the new volume MG sports car were to take off.

The momentous decision to proceed with 'Project Phoenix', which would ultimately lead to the MGF, had been made in 1989, with design work continuing alongside the development of the RV8. As one would expect, much consideration was given to the engine/chassis layout. A front engine with front-wheel drive, a front engine with rear-wheel drive, and a mid-engine with rear-wheel drive were all possibilities. Styling proposals for the new car had been sought from three design establishments, each being given the basic layout and the brief that the car had to be unmistakably an MG. The style chosen as a starting point was one proposed by MGA Developments, and it was their basic model that was refined and prepared for production by the Rover Group Canley Design Studio under the direction of Gerry McGovern.

Final sanction to proceed was given by Rover management in 1992, although much preliminary work had been done and a number of prototypes had been constructed. Having decided that the car was to have a mid-engine layout, much testing was needed to achieve the correct balance between roadholding,

The distinctive design of the MGF, with the low bonnet line and high tail, gives the car a solid, strong appearance. The six-spoke alloy wheels identify this car as the 1.8i.

handling and ride. The solution adopted was to use the Hydragas suspension from the Metro. This has a fluid interconnection between the front and rear suspension units on each side of the car. Gas-filled units take the place of conventional springs and when a front wheel hits a bump this both compresses the gas within the unit to provide springing, and forces fluid down the interconnecting tube to stiffen the rear suspension. Separate front and rear shock absorbers provide additional damping. Modified Metro/Rover 100 subframes are used to mount the double-wishbone, all-independent suspension. This suspension system has proved capable of providing excellent handling allied to ride qualities far superior to those of rival small sports cars.

To be successful the MGF had to use an engine that would give it the sort of performance that drivers of modern sports cars expect. The K-Series engine, first introduced in 1990 for the Metro and Rover 200, utilises light alloy castings and a system of bolting the cylinder head, block and sump together with a single set of bolts. For the MGF the capacity was enlarged to 1,796cc without increasing the overall size of the unit. Two versions were available for the MG. The standard engine in the 1.8i delivered 118bhp, while the VVC engine with variable valve timing produced 143bhp.

The VVC version of the MGF proved a popular choice for enthusiasts, not least because that model came with electric power steering and anti-lock brakes as standard, which were extras on the ordinary MGF. In the hands of the road test teams the standard car was capable of reaching 123mph (198kph) and the VVC 131mph (211kph). The 1.8i took 8.7 seconds to reach 60mph (97kph) and the more powerful model 7.6 seconds. Both cars earned high praise from testers with criticism being directed at cabin finish and a certain blandness about the way the car handled.

MGF 1.8i
1995-2002

ENGINE:
4-cylinder, D.O.H.C. 16-valve
Bore x stroke   80 x 89.3
Capacity   1,796cc
Power   118bhp

TRANSMISSION:
Five-speed gearbox
Final drive   3.94:1

BODY STYLE:
Two-seater open sports

PERFORMANCE:
(from contemporary sources)
Max speed   123mph (198kph)
0-60mph (97kph)   8.7 seconds

LENGTH: 12ft 10.1in (3.91m)

WIDTH: 5ft 10.1in (1.78m)

WHEELBASE: 7ft 9.5in (2.38m)

MGF VVC
1995-02

As MGF 1.8i except:
Power   143bhp
Final drive   4.2:1
Max speed   131mph (211kph)
0-60mph (97kph)   7.6 seconds

TF 115
2002-05

ENGINE:
4-cylinder, D.O.H.C. 16-valve
Bore x stroke   80 x 79
Capacity   1,588cc
Power   114bhp

TRANSMISSION:
Five-speed gearbox
Final drive   3.94:1

PERFORMANCE:
(from manufacturer sources)
Max speed   118mph (190kph)
0-60mph (97kph)   9.2 seconds

LENGTH: 12ft 10.1in (3.91m)

WIDTH: 5ft 10.1in (1.78m)

WHEELBASE: 7ft 9.5in (2.38m)

TF 135
2002-05

ENGINE:
4-cylinder, D.O.H.C. 16-valve
Bore x stroke   80 x 89.3
Capacity   1,796cc
Power   134bhp

TRANSMISSION:
Five-speed gearbox
Final drive   4.20:1

PERFORMANCE:
(from manufacturer sources)
Max speed   127mph (205kph)
0-60mph (97kph)   8.2 seconds

Dimensions as MG TF 115

TF 120 Stepspeed
2002-05

ENGINE:
4-cylinder, D.O.H.C. 16-valve
Bore x stroke   80 x 89.3
Capacity   1,796cc
Power   118bhp

TRANSMISSION:
Six-speed CVT

PERFORMANCE:
(from manufacturer sources)
Max speed   118mph (190kph)
0-60mph (97kph)   9.7 seconds

Dimensions as MG TF 115

TF 160
2002-05

ENGINE:
4-cylinder, D.O.H.C. 16-valve, VVC
Bore x stroke   80 x 89.3
Capacity   1,796cc
Power   158bhp

TRANSMISSION:
Five-speed gearbox
Final drive   4.20:1

PERFORMANCE:
(from manufacturer sources)
Max speed   137mph (220kph)
0-60mph (97kph)   6.9 seconds

Dimensions as MG TF 115

The option of factory-fitted leather seats has been popular with buyers, as have the wooden trim panels for the instruments.

The instrument panel is one of the most attractive features of the car. Cream-painted faces, black markings and red pointers on the instruments help relieve the large expanse of grey plastic on the dashboard.

In spite of the mid-engine layout, the general feel of the MGF is more like a modern front-wheel-drive car than a rear-engined sports car. The handling displays no worrying vices and the ease with which drivers more used to ordinary saloon cars quickly adapt to the MGF does much to explain its popularity in the marketplace. Drivers find that the layout of the controls is very good and that the dashboard layout and instrumentation, although criticised for being unimaginative, works well. The seats are supportive and comfortable, even after long periods at the wheel. The one flaw is

the non-adjustable steering column. For tall drivers, at least for those with long legs, the wheel is set too close to the dashboard, giving insufficient clearance between the brake pedal and wheel rim. Taking the seat right back on the runners helps, but then the driver is sitting so far from the steering wheel that an upright seating position is necessary and headroom can be a problem.

Those more used to the hard ride of their MGB or Midget find the compliant MGF suspension one of the most impressive things about the car. Relatively soft springing and superb body control produce the sort of ride comfort over bumpy roads not usually associated with sports cars. Many highly priced and very fast cars give such a teeth-jarringly hard ride at lower speeds on the average road as to make them unpleasant in everyday use. Not so the MGF. Ride comfort approaches saloon car standards, allowing full use of the available performance. Top down, the cars are

This 1998 MGF has front fog lamps and the optional 16-inch wheels with low-profile tyres. These fill the wheel arches better than the standard wheels.

The mid-engined layout on the MGF makes access difficult. Routine servicing and checking oil, coolant and other fluids is fairly straightforward, but to gain access for major work the panel at the back of the hood can be removed.

thoroughly enjoyable to drive and, especially with the optional deflector fitted, wind buffeting is low.

The MGF, although conceived during the British Aerospace ownership of Rover Group, was actually launched when the company was BMW-owned. Although there had been certain misgivings within Rover that this might see the project's cancellation, in view of the impending launch of the BMW Z3, which was to be built in South Carolina from late 1995, these fears were groundless.

BMW did make a contribution to the PR3 design, initiating the installation of a crash hoop within the windscreen frame. Otherwise the car, launched to such acclaim at the Geneva Motor Show of 1995, was an entirely British production. But BMW's attitude to further development of the MGF seems to have been influenced by the fact that the Z3 occupied the same segment of the market, although the clientele was arguably different. Certainly in dynamic terms the MG was the more sophisticated car, while the BMW's mix of styling details was not to everyone's taste.

Whatever BMW's stance, the MG design team was determined to prove that there were alternative routes to take with the MGF. Highlighting its obvious sporting potential was the low-key but nonetheless successful MG EXF – or EX253 – project. Designed to return MG to its traditional speed-record arena, this was an MGF-based turbocharged 1.4 car, with the cockpit offset to the left and featuring a teardrop canopy. Although encouraged by BMW, the project was not given official status, but when the objective was announced as the Bonneville Speed Week in August 1997, the seriousness of intent was plain. Bonneville had been immensely successful as a venue for MG – the fastest-ever MG was the EX181 of Phil Hill, which recorded 254.91mph on the famous salt flats. Californian Terry Kilbourne, a hugely experienced Bonneville competitor and member of the 200mph club, took the MG EXF prototype to over 217mph, a speed which the MG publicity team made full use of, particularly since the car was based on production MGF components.

Another project was the MGF Super Sports, presented alongside the Earl Howe MG K3 at the Geneva Show in March 1988. The power unit was a supercharged version of the 1.8-litre K-series engine, producing 200bhp, while the suspension was as that of the 1998 MGF Cup race cars. Highly

distinctive in its traditional deep red, recalling Abingdon's works MGBs, and with lightweight aluminium flared side panels to accommodate the wider track and the larger wheels and tyres, this was very much a 'show special' and was billed as a 'weekend race car'. The designer was David Woodhouse, working with Gerry McGovern, and significantly it was Mayflower, whose £24m rights issue had paved the way for MGF production, who produced the one-off body. Despite generating huge interest when exhibited at international motor shows, no production plans materialised. Essentially a track car, the Super Sports could easily have become a state-of-the-art road car, and this was the route followed when it was exhibited at Geneva in 1999 and again in 2000.

The success of the MG EXF project paved the way for EX255, which was intended to better the longstanding Phil Hill record at the 1998 Bonneville Speed Week. This was a far more ambitious project, being a totally new

one-off design using a 4.8-litre Rover V8, and with none other than Andy Green, the World Land Speed recordholder, at the wheel. Sadly, the project was not to be successful, with engine development problems dogging the team before the car was shipped to Utah. Further problems

Above: MG EXF – or EX253 – reached a speed of 217.400mph on the Bonneville Salt Flats in 1997 with Terry Kilbourne at the wheel. Below: Planned to be the fastest MG ever, EX255 awaits a further attempt at Bonneville Speed Week a year later, but engine problems prevented it from running.

The MG Super Sports concept was described as a 'Weekend Racer', drawing on cues from the marque's racing past.

beset the team at its HQ on the former USAF base in Wendover and – despite Herculean efforts by everyone involved – EX255 was unable to run. The car is now an exhibit at the Heritage Motor Centre at Gaydon.

With sales running at consistently high levels, it was not until the 2000 model year that significant changes were made to the production cars and the issue of the perceived lack of character of the cockpit addressed. Announced in August 1999, these were the first major modifications since the car's launch. They included an adjustable steering column and a leather wheel, electric door mirrors, new alloy wheels, and substantial improvements to the interior.

The aftermarket had already been supplying such accessories as wood dashboard kits and chrome trim – to the distaste of Gerry McGovern and the design team, who considered that the contemporary nature of the MGF design was being diluted, at the very least. But marketing needs overruled this stance and in addition to new seats with a full range of trim choices, an optional walnut dashboard was now offered as an alternative to the standard Ash Grey. The cream instrument dials of the original cars gave way to silver, the odometer became electronic, a new alloy gearknob inspired by the fuel filler cap design made its appearance, the door case panels were given brushed aluminium finishers, and a high-specification audio system was introduced. Externally the windscreen surround was now body-coloured, and smoked indicator lenses became standard, while Alumina Green and Sienna Gold joined the colour line-up.

There had always been the possibility of an automatic transmission for the

MGF, and so it was no surprise when the MGF 1.8i Steptronic made its appearance for the 2000 model year. The system chosen for the MGF was based on a continuously-variable transmission (CVT) linked to an advanced electronic control system. This operates in either conventional CVT 'stepless' fashion or with six predetermined steps or fixed ratios, in virtually the same manner as a six-speed manual gearbox. In the MGF two programmes (normal or 'Sport' and 'Manual') can be selected by the driver. In 'Manual' mode the six ratios may be selected either by using the gearlever or via two steering wheel switches.

In use, Steptronic – renamed Stepspeed under MG Rover – is a decidedly user-friendly system. The ability to use the car as an automatic, with the normal CVT selector pattern of PRND, proves ideal for urban driving, while back on the open road the MGF can be driven in true sports car style, using either the steering wheel buttons or the gear lever. The MGF Steptronic proved very rapid as a point-to-point machine, belying its slower 0–60mph time of 9.5 seconds and its 118mph top speed. The downside was the economy, with the combined figure dropping to 34.0mpg, against the 38.3mpg of the standard 1.8i.

Throughout the early part of 2000, BMW's intentions to divest themselves of Rover Group dominated the headlines. When a sale to venture capitalists Alchemy Group seemed done and dusted – with attendant heavy job losses at Longbridge – the deal collapsed. As is now history, the Phoenix consortium, which included both John Towers and Nick Stephenson, who had been instrumental in bringing the MGF to market, once again returned the MG marque to British ownership. The immediate review, particularly of the MG marque, concluded that MG was ripe for further development, and

ultimately led to the largest-ever model line-up in the octagon's history.

In July 2000, within two months of the Phoenix takeover, the MGF SE was launched. A high-specification model, its distinctive Wedgwood Blue paintwork made it a showroom star, and focused attention on the MG marque. Standard equipment included a full-leather interior, 16in multi-spoke alloy wheels, chrome door handles, a wire mesh grille and matching side intakes, a rear boot spoiler, a wind-stop, and a CD tuner. Just 500 models were produced.

In September, the change of name of the company to MG Rover Group was announced, together with the news that the MG model range would be expanded. Peter Stevens, one of the most respected names in automotive design, whose work included the McLaren F1, was now the company's product design director, while Rob Oldaker had rejoined Longbridge after spells at Rolls-Royce and Cosworth. His role as director of product development would prove to be fundamental to the refining of the existing range and the formulation of new models.

The general consensus of the new team was that the MGF needed 'hardening up' – and with more than a nod in the direction of the Super Sports concept, the MG Trophy 160 made its appearance in January 2001. Its specification owed much to the race versions of the MGF, notably the MGF Cup, with the Hydragas suspension having competition-based spring and damper rates and a lower ride height, and with the 16in alloy wheels completely filling the wheel arches and giving the car a purposeful and aggressive stance. Front brakes were AP Racing units, with ventilated discs and red-finish MG-branded aluminium calipers. A tuned version of the K-series 1.8-litre VVC engine was used, with a wide-bore exhaust system, this resulting in an output of 160bhp, over 10 per cent more than

the 143bhp of the then current VVC model. There was a new bib spoiler and a rear aerofoil, and special paint finishes of Trophy Blue and Trophy Yellow were introduced, along with body-coloured inserts for the door casings and centre console, a colour-coded steering wheel, special leather/fabric seats, bright mesh grille and side air intakes, and an alloy/leather gear knob. This was the most distinctive MGF variant yet, and the performance more than matched the looks, with a top speed of 137mph and a 0–60mph time of 6.9 seconds.

On the road the MGF Trophy did not disappoint. The handling was far removed from any previous MGF and recalled the prototype MGF Cup car which was tested at Castle Combe circuit. The ride was decidedly firmer and the impression was of a car where the dynamics had received careful honing. The steering was

utterly precise, with turn-in sharper than ever, and the brakes were a revelation. An incredibly quick point-to-point car that was hugely involving and enjoyable to drive, the MGF Trophy had serious attractions as a track-day car, one which could be driven to a circuit and back home at the end of the day.

Above: After the Phoenix takeover in 2000, the first development of the MGF came with the high-performance Trophy 160 model, clearly inspired by the Super Sports project. Below: The Trophy 160's specification was related to cars raced in the MGF Cup, the official MG race series run in the UK from 1998 to 2000.

What MG Rover had done with the MGF Trophy 160 was to plug the high-performance gap in the range. Yet a far more pressing need was to offer an entry-level model, as arch-rival Mazda had continued the aggressive promotion of their basic 1.6-litre MX-5. The MGF, which had always been a 1.8 model, was losing out among first-time buyers of sports cars and so the MGF 1.6i was created in response, with a 112bhp version of the K-series giving a top speed of 116mph (just 4mph short of the contemporary 1.8i) and a 0–60mph time of 9.3 seconds. Far from being a stripped-out variant, the 1.6i retained an adjustable steering column, electric speed-sensitive power-assisted steering, electric windows, heated door mirrors and alloy wheels, making for an exceptional-value package.

When MG Rover revealed their plans for the MG range, they said that each model would have an 'Extreme'

version. The first of these was the MG XPower MGF. MG XPower was to be the performance brand of the marque, rather as AMG is to Mercedes-Benz and the 'M' cars are for BMW; it was further developed to market performance parts and to develop a complete car in the form of the MG XPower SV and SV-R.

The MGF XPower 500 was a one-off demonstrator, powered by the 2-litre engine of the Le Mans cars and fitted with a sequential gearbox. Making its display début at the 2001 24-Hours, this ultimate MGF with its special bodywork, headlight treatment and aerodynamics hinted at possible future directions for the model. These, though, were for the future, as the production MGFs continued their steady sales both in the UK and overseas, as new post-BMW distribution arrangements were established. By the time the last MGF had been built, production had reached 77,269 vehicles.

The MGF XPower 500 used the 2-litre engine of the Le Mans cars, together with a sequential gearbox, and was street legal.

EX257 and Le Mans

MG's decision to return to international sports car racing was followed by plunging in at the deep end with the MG-Lola EX257 LMP675. This had an MG-sponsored 2-litre turbocharged engine developed by AER. Two cars were entered in both the 2001 and 2002 Le Mans 24-Hours races, driven by Mark Blundell, Anthony Reid, Warren Hughes, Kevin McGarrity, Julian Bailey and Johnny Kane.

In 2001 the number 34 car of Reid, Hughes and Kane set class pole before being forced out with low oil pressure after 4½ hours. Car 33, shared by Blundell, Bailey and McGarrity, ran as high as third overall in the early stages, before retiring with an oil leak and subsequent overheating after some 12½ hours. In 2002 the same driver pairings returned, car 26 being the mount of Reid, Hughes and Kane and car 27 being driven by Blundell, Bailey and McGarrity.

Qualifying saw a class 1–2, while Hughes took car 26 to fourth place

before being forced out with gearbox/transmission failure. Car 27 looked set for a top-ten finish and a class win, but succumbed to a similar failure just before 8am on Sunday morning. Privateer entries for US teams KnightHawk (2002) and Intersport (2003) also ended in retirement.

Owner-driver Mike Newton acquired one of the works cars and this was prepared under the RML banner for 2004, successfully contesting the Le Mans Endurance Series (LMES), in addition to the 24-Hours, where a superb run frustratingly saw the MG-Lola the final retirement, with a holed piston, with just over four hours to run.

MG's return to international sports car racing saw two MG-Lola EX257 cars entered for Le Mans in 2001. Both performed well until their retirement, this one – driven by Anthony Reid, Warren Hughes and Johnny Kane – having led its class in qualifying.

MG TF

Quite why MG Rover chose to give the next version of the MGF the TF designation – as seen on the final T-type Midget of 1953–55 – remains something of a mystery. It did however clearly differentiate the new model, launched at the beginning of 2002, from the previous one, while the Peter Stevens design treatment was to be the precursor of a new MG face, first seen on the MG X80 supercar and which would ultimately encompass the entire range.

The changes to the 'F' were far-reaching, going well beyond the traditional parameters of a mid-life facelift. By far the most fundamental was the scrapping of the interconnected Hydragas suspension in favour of a completely new coil-spring suspension and multi-link rear axle, with both the front and rear subframes now solid-mounted, as on the MGF Trophy. In addition the electric power-assisted steering (EPAS) was given faster gearing to provide quicker and sharper responses.

The MGF had been the last model to use Alex Moulton's Hydragas system, which gave the car such excellent ride and handling qualities. The prospect of renewing ageing tooling for a single model had been decided against, however reluctantly, but the change divided drivers. Those who wanted a more involving suspension package – an optional sports Handling Pack was also available – discovered it with the new TF, but others wedded to the softer suspension of the MGF found it less welcoming, feedback which MG Rover was later to act upon.

The restyling initiated by Peter Stevens hardened the soft lines of Gerry McGovern's MGF. But it was not change for the sake of it, as additional body stiffness and improved aerodynamics were part of the objective. The new front bumper, shaped to reduce front-end lift, had a

framed lower air intake and provision for fog lamps, and new projector lamps and prominent badging completed a very different frontal aspect. At the rear, the bootlid was modified to incorporate an integrated lip spoiler, complete with a high-mounted stop lamp.

The side elevation showed another fundamental change, the introduction of a one-piece outer sill and rear wing pressing which, combined with additional bracing to the bodyshell, resulted in a 20 per cent increase in torsional stiffness and a reduction in scuttle shake on bad surfaces. Significantly, the Euro NCAP tests revealed the MG TF to be the safest sports car available, with a four-star occupant safety rating and a class-leading three-star pedestrian protection score. The revised styling also received accolades, the TF being named 'Cabrio of the Year' at the 2002 Geneva Motor Show and the

'World's Most Beautiful Cabriolet' in 2003, awarded by L'Automobile più Bella del Mondo, in Milan.

The model range remained at four, but with marked power and specification improvements to the two top-range models. The entry level model was the TF115 1.6-litre (115bhp), then came the 1.8-litre TF135 (135bhp) which would account for the highest proportion of sales. The TF120 Stepspeed 1.8-litre with multi-function CVT and 120bhp provided the automatic option, while the range-topping TF160 1.8 litre VVC (160bhp) had fast-road and obvious track-day potential. The TF135 now had a power output approaching that of the original MGF VVC and the TF160 now had identical power output and performance to the MGF Trophy.

New colours included XPower Grey, the base colour for the motorsport programme, Le Mans Green, and

Launched early in 2002, the MG TF featured many changes, including the use of coil-spring suspension instead of Hydragas. Pictured with Cecil Kimber's 'Old Number One', this TF is the 1.5 millionth MG and came down the Longbridge line on 16 April 2002. Its colour was chosen to celebrate the Golden Jubilee of Her Majesty the Queen.

MG's 80th anniversary in 2004 was celebrated with a special limited-edition TF.

Trophy Blue and Trophy Yellow. New interior colours and materials, improved instrumentation and new fabrics, including Alcantara and leather options, completed what MG Rover described as 'the new generation TF'.

Just as with the MGF, the MG TF was a 'real world' sports car, as was its Mazda MX-5 rival, with useable boot space and acceptable fuel consumption. Where the TF undoubtedly scored was in the sophistication of its chassis and the driving pleasure this engendered. "Outrageous fun for all" was how Rob Oldaker defined the MG ethos, and this the MG TF certainly delivered.

Personal ownership experience of both the MGF and a TF135 as sole cars, and therefore daily drivers,

reveals considerable differences between the two cars. The MGF is both hugely entertaining and rapid, and its economy, always returning around 40mpg however hard it was driven, is most impressive. The TF, however, moves the game on. The immediate impression is of its sheer rigidity, it feeling squarely planted on the road whatever the surface or camber. The fact that there are no shakes or rattles attests to the effectiveness of the body changes. The engine provides prodigious amounts of torque, the real key to sports car performance, while the gear ratios, from the previous VVC, are perfectly matched to the performance. The steering is noticeably sharper, right through the speed range, roadholding is even better than that of the MGF, and the uprated brakes are particularly effective.

Maintaining interest levels, several special edition MG TFs were

launched, notably the high-spec Sprint model, with its coloured hood, and the MG 80th Anniversary model with its individually-numbered plaques. Undoubtedly the most famous TF was the gold-finished example, the 1.5 millionth MG to be built and a fitting commemoration of Her Majesty the Queen's Golden Jubilee.

While the MG TF continued to be the UK's best-selling roadster, a number of significant changes arrived for the 2005 model year. The most radical of these was revised suspension to provide a more compliant ride. Front and rear spring rates were reduced (20 per cent at the front and 30 per cent at the rear) and different damper settings gave more control throughout the wheel travel and made the handling more progressive. Additionally the diameter of the front anti-roll bar was increased, while the suspension was tuned to the Continental tyre used, the Conti

Premium Contact. It works: the chassis inspires such confidence that you can drive deeper into a corner than before, yet previous criticisms about the harshness of the ride have become redundant.

A long-awaited change was the introduction of a heated glass rear screen for the hood, as fitted to the MX-5 several years previously. Of smaller area than the previous MGF/TF rear screen, it provided clearer vision and removed the necessity of zipping out the rear window when folding the hood. Cockpit changes included new illuminated heating and ventilation controls, and new finishes for the centre console, doors, instrument binnacle and seating – while new model badging brought the TF into line with the MG saloon range.

Where – if anywhere – the TF range went from here was difficult to predict with MG Rover in administration and the future of the MG marque unsure. An intriguing

prospect was the MG GT show car, a fixed-head coupé version of the TF using the existing platform and powertrain but with the possibility of having the KV6 engine – which would have given a substantial power hike. The success of the Audi TT coupé and the past sales record of the MGB GT indicated a considerable potential demand for such a model.

The MG GT concept recalled the MGB GT. Prior to MG Rover's insolvency in April 2005, strong buyer interest had looked likely to see it reach production.

For the 2005 model year the TF received more compliant suspension and a glass window for the soft top.

The MG
performance saloons

It was under the Rover Group chairmanship of Graham Day that a decision on MG's future was made. Despite the success of the MG-badged Metro, Maestro and Montego saloons, it was decided that the octagon badge would in future be used only on sports cars. Part of the Phoenix strategy for MG Rover, however, was to broaden the MG range, and this implied reversing this policy.

In any case, even in the days of BMW ownership some 'under the radar' work on such models was carried out. At Geneva in 2000, as the storm clouds were gathering over the BMW/Rover alliance, the high-performance Rover 75 Design Concept was shown, squarely positioning the model in BMW territory. With an MG badge this could have been a latter-day Magnette – as

indeed one 'April Fool' magazine story rather less than foolishly suggested. Equally, going further back, the development potential of the Rover 200 had been shown in the Rover 200 BRM limited edition of 1997.

The MG Rover team lost no time in developing models based around the Rover 25, 45 and 75, and announced the range at the end of January 2001 – with sales beginning in July the same year. This was a remarkably short gestation period, considering that Phoenix had only assumed control in May 2000. Launched under their internal code numbers of X30 (MG ZR), X20 (MG ZS), and X10 (MG ZT), they were described by MG Rover's director of product development, Rob Oldaker, as "uncompromising driver's cars."

For once this was not PR baloney: whilst keeping the essentials of the Rover chassis in question, everything was re-calibrated. The lowered

Distinctive face of the original MG ZR: lowered suspension and alloy wheels linked with superlative handling and competitive pricing created a formula for the biggest-selling hot hatch in the UK.

suspension was firmer, the anti-roll bars were increased in stiffness and the brakes were uprated, while re-valved and quicker steering, a shorter-throw gearlever and special exhaust systems further enhanced the sporting feel of the cars, as did engines retuned for better throttle response and a move to a lower final-drive ratio. Taken with the aerodynamic add-ons – and these weren't purely cosmetic, it should be stressed – the result was three cars of widely different character from the Rovers on which they were based. Perhaps in one or two instances the difference was too great, as in July 2002 the ZT – distinguished in V6 form by a higher power output than on the equivalent Rovers – was given softer suspension, with the original more sporting set-up banished to the options list.

The MG ZR was the biggest possible success in the range. By February 2005,

it had sold in excess of 75,000 examples, making it the UK's best-selling hot hatch. With strong youth appeal, the entry-level 105 – with a 103bhp 1.4-litre engine – was both quick and affordable and had undeniable 'cool', in addition to being

New for 2005, the MG ZR Trophy had a higher specification and revised styling, but the involving driving experience remained undiluted.

Above: The staid-looking MG ZS in turbo-diesel guise was one of the most successful additions to the MG saloon range. Below: During the 2004 model year a restyling exercise provided a much-needed image lift; changes included a bodykit with vented front wings (mirroring the MG XPower SV), standard on the ZS 180 seen here.

insurance-friendly. The 1.8-litre ZR 120 remained probably the best-value package of all, with performance allied to exceptional economy. The ZR 160, with the 160bhp version of the 1.8-litre engine, was the ultra-high-performer, while for the economy-minded the 2-litre turbo-diesel version delivered 117bhp yet could turn in more than 50mpg. With a

Stepspeed version also available, MG had all its bases covered.

On the road, the MG ZR impressed as being a total driver's car, with handling and performance that few could match. With the sharpest of throttle response, powerful brakes and impeccable road manners, this was genuinely a car for sheer driving fun. The mid-2004 facelift with revised grille and tailgate treatments – but unchanged mechanicals – gave the ZR an even stronger road presence than before.

Based on the Honda-derived Rover 45, the MG ZS, meanwhile, had what was surely one of the finest sports-saloon chassis: in fact SV chassis engineer Giordano Casarini said the final wide-track ZS180 was the best-handling car in the MG Rover range. Roadholding was exemplary, and the poise and balance of the car utterly outstanding. The ZS was dubbed the best-handling chassis in the BTCC and the fact that this was translated into the road car made it more than

The MG Metro, Maestro and Montego

The Metro was the small car launched in 1980 in a last-ditch attempt to revive the flagging fortunes of Britain's major volume-car producer. Built in a new factory at Longbridge, it quickly gained public acceptance and in May 1982 an MG 1300 version was announced. The power output of the 1,275cc A-plus engine was increased by 12bhp and the interior trim was upgraded. To add to the sporting image, alloy wheels, lower-profile tyres and a rear spoiler were specified, and the MG Metro gave good performance, with a top speed of around 100mph (161kph). An even higher-performance version, the MG Metro 1300 Turbo, was released a few months later. This had its engine modified to produce 93bhp, with improved cylinder head cooling, a lower compression ratio, stronger crankshaft and solid-skirt pistons. The turbocharger was mounted between the engine and the bulkhead. Wider alloy wheels, stiffer anti-roll bars and uprated Hydragas suspension units helped keep the car on the road, and bigger brakes were fitted to stop it.

A BL-designed medium-sized car, the Maestro, appeared in 1983 and there was an MG Maestro 1600 version for those seeking extra performance. These cars had electronic instruments and a synthesised voice that issued warning messages and instructions to the hapless driver. As with the Metro, the MG Maestro had an uprated engine, initially a poorly developed 1,600cc unit with different carburettors and manifolds that boosted power to 102bhp; later this was replaced by a revised S-Series engine with a greater power output. In October 1985 the 2 litre O-Series engine with 115bhp was fitted, mated to a Honda gearbox.

The Montego, the 'three box' saloon car launched by Austin Rover in 1984, was designed to appeal to company car buyers, and the MG version was given the 2 litre O-Series engine later fitted to the Maestro. Like the other MG saloon cars sold by the company, the interior trim was given a sporting image with grey and red the predominant colours, and had a

liberal sprinkling of octagonal badges. A turbocharged variant had a 150bhp engine and suspension and braking modifications to control the extra power. The Montego turbocharged engine was also fitted to a limited edition Maestro with the exterior appearance transformed by Tickford coachbuilders, who added side skirts and deeper spoilers painted to match the body colour. These were potent cars with an acceleration figure to 60mph (97kph) of 6.7 seconds. The large 'Turbo' badges on each side of the car ensured that other road users were aware of what it was that had just passed them!

The MG versions of the Metro, Maestro and Montego saloons may have been little more than a marketing exercise, but the cars themselves do have merit – although the early version of the Maestro 1600 is to be avoided. Enthusiasts wanting saloon car transport that is both a little out of the ordinary and acceptable at MG events could do worse.

The MG Metro Turbo: a small performance saloon in the best MG tradition.

MG ZR, ZS and ZT in Competition

For 2001, MG announced an ambitious motor sport programme encompassing Le Mans, the Junior World Rally Championship and the British Touring Cars Championship. The ZR, carrying the MG code EX258, would be the rally contender in Super 1600 guise, and the ZS would wear the octagon in the rough and tumble of touring car racing, powered by the KV6 and tagged EX259. The motor-sport programme, with its distinctively liveried cars and team personnel, attracted a strong following, and did much to raise the profile of the MG marque and stimulate sales.

The West Surrey Racing (WSR) works team for the BTCC was to taste early success in only its third race in October 2001, with a pole position and outright victory and with established drivers Anthony Reid and

Warren Hughes right on the pace. Both would post race wins in 2002 and 2003, when they were joined by rising star Colin Turkington, first in the Atomic Kitten 'shadow' team with Gareth Howell, and then as part of a three-car team for the final year of works support. Despite good results with the ZS, Vauxhall took the championship honours. For 2004, WSR ran two cars – now with 2-litre, four-cylinder K-series engines – for Reid and Turkington, running for the Independents' Trophy. Both drivers were impressive throughout, posting class and outright wins and Anthony Reid was still a championship contender going into the final race. He was to win the Independents' Trophy outright.

The JWRC performances of the Super 1600 MG ZR were disappointing, but

In racing regular podium finisher and winner of the BTCC Independents' trophy in 2004 was the hugely experienced Anthony Reid. Meanwhile, in rallying the MG ZR proved a potent rally car in the hands of Gwyndaf Evans.

not so its appearances in the British Rally Championship, with Gwyndaf Evans at the helm, where it proved a rapid contender. But it was on long distance events that the car showed its mettle, with two successive runner-up positions on the World Cup Rally, which is limited to 1.4-litre production cars. Similarly, the 2004 London–Sydney Rally also saw a strong MG finish. Internationally, Gwyndaf Evans and Tony Jardine have both won their classes on the Network Q RAC Rally/Wales Rally GB. The F1 media pundit is a regular and successful competitor in the MG ZR, with an outright victory on the Norwegian Mountain Rally in 2005 to add to his many class wins.

On the racetrack, the ZR of John and Mark Hammersley took outright honours in the 2004 Britcar series. In the MG Car Club MG Trophy series the car is pitched against the MG TF, and former MGF Cup competitor Barry Benham won the title outright in 2003. Rob Oldaker was a regular competitor in this championship, incidentally, and his feedback undoubtedly influenced future development policy.

The ZT-T took the spotlight in August 2003 with MG returning to Bonneville for the 55th Speed Week, with an MG ZT-T prepared by So-Cal and running a 765bhp Roush-modified Ford V8. Driven by Pat Kinne, the ZT-T became what is thought to be 'the world's fastest wagon', with a speed of 225.609mph. For 2005, it was the turn of the MG ZT V8 260 to move into the limelight, a two-car entry being announced for the high-profile and spectacular German DTM series. Running under the MG-Zytek banner, MG was set to join Audi, Mercedes-Benz and Opel, with a car specially prepared by Zytek.

surprising that this model always lagged in sales terms. The 2004 facelift gave the ZS a much-needed freshening, the SV-style wing vents of the optional body kit being particularly successful, while the revisions to the cabin much improved the car. The ZS remained the most underrated car in the MG range, yet conversely it was the most rewarding to drive. If prejudice can be overcome, the 50mpg of the 2.0 litre Turbo Diesel in 117bhp guise is matched by massive torque and a 0–60mph time of 9.5 seconds, which is impressive by any standards.

As for the MG ZT and the ZT-T, there is no doubt that these models gained immeasurably from their transformation into MGs. With a range that encompassed every variation from tax-busting turbocharged 1.8-litre versions and economy-conscious diesels through to the mighty V8 rear-drive 260, these were cars which combined both style and practicality with outstanding performance. The build quality of the ZT, as on the Rover 75 from which it derived, was particularly impressive, and it is also

significant that in re-engineering the model for the rwd V8 none of the Rover's refinement was lost. On this most powerful variant, any reservations a driver might have about such power outputs making the car difficult to drive can be quickly dispelled. The author can report that

Above: Development of a sporting version of the Rover 75 began under BMW ownership, and the MG ZT was indeed much more aggressive-looking. This is the tax-efficient ZT 1.8 Turbo. Below: The MG ZT-T is an elegant Tourer version – a superbly equipped and desirable estate car.

even in the streaming wet road conditions which his road-test involved, the ZT 260 remained totally surefooted.

The Rover-based MGs in all their guises successfully revived the MG values of affordable, involving performance motoring. In the dying days of MG Rover the MG marque became the company's dominant brand, and if anything was to be salvaged from the wreckage it was likely to be the MG name, given a perhaps unexpected lustre by the range of badge-engineered Z-cars. In his grave Cecil Kimber may well have permitted himself a wry smile.

Above and right: As launched, the MG ZT 260 V8 was very much a low-key high-performance saloon, with discreet badging and only a modest spoiler at the rear. Extensive changes to chassis and drivetrain were required to accommodate rear-wheel drive and Ford V8 power.

The MG ZT 190 as it looked when production sadly ceased in April 2005: the stronger corporate grille treatment transformed the appearance of the car, which in this case was finished in the 'flip colour' Chromescent paint treatment 'Shot Silk' from the MG Rover bespoke Monogram programme.

MG XPower SV and SV-R

The concept of an MG supercar might seem at odds with the affordable sports car image the MG marque has cultivated over the years. But it was always the aim of the new MG Rover team to create such a vehicle as a flag-waving project. In 2001 the opportunity to take a short cut presented itself: MG Rover acquired the assets of the Italian subsidiary of the Qvale Automotive Group.

This Modena-based company, in the shadow of Ferrari and other supercar manufacturers such as Lamborghini and Maserati, was manufacturing the Mangusta sports car. This was a traditional front-engine rwd design powered by a Ford V8, and had originally been shown as a De Tomaso concept car at the 1996 Geneva Motor Show. Qvale Automotive of San Francisco acquired the rights to the car some four years later and put it into production. The car was not only certified for European markets but also for North America – a great attraction for MG Rover.

The advantage of acquiring the rights to the Mangusta was its existing compliance with regulations; therefore, if the basic chassis and running gear arrangements were unchanged, the MG version would not require recertification. Initial plans thus called for nothing more than a reskinning of the Mangusta, so production could start as soon as possible. But after being shown in concept form at the 2001 Frankfurt Motor Show the design was dramatically reworked by Peter Stevens, emerging with a substantially changed carbonfibre body.

The decision for the body to be in a carbonfibre composite was prompted by a need to reduce the car's weight relative to the Mangusta. Another decision was that the MG would be built to rolling-chassis stage in Italy, using the local network of specialist companies – although the carbonfibre was developed and sourced in the UK.

The engines for the SV and the SV-R are both Ford-derived V8s, developed from the Mustang power unit. The 320bhp 4.6-litre version of the SV is modified by Roush Industries in the USA, while the SV-R uses a 5.0-litre engine, bored and further modified by Sean Hyland in Canada to produce some 385bhp. There is a Tremec five-speed manual gearbox, although an option on the SV-R is a four-speed dual-mode Ford automatic 'box. Each built-to-order car made under MG Rover was finished to customer specification in a separate facility within MG Sport & Racing at Longbridge.

Performance of both the MG XPower SV and SV-R is in genuine supercar territory, with 0–60mph times of 5.3 seconds and 4.9 seconds respectively and top speeds of 165mph and 175mph. Despite the huge performance potential, this is the easiest of cars to drive on the road, with huge reserves of roadholding, phenomenal brakes and exceptional handling – although unlimited continental roads and track days clearly beckon if you want to experience the searing acceleration to the full.

The MG XPower SV-R moved the MG marque squarely into supercar territory.

Collapse *and* Rebirth

The darkest day for MG Rover was 15 April 2005 when PriceWaterhouseCoopers announced the company had entered administration, the majority of the 6,000 workforce were to be given notice and production had ceased.

From the formation of MG Rover in 2001, the company had realised that its future could not be as an independent company and that in order to survive it must seek alliances with other manufacturers. This was one of the motives for the high-profile motor sport campaign, notably the Le Mans forays with MG EX257 in 2001 and 2002. 'Setting out our stall,' was how deputy chairman Nick Stephenson described it. Logically, the ideal partner would have been Honda, with whom Rover had excellent relations in the past when John Towers was at the helm. But the government-initiated takeover by British Aerospace had left the Japanese company both cold-shouldered and deeply offended; there was no way that there would be any future co-operation.

Consequently, with no Japanese link, MG Rover's board looked further afield, outside the traditional European industry base. Negotiations took place with Malaysia's Proton and, more significantly, Brilliance China Automotive Holdings. While the Proton collaboration came to nothing, the link with Brilliance looked far more promising, until the then chief executive was alleged to be involved in criminal activity and what looked to be a done deal collapsed.

What the Brilliance negotiations had demonstrated however was the burgeoning strength of the nascent Chinese auto industry, which would have far-reaching ramifications for the MG marque. But by 2004 it became clear that MG Rover was running out of money and an alliance was now a matter of pressing urgency. There had been a long period of negotiation with Shanghai Automotive Industry Corporation (SAIC), one of the top three Chinese auto manufacturers who had links with GM, BMW, Mercedes-Benz and Volkswagen. There was a tentative agreement for them to acquire 70% of MG Rover and, later in the negotiations, China's oldest automobile company, Nanjing

IAN POWELL

MG tastes double Le Mans glory – with RML

MG's 2001 and 2002 campaigns with the two MG Lola EX257 cars had, despite ultimate disappointment, demonstrated the huge potential of the distinctive sports racers, which US team Intersport were to demonstrate with customer cars. Both the ex-Works EX257 cars were acquired by Mike Newton, CEO of the AD Group, and one of these ran under the RML team banner in the Le Mans Endurance Series in 2003 and 2004, narrowly failing to finish the 2004 Le Mans 24 Hours.

But the endurance tide had now turned for the octagon marque and shortly before the MGR collapse, MG Sport & Racing agreed a designation of EX264 for a development of the EX257 design, to be carried out by Lola Cars and RML. This was built around the Lola B05/40 chassis, fitted with a normally aspirated Judd V8 MG-badged engine. The team comprised Thomas Erdos, Mike

Le Mans glory at last for MG as drivers Tommy Erdos, Mike Newton and Warren Hughes celebrate their 2005 LMP2 victory in the RML MG Lola EX264.

Newton and former MG Works driver Warren Hughes. At last MG was to taste Le Mans glory as MG Lola EX264 won the 2005 LMP2 class with the most memorable of performances, overcoming setbacks that would have driven a lesser team into retirement.

More was to follow in the 2006 24 Hours with a further class win

After the most eventful of races, the RML MG Lola EX264, powered by a Judd V8, brought Le Mans glory to the octagon with outright victory in the LMP2 class at the 2005 24 Hours.

for the second MG Lola EX264, now again fitted with the AER Turbocharged engine, with the Erdos/Newton pairing joined by Andy Wallace that netted a superb 8th overall. The distinctive red, white and blue liveried cars with the MG octagon dominant, were a familiar sight throughout the 2006 season and in 2007 as MG Lola EX264 secured the Le Mans Series win.

As competition intensified for the 2008 season, MG Lola EX264 was further developed, so much so that it had to be re-homologated as MG Lola EX265, although still running an AER 2.0 litre turbocharged engine. But competing against the new and dominant Porsche Spyder proved a major task and RML converted the car into a svelte coupé which ran as MG Lola EX265C, taking 4th place in its race debut at the 2008 1000km Silverstone event.

On 22 February 2006 there was a new dawn for MG as Mr Wang Hongbiao, chairman of Nanjing Automobile Corporation UK Ltd, is congratulated by Cllr Mike Whitby, leader of Birmingham City Council, following the signing of a 33-year lease with St Modwyn Properties PLC for 105 acres of the Longbridge site. St Modwyn chief executive Bill Oliver (centre left) and Richard Burden MP (left) look on.

Automobile Corporation (NAC) were also involved. But by early 2005 doubts about the solvency of MG Rover were voiced in many quarters, including a consistently aggressive and hostile media, and the deal collapsed. There was now no alternative but for the MG Rover board to put the company into administration and not receivership, as erroneously stated by a minister in the Labour government.

When, on 8 April 2005, PriceWaterhouseCoopers (PWC) were appointed as Administrators for MG Rover, the future looked decidedly grim. One week later the 6,000 Birmingham workforce was cut to just a tiny number to keep the Longbridge site ticking over. All production had now ceased – with the exception of the completion of a handful of cars already on the line – and PWC set about the task of seeing whether a buyer could be found for all or part of the business. As part of the previous negotiations, SAIC had already acquired the intellectual property rights to the various MG Rover models, including the new mid-range car, which meant that they were able to put cars back in production in China. This they did under the Roewe brand, the Rover name having reverted to Ford, via Land Rover, having only been used under licence by MG Rover.

Although many industry names were reportedly canvassed, no European carmaker was interested in acquiring the assets of MG Rover. Now, SAIC renewed their interest, aligning themselves with Magma, a consortium including former North American executives from Ford and GM, but surprisingly it was NAC who were victorious on 22 July 2005. Not only did they acquire the MG brand but also the dormant marques of Austin, Morris, Wolseley and Vanden Plas. They rapidly embarked on a 'Lift and Shift' of the Longbridge production lines, including the Powertrain engines division, for a brand new MG factory in Pukou, Nanjing. The rump of the Longbridge factory was retained, including the Rover 75 line and the new paint shop.

Throughout, NAC had been afforded considerable support from Birmingham City Council – who became the Chinese company's strategic partner and were determined that some form of manufacture would remain at Longbridge. The intention was that the MG TF would continue to be produced in Birmingham, while MG versions of the Rover 75 (MG7) and MG ZR (MG3) would be produced in China. A further diversion was the ongoing negotiation with GB Sports Cars who had ambitions to revive the Austin-Healey marque beside MG at Longbridge, but this was not to materialise. Similarly, a proposal to build MG cars in Ardmore, Oklahoma, USA, was also stillborn.

MG Sport & Racing had reputedly interested a potential US purchaser but this failed to materialise and the 13-hour auction of the competition/support fleet and a number of MG SV cars on 25 March 2006 brought the curtain down on the MG 'Works' operation.

This was not, however, the end for the successful MG ZS BTCC cars. WSR continued to enter them in both the 2005 and 2006 seasons, latterly under the Team RAC banner.

On 29 May 2007 NAC announced the resumption of MG TF production at Longbridge at a high-profile event. In reality, the cars shown were pre-production versions of the revised MG TF LE500, and subsequently NAC executives were on record as saying that volume production would not resume until further rigorous testing and development had taken place, clearly mindful of the reputation for unreliability that had bedevilled the MGF/TF over the incidence of head gasket failures. In the event, this proved to be the correct route, for quality and reliability issues of the Sino-British cars were to prove impressive.

Longbridge celebrates the return of MG to Birmingham. The first production MG TF LE500 cars were given an ecstatic welcome at a high-profile launch ceremony at a now much-truncated Longbridge on 29 May 2007.

2007 saw the launch of the MG ZR/MG3-based MG S2000 Sport, a 270hp 4WD rally car for the Super 2000 category of the International Rally Challenge. The 2.0 litre Twin Cam DOHC engine was developed from the MG ZS BTCC cars and the entire project carried out by Motor Sport Developments, with NAC/MG endorsement.

The extent to which NAC's quality commitment extended was typified by the approach to the K-series engine design, which they had inherited from MG Rover. This engine design, while delivering excellent performance and economy in both the MGF and subsequent TF, had a not-undeserved reputation for unreliability in the context of overheating and consequent head gasket failure. The problem was addressed by Land Rover, who used the engine in the Freelander, with a new design of gasket and through-bolting, but the fact that MG Rover had always been reluctant to concede that a problem existed had proved very damaging in the long term.

To NAC's credit, they were determined to ensure that there would be no repetition of such problems and extensive development work and the most arduous of testing regimes were put in hand for what was now known as the N-series engine. That this has subsequently been proven in the remanufactured MG TF and the other models in the China-built MG range, demonstrates the correctness of this decision.

NAC needed to relaunch the MG range in the UK with the MG TF, but there would be no VVC variant and nor would the MG GT prototype see production. Back in China the MG range included the MG7, a ZT derivative, and the MG3SW, based

around the Rover Streetwise, but with MG badging. The UK promotion was based around the premise 'MG – a New Journey' and around a considerably updated MG TF, the LE500. This was an exceptionally high specification model that included as standard, air conditioning, hardtop, parking sensors, leather trim and many other items that had been deleted from the last MG Rover TFs on the grounds of cost saving. Exclusive colours added to the desirability of the model. Pricing proved a real eye-opener, for under MG's previous custodians this specification would have been priced at around £23,000. The NAC car was priced at £16,999, the sourcing of components from China enabling a

significant price advantage, particularly over its sole competitor, the Mazda MX-5.

Nor was the price advantage restricted to the LE500. The mainstream TF135 was now sold at £13,995, the first 100 cars being offered with leather seats at no extra cost. Compared with the original MGF, which was priced at £15,995 at launch in 1995, this represented

The 2010 MG TF model range. MG TF LE500 (left), MG TF135 (centre) and MG TF 85th Anniversary with optional hardtop striped in model colours. Just 50 cars of this commemorative edition were produced, of which this was the final one.

MG TF 135 cars on the Longbridge assembly line where there was a considerable element of individual build, evoking memories of MG RV8 production at Cowley in the early 1990s.

astonishing value. All models now had a restyled nose that harked back to the original Gerry McGovern MGF rather than the later Peter Stevens styling. Press comment was generally favourable, although adverse

comment on the age of the design was a recurring theme. The build quality of the first MG to be manufactured outside the UK in recent years elicited little comment.

Back in China, the logic of two auto companies producing near identical versions of the same models under the MG and Roewe marques was increasingly questioned and pressure was brought to bear from national government level for the

operations of NAC and SAIC to be combined. This was announced as a merger, taking place on 26 December 2007. But in reality it proved to be SAIC taking over its smaller rival and subsuming its operations, although MG production continued at Pukou and Roewe in Lingang but with an increasing cross-pollination between the two plants. SAIC now had two state-of-the-art manufacturing centres at its disposal.

TF LE 500 sales brochure on the 'New Journey' theme.

Despite being limited to just 50 cars, the MG TF 85th Anniversary model merited its own brochure.

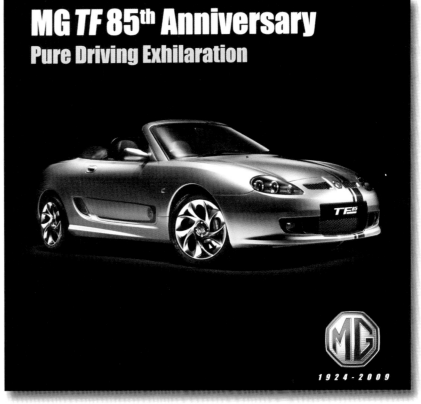

Production returns to Longbridge

As planned, the MG6 has returned potentially large-scale production to Birmingham and on 13 April 2011 the first production MG6 left the lines in Longbridge's Car Assembly Building 1. To a tremendous reception Lisa Ponter, the only female MG Motor UK production line operative, drove the first customer MG6 off the line, through a triumphal arch, dry ice and the cannon-fired confetti that has now become something of an MG tradition.

MG Motor UK sales and marketing director Guy Jones stressed that the past six years had been about creating a centre of manufacturing excellence but that it had now

moved forward to the next stage of volume production returning to Longbridge. He told his media-dominated audience that the MG6 was only the first of the new MGs to come out of the Birmingham plant and that it would be followed in 2012 by the MG3 and possibly the MG5.

The subsequent huge media exposure included radio, regional and national TV, social networks, and national, regional and specialist press, with coverage that the brand had not seen since the MGF launch in 1995. The underlying message was that the MG brand was back, as part of the world's eighth largest vehicle manufacturer. The leader of

Birmingham City Council, Mike Whitby, one of the staunchest supporters of MG's rebirth at Longbridge, said: 'This is a great day for the city and Birmingham's pre-eminent brand and its significance cannot be underestimated with SAIC's commitment. This sees the creation of highly skilled jobs in engineering and major R&D here in the city. This is a new chapter for a very powerful brand.'

The welcome sight of a full assembly line of completed MG6 cars where eerie silence had prevailed for so long.

SAIC continued the commitment to Longbridge. NAC had signed a 33-year lease with St Modwyn Properties – to whom MG Rover had concluded a sale and leaseback deal before the company's collapse in order to provide much needed funding – and announced that it would be the major R&D centre for the company. It would, as NAC had originally intended, also be a production facility. TF production confirmed this, but not at the 10,000 vehicles per annum as originally envisaged. Instead it was to continue on a limited batch basis, but with all major components, including body and drivetrain, being shipped in from China for final assembly. This would be the policy for future models, starting with the MG6. The NAC 'Lift and Shift' operation for the purpose-

built Pukou plant had seen Longbridge retaining the former Rover 75 production line and its capability for UK manufacture, with a higher proportion of local content. In the future, Birmingham would be seen as the European – and potentially world – bridgehead for MG.

The year 2011 would, however, see the termination of MG TF production. The sports car concept had remained alien to the Chinese market, with disappointingly low sales, despite high-profile usage by the China Police force, while UK sales – through the small but enthusiastic dealer network – were hampered by the brand's low public perception. The forthcoming Euro 5 requirements would have meant major further investment for what was now a niche product and

SAIC judged this to be an uneconomic route. The final MG TF 135 models were due to leave Longbridge in spring 2011.

While an MG range without a sports car is not without precedent, as in the Austin Rover years, for the brand's perception such a model is viewed as essential and a successor roadster is definitely on the agenda for the future. But with all SAIC

Following the abandonment of the British International Motor Show, the Goodwood Festival of Speed pioneered the 'Moving Motor Show' format in 2010. This highly successful innovation saw the new MG6 coming face-to-face and being driven by its public for the first time.

MG Zero concept show car made its debut in Beijing in April 2010. External design links with MG6 but the interior is particularly striking and designed to appeal to young style-conscious buyers.

energies being initially concentrated on high-volume saloon cars, particularly for the China home market, this has appeared a seemingly low priority. Preliminary design work has reportedly been carried out at Longbridge, now known as MG Birmingham, and indications are that for the new model SAIC will eschew the mid-engine layout of the MGF/TF in favour of the more conventional layout of front engine/rear wheel drive. Indeed, such a layout was

viewed by SAIC as vital 'to invoke the spirit of the MGB'. This platform would provide much greater scope for variants, the most likely being a GT model in addition to a traditional roadster.

Appealing though such a roadster concept sounds, its exact position in the SAIC product plan remains uncertain, although the emphasis on MG's sports car heritage in the 2011 promotional campaign may provide an indication of sooner rather than

later, despite statements to the effect that 2016 would be the earliest that such a model would be seen.

There is little doubt that if, and when, a return of the MG brand to North America takes place, an MG sports car will be pivotal to its success, the MG marque still enjoying the strongest of followings, despite the last new MGBs being sold over 30 years ago. Like other Chinese manufacturers SAIC will clearly have long-term aspirations

for this market but at the time of writing (2011) all efforts are directed towards SAIC's home market, with MG Motor UK being the bridgehead to Europe and other selected markets.

NAC and subsequently SAIC always intended that Longbridge would become the R&D heart of their operations, with Birmingham being the European hub. Much of SAIC's design and development took place alongside Ricardo in Leamington Spa,

Mr William Wang, managing director of MG Motor UK (centre) with leader of Birmingham City Council Mike Whitby (right) and Richard Burden MP (left), two of the major driving forces in the rebirth of MG production in the West Midlands following the MG Rover collapse in 2005.

Lisa Ponter of MG Motor UK, currently the only female on the MG6 assembly line, has just driven the first MG6 customer car through dry ice, cannon-fired confetti and blazing spotlights into a media frenzy on 13 April 2011 at a rejuvenated Longbridge.

with many former MG Rover engineers as part of the team. The entire operation transferred to Longbridge (as the SMTC UK Technical Centre) and a 250-strong team was tasked with the future design and engineering direction of MG and Roewe products.

In 2010 the new, dedicated Design Centre, under the leadership of Tony Williams-Kenny, was revealed to the world's media. Subsequently Williams-Kenny was promoted to

head the entire design operation for both MG and Roewe. Bringing new designs rapidly to market is a particular strength of the Anglo/Chinese operation, with 24-hour working between the two design and engineering operations uniquely facilitated by the differing time zones of the two countries. This means that the UK and China teams can each download their output on a daily basis, providing SAIC with an invaluable fast-track resource.

The SAIC product plan for the MG brand in the UK – and ultimately European and other world markets – is based around clearly defined market segments but always underpinning the range with the key MG attributes of sporting driving and affordability. According to MG Motor UK sales and marketing director Guy Jones it is not the intention to transform MG into a mid-range 'value' brand, but instead to build on the 'affordability' theme.

Equally, there will be no further excursions into supercar territory with a vehicle like the MG SV. Nor is there any intention to move into traditional non-MG areas, typically MPVs, that would dilute the brand ethos. In taking this approach, SAIC has endeavoured not only to redefine the brand's DNA but also to build upon its traditional strengths and 'British-ness', as has been seen in China's international auto shows.

When SAIC acquired the MG Rover intellectual property rights, the most significant design was that of the mid-range car, known as RDX60. After further design and engineering input this emerged as the Roewe 550 and was launched at the Beijing Motor Show in 2008. MG Rover had always envisaged that RDX60 would also spawn an MG version and this is the route followed by SAIC. The MG6 was revealed at the 2009 Shanghai Auto Show.

The significance of the MG6 in the MG product plan cannot be underestimated. It is positioned in the C-segment in terms of price (ranging at launch from £15,495-18,995) with its competitors falling into the Ford Focus/VW Golf and similar European and Far Eastern models. Launched initially as a fastback, with the MGB-linking GT moniker a surprise addition, the MG6 has very quickly seen a saloon variant, also reprising history as the Magnette, added to the range. Both models have impressive interior space and are well specified in terms of standard equipment.

This is an entirely new design, with just a single carry-over suspension part from the Rover 75/MG ZT. All the design and engineering work was carried out at Longbridge, with considerable input in the area of vehicle dynamics. Past owners of the MG ZR and ZS will feel very much at home with the handling of the MG6, which continues the tradition of being a rewarding driver's car. In its initial test, *Autocar* described the car as 'a spirited and willing performer' and a 'value for money hatchback'.

Power comes from the turbocharged 1.8 TCI-Tech four cylinder petrol engine, which develops a power output of 160ps. The UK cars are offered with 5-speed manual transmission with ABS and EBD as standard. Suspension is McPherson struts at the front and multi-link at the rear. SAIC is developing its own 1.9 litre turbocharged diesel for the MG6 and subsequent MG models and will doubtless offer other power units within the lifetime of the model. The design and engineering for the new diesel has been carried out at MG Motor UK and its introduction will avoid dependence on a third-party manufacturer.

What has set the MG6 apart from its competitors and already been favourably commented upon in pre-production road tests is its handling, which has been developed by the renowned Longbridge team of chassis designers. If the MG ZS became the benchmark for the handling of the Z saloons in MGR days, it is clear that the MG6 has continued in similar vein and this will be fundamental to underpinning the sporting ethos of the brand.

Of all the MG variants of the Rover saloons, by far the most successful was the MG ZR. As a hot-hatch in both three- and five-door form, the combination of a compact and rapid model with excellent handling appealed across a broad spectrum of

buyers, both male and female and from young to mature drivers. Testament to the 'rightness' of this MG is the fact that good examples remain highly sought-after on the used market.

None of this was lost on SAIC/MG Motor and a successor MG, the MG3, was an early addition to the product plan. Designed around a new platform it is, like its larger MG6 sibling, planned for assembly in Birmingham. Again, this MG variant has had considerable input from the Longbridge engineers and by all accounts should prove a worthy ZR successor in this fiercely contested market sector. Pointers to the production version of the MG3, scheduled for its UK launch in 2012, may be gleaned from the striking MG Zero concept, launched at the Beijing Auto Show in 2010. This was a design concept created in Birmingham under the direction of Tony Williams-Kenny.

The reveal of the MG5 concept at the Auto Shanghai 2011 show was a further indication from SAIC that a full family of models is intended for the MG brand. A Focus-size hatchback, it was promoted as a British design concept to its international and China audience with the Morris Garages name prominent on the stand, yet more emphasis on the origins of the MG marque. Although no production details were released it would appear that the intention is that the MG5, together with a new version of the MG7, will join the MG6 and MG3 in SAIC's overseas brand portfolio away from its domestic market and possibly be assembled in Birmingham.

The question as to how far the MG brand can be stretched and still retain its credibility is a difficult one to answer. From once being essentially a sports car brand, albeit one with a worldwide reputation, MG has been transformed into a volume producer of saloon vehicles. How

Striking concept MG5 was revealed at Auto Shanghai 2011 and may indicate the production version, likely to be assembled at MG Birmingham.

could the brand develop further? It appears that an SUV/crossover model is on the agenda. The fact that brands like Porsche, VW and BMW have successfully adopted this route without compromising their marque's DNA is cited as an example.

What is significant about this

proposal is that it would take advantage of the access to General Motors technology as a result of the Chinese Joint Venture with SAIC, in which the China company has the dominant share. This could see the new model built on the same platform as the Vauxhall Insignia. The SAIC/GM JV also includes the

With the exception of the relaunched MG TF, and until the resumption of MG production at Longbridge, the public's brand perception of MG has been low-profile. However this started to change in 2010 when MG Motor UK participated in the first Moving Motor Show at the Goodwood Festival of Speed. With the demise of the British International Motor Show, the concept of an event where vehicles could be both seen and driven by potential customers proved a resounding success. For MG it showcased the cars to an influential audience and the brand was scheduled to return in 2011. A national TV advertising campaign from renowned film maker Ridley Scott was also planned to raise brand awareness.

Motor sport and MG have been inseparable since the earliest days of the marque and the high-profile activities of the MG Rover years did much to reawaken the brand in the public mind. Since 2005 there has been successful participation in rallying in China and considerable enthusiasm for motor sport activity, while in Europe there has been MG participation in the Intercontinental Rally series, activity at National level and keen club level motor racing championships run by both the MG Car Club and the MG Owners Club. The continuing high-profile appearances of the MG marque with the AD Group and RML are the subject of a separate section. Looking ahead, MG Motor UK would clearly like to be involved with the British Touring Car Championship (BTCC) for which the MG6 would be ideally suited and there must be a strong possibility of future participation.

The motor sport arm of MG Rover was MG Sport & Racing. The high profile that the MG marque enjoyed was arguably as much about its branding as MG X-Power as a performance brand in its own right, with parts and performance add-ons, and the MG SV and SV-R were an

integral part of the operation. SAIC/MG retain the rights to the MG X-Power brand and there is the potential that in the future this could become the performance arm of MG, just as AMG is for Mercedes-Benz.

Six years on from the MG Rover collapse, and in a much changed global automotive scene where influence has inexorably moved eastwards, the MG brand would appear to be in stronger health than anyone could have predicted. Few would have believed that the MG octagon would again be one of the most coveted badges in the automobile world. The brand's owners, initially NAC and now SAIC, have both taken on board the heritage and ethos of the MG marque and clearly have every intention of building upon it and there is huge ambition within SAIC – now the eighth largest world manufacturer – to further consolidate this. SAIC has publicly stated that the intention is to triple MG and Roewe sales up to 700,000 units per annum by 2015. The MG Motor UK operation will undoubtedly have an important role to play here, for in addition to its key design and engineering role, Longbridge still retains the capacity to produce 100,000 vehicles annually.

The intention that in future MG will encompass a full range of vehicles is a far-reaching one and acknowledges its strength as a world brand, upon which SAIC will realise much of its global ambitions. Traditionalists may bemoan the fact that there is currently no MG sports car in the range, but the fact that one is definitely on the way should allay fears in this regard. But however the model mix may develop and whatever the primary energy source becomes, what remains certain is that future MGs will continue to provide affordable driving fun in the true 'Safety Fast!' tradition and remain true to Cecil Kimber's vision.

development of a new family of engines, ranging from 1.0 -1.5 litres capacity, together with alternative energy power units. MG reportedly has plans for both hybrids and EVs in the future, while SAIC's all-electric E1 concept, unveiled at Auto Shanghai 2011, will almost certainly have ramifications for MG.

Acknowledgements

First Edition

I do not know how to attempt to give credit to all those who have knowingly, or unknowingly, helped me to enjoy and learn about MGs during the 36 years I have been involved with the cars. I suppose the real credit for my conversion from seeing an MG sports car as just a nice thing to have, to them becoming a hobby that has absorbed most of my spare time, must be due to the enthusiasm of the people I encountered when I joined the MG Car Club in 1962. Membership brought with it the privilege of many visits to Abingdon and of meeting many of the people most closely involved with building the cars, and those who drove them in competition.

What I remember most about these encounters was the enthusiasm for the marque, the dedication to the cars and the other people who worked with them, and their patience when dealing with MG owners, like me. The sheer quality of the people involved with MGs, then and now, is what makes them so special. I can honestly say that I have met almost nobody in MG circles whom I disliked, but I have made a great many friends whose lives have also been enriched by their membership of MG clubs. Who could ask more?

As far as this book goes, I have drawn heavily on the experiences of others and on the goodwill of those owners who have let me loose with their cars. For any technical queries I have been able to speak to many of those involved with supplying parts and services for MGs, a service that is better in most cases than that enjoyed by people running ordinary modern cars. I am grateful to the help and advice given by Jon Pressnell, who kindly read the manuscript and added many useful comments based his experience of the cars.

A special mention must also be made for the assistance given by the following owners who made their MGs available for photographing, always a time-consuming exercise: Christopher Banton and Trident Garages, Ottershaw (MGF), Philip Bayne-Powell (ND), Mike Beale (TF), Michael Bean (MGB GT V8), Roger Chamberlain (TC & MGB), Chris Deacon (Midget), Paul Garett (MGB), Peter Green (TF), Gerry Hiorns (Police MGB GT V8), John King (MGB), Ken McGowan (Midget), Eric Nicholls (ZB Varitone & LE MGBs), William Opie (NB), Rob Overington (MGC), Keith Portsmore (NA Allingham), Garry Stafford (MGB), Roger Taylor Classic Cars (Midget 1500) and Ken Wilbraham (MGA Coupé).

MALCOLM GREEN, November 1998

Second Edition

With preparation of the copy and illustrations for the second edition being concluded in parallel with MG Rover Group entering administration in April 2005, I would nevertheless gratefully acknowledge the help and assistance of the company's personnel. In particular: Nick Stephenson, Deputy Chairman who experienced Bonneville disappointment and triumph; Rob Oldaker, Product Development Director and Managing Director MG Sport & Racing, who was always accessible and supportive in addition to being a true driving enthusiast and who led the delivery of some superlatively handling MGs; Peter Stevens, Product Design Director, inspirational and again tremendously accessible and communicative; Kevin Jones, UK Brand and Product Communications Manager, an incredibly dedicated and loyal PR, who unfailingly met every request and organised test cars. To the countless MGR staff who have helped and advised go grateful thanks, together with the MG Works drivers, particularly Mark Blundell, Anthony Reid, Warren Hughes, Gwyndaf Evans, Colin Turkington, Tony Jardine and WSR team principal Dick Bennetts. David Knowles, as ever, provided invaluable information resource.

ANDREW ROBERTS, May 2005

Third Edition

Any marque publication must draw on the parent manufacturer so thanks are due to NAC MG and their successor MG Motor UK Ltd, in particular sales and marketing director Guy Jones and ever-helpful colleagues Doug Wallace and Ian Pogson. Patrick Warner of Sterling Automotive provided photographic cars and constant support, while David Knowles' information resource and input again proved invaluable and is gratefully acknowledged.

ANDREW ROBERTS, October 2011

All photographs are courtesy the LAT Archives except as follows:
Magna Press Photo Library pages 6-16, 18-22, 23 (top), 24-5, 29-30, 32, 34-5, 40-2, 45, 48, 50, 53, 55, 56-7, 60
(lower), 62-4, 72 (top), 73, 86-7, 89, 91-4, 96, 98, 100-6, 108-11, 113-4, 116, 119-22, 126-30, 134-40, 142, 145, 154-5.
Andrew Roberts pages 88-9, 157, 160-161, 162, 168, 170-171, 172-180, 182-186.
MG Rover Group pages 157-158, 160, 163, 164-165, 166-167, 168.
Headlineauto page 188.
Cover picture by Neill Bruce.

Index